Longman Handbooks for Language Teachers
General Editor: Donn Byrne

Jane Willis

Teaching English through English

A Course in Classroom Language and Techniques

Longman

LONGMAN GROUP UK LIMITED
Longman House, Burnt Mill,
Harlow, Essex CM20 2JE, England
and Associated Companies throughout the world.

First published 1981
Eighth impression 1987

ISBN 0-582-74608-6

Produced by Longman Group (FE) Ltd
Printed in Hong Kong

Acknowledgements My sincere thanks are due to the many staff and trainee teachers at the
British Council Teaching Centre in Teheran from 1974 to 1978 who encouraged me in the
early stages of this project, especially Tim Cockburn and Alan Mountford; to all my
colleagues from different parts of the world who subsequently offered advice and ideas; to
John Sinclair, for his insights into the language of the classroom; to Jean McGovern who
painstakingly read and commented on the final version of the manuscript; to Malcolm
Cooper and Mike Fox for their permission to reproduce some pages of *Junior English
Reading* (Longman 1978); to Mavis Sharp who deciphered and typed the last five Units; to
all the staff in Longman through whose hands this book has passed—in particular to the late
Peter Clifford for his encouragement in the early stages—and to Donn Byrne who has been
constructively enthusiastic all along. I would also like to thank the professional actors who
made the taped material so lively and the friendly staff and students of Selly Oak Colleges,
Birmingham, who made the classroom recordings possible. Last but by no means least, I
wish to thank my family for their continual patience and encouragement: my daughters,
Jenny and Rebecca, who have often and unbegrudgingly managed without me during the
writing of this book, and my husband, Dave, who has been a constant source of inspiration,
critical evaluation and linguistic advice ever since the beginning of this project.

Birmingham, 1980
JW

Illustrators: Sally Foord Kelcey
pages 1, 2, 3, 6, 7, 13, 14, 19, 20, 25, 26, 32, 33, 39, 40, 45, 46, 52, 53, 58, 59, 63, 64, 69, 70, 75, 76, 82, 86, 87, 110, 111, 117, 126, 127, 136, 151, 158.
Chris Williamson
pages xii, 10, 17, 23, 24, 37, 43, 49, 67, 74, 81, 84, 92, 94, 103, 104, 114, 122, 124, 134, 142, 151, 152, 156, 157, 164, 172, 173.

Contents

Introduction

1 Who is it for?

This is a practical training course for teachers or intending teachers of English as a second or foreign language, designed to give them practice in effective use of classroom English and to extend their language teaching skills and techniques, with the aim of helping their students[1] learn how to communicate successfully in English.

Non native-speaker teachers of English can use the course in many different ways:

(a) mainly as a language course

(b) as a language and methodology course combined

(c) as the basic course leading to the Royal Society of Arts examination, the Certificate for Overseas Teachers of English (C.O.T.E.)

(d) as a reference book, both for language and ideas for teaching and materials writing

Native-speaker teachers of English can use it as follows:

(a) mainly as a methodology course, including relevant language work, e.g. analysing a teaching item, or elicitation techniques

(b) as a basic course leading to the Royal Society of Arts 'Preparatory Certificate for the Teaching of English as a Foreign Language to Adults'

(c) as a preliminary course for experienced teachers wishing to sit the Royal Society of Arts examination for the 'Certificate in the Teaching of English as a Foreign Language to Adults'

The course can be used flexibly and selectively:

– the twenty-one Units need not be covered in the order they appear

– the practical teaching exercises can be used in conjunction with teaching materials available locally, whatever the style of textbook or type of syllabus at present in use in schools or colleges

– this course can be adapted to meet local needs and to suit teaching conditions everywhere

– no expensive equipment is necessary, apart from a cassette tape recorder for non native-speaker teachers to use with the accompanying tape

2 What are the aims of the course?

(a) Language aims[2]

(i) to develop teachers' insights into the form and use of English, and to give

---

[1] By students, I mean pupils, i.e. children, as well as adult learners.

[2] This course is *not* a grammar book for teachers. A very useful book to have with you while using this course would be *A Practical English Grammar*, by Thomson and Martinet, Oxford University Press, new edition 1980.

practice in linguistic analysis necessary for lesson planning and materials writing

(ii) to help non native-speaker teachers become fluent and accurate in the use of the specialised and idiomatic forms of the English used when teaching English

(iii) to give teachers practice in the language skills specific to language teachers, e.g. providing examples on the same pattern, eliciting particular structures, or dealing with errors

(iv) to enable all teachers to use English effectively and imaginatively when teaching, in the following ways:
– as a means of instruction
– as a means of class organisation
– *and* as a means of communicating with their students as individuals, who have a life of their own outside the classroom

(v) to show teachers how to exploit genuine situations that occur in the classroom (e.g. a student arriving late) for meaningful and authentic language practice, so that students use English for communication and gain confidence in speaking English

(b) Practical teaching aims

(i) to help teachers to identify the needs of their students, and to plan their teaching so as to fulfil those needs as far as possible

(ii) to help teachers to evaluate in a constructive way their own methods and materials, and to give guidance in writing supplementary materials where necessary

(iii) to encourage teachers to use a wider range of teaching techniques in order to promote meaningful language practice, thus encouraging and motivating students to speak and use their English

(iv) to enable teachers to plan and stage their lessons, organise their classrooms and 'manage' their students in such a way as to promote maximum language learning and active communication among their students

(v) to help teachers cope with problems like over-large classes, or lack of equipment

(c) A summary of the aims of the course

The most important thing of all is that by the end of this course, teachers should be able to teach their students how to communicate in English, not just how to do grammar exercises or choose A B C or D as the correct answer. To do this, teachers should aim, not only to teach English in English, but to exploit the genuine communicative situations that arise in the classroom for meaningful language practice, and to allow plenty of time for oral production activities after the practice stages of the lesson.

3 What does the course consist of?

The course consists of this book, together with recorded materials on a C90 cassette. The tape is essential for non-native speakers who wish to concentrate on improving their language.

The book is divided into two parts containing twenty-one Units in all. See list of Contents, page iii.

Part One, Units 1–12, covers the use of social, personal and organisational language in typical classroom situations (e.g. enquiring why someone is absent), and helps teachers to see how these situations can be used for presenting, practising and reinforcing target language.

Part Two, Units 13–21, deals with the main areas of methodology, (e.g. oral practice activities, teaching reading,), and the language and teaching skills needed for each.

Each Unit is divided into five or six Sections.

The **Sections** in the Units in Part Two differ slightly from those in Part One, but generally they progress as follows:

ⓐ preliminary discussion

ⓑ an intensive study of a teacher◂▸student dialogue or a lesson extract (on tape)

ⓒ classroom language in the form of substitution tables

ⓓ the exploitation of classroom language, and practice in a varie⁺y of teaching skills. Taped materials are available for some of these Sections

ⓔ role play or teaching practice, followed by an evaluation session

ⓕ suggestion for further reading

For a detailed breakdown of these Sections, see Section 6 of the Introduction.

4 Is the course graded?

(a) Generally speaking, the earlier Units in each Part are somewhat easier, and Part One is less demanding than Part Two.

(b) Less experienced teachers intending to follow the greater part of the course, should start at the beginning of each Part; either completing Part One, then continuing with Part Two, or taking Units from both Parts alternately, i.e. Unit 1, Unit 13, Unit 2, Unit 14, etc., thus including methodology from the beginning.

(c) Teachers with some English teaching experience should have no difficulty in using these Units in any order, after completing Unit 1, as long as the cross references to other Units are followed up. Unit 1, however, would be best done first.

5 How long will the course take?

The timing is difficult to assess, because it depends on the time available, what teachers' aims are, how much practice they need and how selective they wish to be. It is unlikely that any teacher will find every Section relevant to his needs; examination candidates, for example, may need to spend more time on some aspects than other trainees. Very approximately, it could be estimated that an average Unit in Part One may take between 3 to 6 hours to cover fully, whereas an average Unit in Part Two could take between 6 and 12 hours. These estimates include the minimum role play and teaching practice, and give a total of between 100 to 200 hours for the whole course, including both language and methodology. However, the book can be used in other ways, for example:

– a 30 hour methodology course could be based on the Units in Part Two, omitting all Sections **b** or **b** and **c**.

– alternatively, a 30 hour course on the teaching of reading and writing could be based on the final three Units completing all relevant materials writing tasks in Section **d**, and following up all cross-references to earlier Units.

– a 20 hour language course could be based on relevant Units of Part One, especially those including Exploitation Sections, and the remaining Units could be used as reference sections for teachers to use on their own, or on a subsequent course.

6 To the user of the course

If you are participating in a teacher training course, your tutor will probably already have selected the areas of this course relevant to your work.

If you are studying on your own, find at least one, preferably two or three colleagues to study with you, then you will profit from the pair and group activities, and learn much more. The tape will give you a lot of help. Try to arrange to watch each other teaching too and discuss the lessons afterwards.

If you are planning a course remember to be selective, and choose Units and Sections that are relevant to everyone's needs. Be prepared, too, to make adaptions both to the language and to the techniques so that they suit *your* teaching conditions, and interest *your* students. Allow plenty of time for the practical work and for follow-up discussion.

A detailed account of how to use each Section follows. **L** denotes mainly language work, **M** denotes method work, **L + M** can be used both for language and method combined.

Other SYMBOLS used here are repeated throughout the coursebook, namely:

   work on your own

work in pairs

small groups

whole class

   group discussion before class discussion

use the tape

suitable for written assignment for examination practice

How to use each section

Part One

Social, personal and organisational classroom language

(These Units can be taken in any order after completing Unit 1. Omit Unit 7 if you have no chance of using tape recorders or taped materials.)

The **CARTOON** is designed to 'set the scene' for the theme of the Unit.

Part Two

Language of instruction and teaching techniques

(These Units progress through the presentation practice and production stages of oral work, to listening, reading and writing. They gradually get more difficult. It is advisable but not essential to take them in the order they appear. Cross references to other Units are included for users who wish to 'jump around'. Unit 16 can be done at any point.)

The **FOCUS** page is designed to indicate the various teaching activities for which specific language is needed; in some Units it identifies problem

Part One

Part Two

areas and offers possible solutions.

Use it as a reference page, especially during the Preliminary Discussion, and for Sections **c** and **d**.

ⓐ Preliminary discussion

The aim of this preliminary discussion session is not necessarily to find answers for all the questions at this stage. It is to share experience, exchange ideas and to bring problems to light. It is to be hoped that by the end of the Unit most of the discussion points you originally find obscure or unanswerable will be clarified or solved as a result of working through the Unit carefully.

L + M   The six or so discussion points normally begin fairly generally, then focus in on the themes of the Unit. Some are concerned with questions of theory and methodology, others raise language points, like appropriacy and social register in language use.

They should be taken in order, each discussed first in small groups before being discussed as a class. The small group work ensures that you *all* get practice speaking about teaching English.

The points can be discussed briefly by those of you who are mostly concerned with language work, or more fully if you are also concerned with theory and methodology.

The points marked ⬤ are suitable for written assignments for those of you taking TEFL examinations. They should not be written until the Unit has been completed and revised thoroughly. Some questions need to be reworded slightly to make them more specific, e.g., 'Discuss *two* ideas for . . .' rather than 'Discuss *some* ideas for . . .'.

ⓑ Dialogue practice

ⓑ Lesson extract

These have been recorded on tape so that you can hear and imitate native-speaker teachers talking to their students in a classroom situation.

You should first read the instructions above the scripts; normally they tell you to play the tape once, straight through, to get the gist, and then play the tape through again, stopping it after each phrase or sentence so that you can repeat the teacher's part. Pauses for repetition have *not* been left on the tape. Stop the tape yourself (or your tutor will stop it for you) while you repeat. Repeating the teacher's part should improve your pronunciation and help to make you more fluent. After that you should work in pairs without the script but referring to relevant aids or teaching materials seeing how much you can remember.

L   The two **DIALOGUES** are short enough to be practised and learnt thoroughly, comparing your pronunciation with that of the teacher on the tape. Choose the one relevant to your teaching situation. If you do not have the tape, try to get a native speaker to help you with them, and correct your pronunciation if necessary.

L + M   The **LESSONS**, longer than the dialogues, are designed to give controlled practice in use of language as well as pronunciation. In some Units there are two extracts for you to choose from: one set in a school and one in a college. Where the language and methodology is appropriate to either, only one extract has been included.

Part One

L + M   The **LANGUAGE ACTIVITY** gives practice in one or two specific skills necessary for English teachers. Sometimes there is a short exercise on tape to accompany it. Each Unit deals with a different skill. If you feel you need some more practice, help each other to make up some more examples along the same lines.

Part Two

Read the notes on the left before you begin. These put the extract in its context, so that you can understand the purpose behind what the teacher is doing and saying, and know why certain words are stressed. The follow up notes also help do this. For those of you concerned also with methodology, the lessons outlined here can be discussed in detail, with reference to your own teaching situation. They could also be adapted for use in teaching practice if you have students of a suitable level.

👤or👤👤   **M**   The **TEACHING HINTS** are designed to make you think about the reasons behind the teacher's actions and choice of words. They may give you some ideas that you could try in your classes. There is a **KEY** to the teaching hints in Appendix D, pages 183–185.

🅒 Classroom language

👤👤   This Section was designed primarily for the non native-speaker teacher of English, however native speakers could use these sections in conjunction with the Exploitation Section and Appendix A for some extra linguistic analysis practice, analysing the forms, meaning and use of suitable teaching items. Just to read through the tables in Part Two rapidly also gives some idea of how a lesson can progress.

I have tried to make the language in these tables as comprehensive and as self-explanatory as possible. As a result I am sure that you will already be familiar with some of this language. Do not waste time practising what you can already use effectively. Begin by skimming through the substitution tables, identifying what the teacher is trying to do in each case. Practise some of the language concentrating on pronunciation and fluency. Ask your neighbour to listen to you critically. Then pick a group of tables which contain idioms or phrases which are new to you. Make sure you know what they mean and when to use them, adapt them to suit your teaching situation, and then practise in pairs, *not* reading from the tables, but *memorising* a sentence and saying it as naturally as possible. Your partner should act the role of the class, and ask questions or react in a manner typical of your students. You should add your own ideas, if you can, to create a meaningful classroom conversation. Try to use, where appropriate, the intonation and stress patterns that you heard on the tape in Section **b**. Practise from one table or set of tables until the patterns come naturally to you.

Sometimes possible student responses are suggested in brackets but you will be able to think of many other things your students will need to say. Make and keep a list of these, for reference, then you can gradually teach them to your students when the opportunity arises.

The language tables in Part One are

Certain sets of tables, e.g. those applying to one technique, or those progressing through stages of a lesson, should be practised consecutively if they are to make sense. Make specific references to your teaching materials wherever necessary. Some Units contain over 20 tables. Do not try to practise all of them in one session. You

Part One

followed by an exercise called **TEST YOURSELF**. You can do this in pairs, orally, testing each other, or you can write down what you think is suitable then look back through the tables to check your work.

Part Two

can use them in conjunction with Sections **d** and **e**, practising tables relevant to that particular activity. You can always go back to the tables later and use them for reference.

ⓓ Exploitation

L   Units 1, 2, 3, 6, 7, 10 and 12 contain Exploitation Sections, with recorded material.

The Exploitation Sections give the opportunity for less controlled practice in classroom language, before the free oral production required in Section **e**.

The aim of this Exploitation work is to give you practice in recognising and using the opportunities for genuine communication in English that arise in the classroom.

All these situations can be used to present, practise or reinforce particular structures or language items commonly used in these circumstances. Practice is given in identifying these structures, and analysing them for teaching later on. Appendix A contains more ideas for language items that can be practised in these situations

The taped material consists of extracts from an EFL lesson recorded live and unrehearsed at Selly Oak Colleges in Birmingham. The students from various overseas countries were new to Britain, and had had about 200 hours of intensive tuition in English by the time the recordings were made. The teacher had taught the class only once before. The extracts are not for intensive practice, as were the scripted dialogues in Section **b**. They should be considered as a target performance, purely to illustrate the kind of teacher ◄─► student and student ◄─► student interaction which can take place meaningfully in a classroom. The willingness and the ability to communicate are more important than accuracy at this stage.

ⓓ Teaching skills

L + M   The aims of this Section are threefold: to give you opportunities
(i) to think about the purpose behind many of the teacher activities we all do without really thinking why, e.g. asking questions
(ii) to practise the specialised language skills needed by an English teacher, e.g. eliciting, correcting, checking understanding
(iii) to write material and prepare visual aids to supplement your present text books where necessary. If there are enough of you together you can pool your work and produce a complete set of materials after each session; these you can have duplicated so you can all take them away with you and use them in your schools or colleges with no further preparation.

In some Units this section is quite long because of the differing needs of different levels of students. Select the activities or tasks which seem most relevant to your teaching situation and/or those which you know least about and therefore need to practise.

Very often the Teaching Practice in Section **e** is based on one of the tasks in this Section, so it is a good idea to look ahead at the Teaching Practice **PLANNING** before you make your selection from Section **d**.

Part One

Units 4, 5, 8, 9 and 11 include a variety of language teaching activities workshops. These should be adapted to suit your own teaching situation.

GAMES   In some Units, a game is suggested at this point. These are for both native speakers and non-native speakers. As well as giving practice in specific language skills relevant to teaching English, they should provide some light-hearted fun and entertainment. They can all be adapted if necessary and can be used at any stage in this course, not solely in the particular Unit where they are found. Some can be played many times and still remain fun. An Index of games can be found on page 192 at the end of the book.

Part Two

ⓔ Role play

ⓔ Teaching practice

In this Section, you have the opportunity to put together the language and skills that you have been practising in Sections **a–d**, and actually use them in situations similar to those you will meet in your own classroom. The practical work is planned in groups, executed, then discussed and evaluated; the Unit ends, as it began, with discussion.

Full instructions are given in each Unit so that you can read them and carry out the Activity without help from your tutor.

The use of 'character' cards or 'role play' cards can make the Activity more interesting, and more realistic. These cards are given out, face down to each person acting in a student's role. Then when the 'teacher' begins to teach he will have normal classroom problems to deal with. Choose typical student characteristics for the cards, and change cards round each time you change 'teachers'.

The instructions under the heading **PLANNING** may need some adaptions to meet your particular needs, so ask your tutor if in doubt. Plan, watching the time carefully, to allow plenty of time for the teaching and the follow up.

Ideally, teaching practice should be with genuine students, so that there are about three teachers to each group of ten or more students. The 'teaching' can be shared out as suggested in the instructions, one teacher teaching while the others observe, making notes which cover the points to be discussed in the Evaluation later, and any other interesting ideas or language queries.

If genuine students are not available, you can 'teach' each other. This is called peer teaching.

Using role play cards for teachers playing the parts of students, see the cards illustrated here (you will need to adapt these to suit your lessons) you can simulate real teaching conditions fairly well. By planning your lesson with one group and then teaching it to members of other groups, you benefit from each others' experience. Before you begin 'teaching', take care to put

Part One

Part Two

your 'class' in the picture; i.e. explain what 'level' they are to act for your lesson, what they have just learnt and can do well and so on. 'Students' should remain as 'students' during a peer taught lesson and resist the temptation to interrupt even if things are going wrong. Everything can be discussed later, during the Evaluation session. Take notes of things you want to bring up in the discussion.

The **FOLLOW UP** and **EVALUATION** session is slightly different for each Unit. Basically it is a time to discuss constructively the previous activity, and also to look back at the whole Unit, to discuss how far the aims of the Unit have been fulfilled and how far the problems raised in Section **a** solved.

Keep all the notes you take during the Evaluation session, your discussion notes, lesson plans, copies of materials produced, lists of ideas for games, new techniques, visual aids and so on, that you get together during the course, so that you can use them again when teaching in your school or college. They should save you a lot of preparation time in the future.

Try to observe as many other teachers teaching as you can. In your schools or colleges, try to sit in on each other's classes, even if only for ten minutes at a time. It's all good experience.

In the **GLOSSARY** at the end of this book you will find a list of words which are used in a specialised way when talking about Teaching English as a Foreign Language. Words which are marked thus* the first time they appear in the text are included in the Glossary. The ELT terms which are not in the Glossary can normally be found in a standard dictionary. Some words that are not actually in the book appear in the Glossary; this is because they appear in the basic books on TESFL* that are recommended in the Further Reading Sections, and because they may come in useful at the Discussion Stage of each Unit.

---

7 What exactly does it mean, 'Teaching English through English'?
Using English in the classroom

Teaching English through English means speaking and using English in the classroom as often as you possibly can, for example when organising teaching activities or chatting to your students socially. In other words, it means establishing English as the main language of communication between your students and yourself; your students must know that it does not matter if they make mistakes when they are talking, or if they fail to understand every word that you say. They must recognise that if they want to be able to use their English at the end of their course they must practise using it during their course. At the early stages it may be difficult both for you and for them, so a lot of praise and encouragement will be needed and correction of mistakes should be kept to a minimum or your students will lose confidence and give up. (Ideally, correction should only occur during the presentation and practice stages of the lesson, if they are getting the main teaching point wrong.) Remember that the main aim of learning a language is to learn to *communicate* in that language; if you understand what a student says despite his mistakes, then he has communicated successfully. Encouraged by his success, he will try again, gain more practice, and his mistakes will gradually disappear. Students will not want to practise if they are afraid of making mistakes which result in interruptions and corrections; then they may never learn how to communicate in English.

Grading your English

You can make it easier for your elementary students if you introduce your classroom language slowly, as suggested in Unit 13. With students who have learnt some English before, it is a good idea to try at first to keep mainly to the vocabulary and structures that they have already covered in their previous work. When they have got used to hearing and understanding these, and perhaps using some of them for themselves, you can introduce other useful phrases. You can also introduce items that you will be teaching them soon, so that they will be familiar with the 'new' item when you come to teach it. (For more on this, see Unit 5, Section **d**, and the Introductory Unit.)

Occasionally L¹ may still be useful

You may not be able to speak English *all* the time, however, unless you have a multi-lingual class or more advanced students. There are times when it is preferable and more economical as far as time is concerned to drop English for a few seconds and use the students' own language. For example:

(i)   If it would take a long time to explain the meaning or use of a new word in English, you could give it to them in L¹, i.e. in the students' own language. You would then need to make sure that plenty of examples are given in English so that students can practise it and remember it.

(ii) You might find it quicker to explain the aims of your lesson or of the next activity in L¹, just to make sure that everyone knows what they are learning and when they can use it. For example, it is very difficult to explain clearly in English that you are going to teach ways of making suggestions. A quick explanation in their own language would save time and make students more relaxed, confident and ready to learn.

(iii) As a check of your students' understanding, after the presentation stage, you could ask them, 'How would you say that in *your* language?' If most get it right, it will boost their confidence and help reinforce their learning. If some get it wrong you will realise in time to save the situation. This helps particularly the weaker students: the shy adults who do not like to admit they have not understood, or the children who do not realise they have not been understanding correctly.

(iv) You might ask an early intermediate class to discuss in L¹, in pairs, the main ideas of a reading passage, but only where the aim of your lesson is to improve their reading skills, e.g. reading for the main points, where subsequent discussion in their own language, in pairs, might help them develop this skill.

As a general rule, it is probably a good idea if you only allow your students to speak in their own language if you give them permission to do so. You then have to make clear when they must stop speaking L¹ and return to English, for example:

T: How can you say that in your language?
 S: *(answers correctly in L¹)*
Ss: *(Begin speaking L¹)*
 T: Yes, good, it's _____, isn't it? OK, then back to English. How can we say that in English? . . .

Danger signal!

If your students begin speaking in their own language without your permission, regard this as a danger signal. Are they bored? Are they not sure of what they are doing or why they are doing it? It generally means that something is wrong with the lesson, and a change of activity is what's needed.

Learning English through English

If you are teaching English overseas, learning English through English in your lessons, in a classroom with an English atmosphere, is, for your students, the next best thing to going to Britain or an English speaking country and learning English there.

If you are in Britain, your students will already have recognised the need to communicate in English and will be happy to do so in the classroom.

Do not, however, expect immediate results. It may take time for your students to improve. But by the end of their course you should have produced students who can not only pass their exams but who can also communicate in English. This is what this course, *Teaching English through English* aims to help you to do.

Finally, remember the English proverb: 'If at first you don't succeed, try, try again'. A lot of teachers have done, and it has worked.

The best of luck!

Notes to tutors and organisers of teacher training courses

1 **How you use this course** will depend on your particular aims and objectives, the length and intensity of the teacher training courses you run and the specialised needs of the teachers who attend. *Teaching English through English* was designed to be as flexible as possible and is intended to be used in conjunction with the English textbooks and teaching materials available locally. You should make sure that teachers bring to each session the books and visuals they use or will use in class as well as *Teaching English through English*. If the courses you organise are divided between Language and Methodology, you could use Part One of *Teaching English through English* as a basis for Language Work, and Part Two as a basis for Methodology, concentrating on the FOCUS Page in conjunction with Sections **a**, **d** and **e**. Teachers could study Section **b** on their own with the tape if they have access to a cassette player, and use **c** for reference.

There are in fact many different ways of using this course; it is purely a question of selecting and adapting the material to meet your needs. See page vii of Introduction.

2 **The teacher-training methodology** suggested in *Teaching English through English* reflects a sound English teaching methodology in many aspects. If you follow the Sections of each Unit through in order, you will find the same controlled progression from controlled to free as you should find in any sound English lesson: Section **a** presents the themes and topics of the Unit, Sections **b** and **c** present and offer controlled practice in classroom language, Section **d** allows for freer practice while Section **e** presents the chance for free production. Your role, as tutor, also changes throughout the Unit; in the early Sections you control the activities, and can insist on accuracy and use of socially appropriate language. By Section **e** you should have gradually withdrawn your guidance, except perhaps for some help at the planning stage, so that the teachers are on their own for the role play and teaching practice. As you sit back and watch this happening you can diagnose areas where remedial help with language or techniques is needed in the future.

The mixture of individual, pair and group work should add variety to the training sessions as well as ensuring maximum participation. Teachers will gain experience in the organisation of group and pair work, and be familiar with the advantages it offers, so that they will be able to handle group and pair work with confidence in their own English lessons.

3 **Using the taped material**. For Section **b**, the **DIALOGUE PRACTICE** and **LESSON EXTRACTS**, the length of the utterance you expect your teachers to repeat will depend on their level of attainment in English. You might find it easier to mark in, thus / , in your book, the places where you will stop the tape for them to repeat, before you play it to them in class. Insist on non-ragged choral repetition, and check individual pronunciation sometimes, just as they should do when teaching a class.

When teachers are practising the language from Section **c** in pairs, you may need to replay the dialogue to remind them of acceptable intonation or stress patterns, so keep the tape and cassette player on hand.

It is to teachers' advantage if they can have their own personal copy of the tape to practise at home or in their own time. Obviously this may not always be possible.

For Section **d**, in Part One, **EXPLOITATION**, treat the **SAMPLE EX-PLOITATION** dialogue in the same way as you would an intensive listening comprehension exercise. (See Unit 18 on LISTENING.) This way teachers will be able to learn by watching your methods. Observing and listening to someone teach makes more impact than just talking about it. (The tapescripts are in Appendix C.)

4 **Miscellaneous organisational tasks for tutors will include:**

(a) organising, where possible, classes of students for teaching practice, for Part Two of the course; this may include grading and testing them and supplying textbooks for them

(b) supplying materials for making visual aids, i.e. card, paper, glue, sticky tape, drawing pins, felt pens, rulers, scissors, boxes for storage, magazines, pictures, etc. Also blackboards or firm card covered in sheets of paper in lieu of a blackboard, chalk etc.

(c) organising rooms with extra blackboards for group work

(d) organising a small library of English Language Teaching books, especially those recommended in the Further Reading Sections. Your nearest British Council Office may be able to help with this, if you are overseas

(e) laying on some system of duplicating to make multiple copies of materials produced by teachers in Part Two, Section **d**, Teaching Skills, so they can each have copies of everything

NB The services of a secretary and a typewriter will be useful if you are concentrating more on the methodology side and the production of supplementary materials

(f) planning the course and time tabling. If you have genuine students for teaching practice, who come at a regular time each day, make sure that there is plenty of time allowed so that a good lesson can be prepared.

5 To find out more about **the Royal Society of Arts qualifications** (Certificate for Overseas Teachers of English etc.) write to: The Assistant Secretary, R.S.A. Examinations Board, (C.O.T.E. Scheme), Murray Road, Orpington, Kent, BR5 3RB, or ask at your nearest British Council Office.

NB You would need to apply for details of the scheme at least nine months before you were planning to begin a course leading to this examination.

6 There are a variety of **films on English teaching** available from the British Council. Some of them may be suitable for your teachers. Contact your nearest British Council Office or write to The Head, C.I.S. (Central Information Service), The British Council, 10 Spring Gardens, London SW1, giving details of your teaching situation.

Introductory unit

For non-native speaker teachers, especially those who have had difficulties when attempting to introduce English as the main language of communication in their classrooms – or who have never taught English mainly in English before – or those who have never taught English at all before now
Native-speaker teachers, turn to Unit 1.

Read

Read the following few pages, bearing in mind the discussion points (a) and (b) on page 3. The words marked * are used in a specialised way and should be checked in the Glossary at the back of this book.

Why use English?

The language used as the main language for communication in the classroom, during an English lesson can be fairly extensive and very idiomatic, particularly at 'intermediate'* and more 'advanced'* levels* of learning. In a beginners' class, gesture and tone of voice* are at first more important than the actual words or phrases used to tell students what to do and how to do it. But if beginners get used to hearing nothing but English spoken during their English lesson, they will very soon understand and later learn to say words like 'good', 'altogether' etc. So as well as learning the specific language items* that are actually being taught in the lesson, they will also be practising unconsciously a number of language skills*, learning how to listen, to pick out key words* and beginning to think in English for themselves, thereby reducing the amount of interference* from L¹*, their mother tongue. So at the end of the year, a class taught English mainly in English, will have learnt how to listen to the flow of English, to infer points from intonation* and stress*. They will be familiar with using the language for two-way communication, asking as well as answering questions; they will have had extra practice in the structures* they have been taught, they will have acquired patterns* and lexis* they have not specifically been taught, owing to the repetitive nature of classroom situations. They will learn to recognise 'advanced' structures at an early stage. This will be a great help to them later when they are asked to produce* these structures themselves. Language is much better learnt through real use than through pattern drills and exercises.

How do I start using English?

Even with a class of beginners starting their first English lesson, it is possible to teach entirely in English. On the other hand a class in its second or third year of English which is used to receiving all explanations and instructions in the native language (L¹) is likely to resent the intrusion of English into the English class and make a fuss. First they must be won over and persuaded of the value of classroom English. Perhaps the best introduction is to appeal to their pride. Now that they have acquired some knowledge of English, they can use this knowledge in the classroom. But the students will only accept this argument if it can be shown to work. For example the instruction 'Would you close your books please?' should at this stage be accompanied by a clear demonstration. The teacher should pick up a book from his desk and close it as he gives the instruction. If only a few students understand and obey, they should be praised – 'Good, you've closed your books'. At this stage other students, perhaps a bit slower, will have

Would you close your books please?

1

understood and obeyed. If there are still students who do not understand, the instruction can be rephrased*, (and the demonstration can be repeated), perhaps in a simpler form – 'Please close your books'. The teacher should not get angry with students who do not understand. Praise and encouragement are much more valuable tools for the teacher than anger and punishment, particularly when students are being asked to do something new.

Stage your language

Whenever a new classroom item is introduced, it should be accompanied by gesture or demonstration to make the meaning as clear as possible. When the teacher says 'I want to collect your exercise books' he can pick up the first student's book and hold his hand out for the second. When it is handed to him he says 'Good. I want to collect all your exercise books'. As he goes round the class he may say 'I'm collecting your books', then perhaps ask a student 'What am I doing?' After this has been done on several occasions he may say 'You've done an exercise for homework. It's in your exercise books. What do you think I want to do?' As he holds out his hand for the first book perhaps a student will offer 'You want to collect our books'. In this way both comprehension and production can be reinforced*. At this stage many of the students still depend on gesture as an aid to comprehension. Before long however, the language will be enough. At the end of the lesson the teacher simply says 'I want to collect your books' and the words themselves are sufficient to make the students pick up their books and offer them to the teacher. A simple extension of this at a later stage would be 'Ali, I want you to collect the books', picking up the first two books and handing them to Ali. The next stage might be 'I want Ali to collect the books', and so on. It is often said that the best way to learn English is to go to Britain or America where you can hear people *use* the language. This is certainly true. Unfortunately many of our students do not have the chance to go to Britain or America, but they should have the chance to hear their teacher use the language in the classroom and to use it themselves.

Praise before correction

Neither teacher nor students should worry too much about small mistakes. The important thing is that students should understand and be understood. If a student asks the question 'You want collect our books?' he should be corrected but first and more important, he should also be praised – 'Good, Well done. Yes, I want to collect your books. *You* ask the question again so everyone can hear it – Listen. "Do you want to collect our books?" Now *you* ask. Good'. In this way the form of the question has been corrected but the student has been given full credit for making himself understood. This method increases student motivation*, he will now be keen to try again and not nervous of making mistakes.

To get your students talking

In early Units, in brackets after the substitution tables and sentence patterns, are the answers the students should be encouraged to make. The teacher will have to say them first, gesturing to show that that is what the class should say. For example, even in a class where the present perfect tense has not been taught, the teacher asks, 'Have you *finished* that exercise?' The class will soon understand 'finished'. Then the teacher can nod, gesture towards someone who has finished and say 'Yes, I have', until he can say it. Then the class can say it, too, if they have finished and they should be praised. After several repetitions of this in following lessons, the class will respond automatically without needing the help of the teacher's gestures. They should be especially praised for this.

The same technique* can be used in getting the pupils to speak English in other circumstances. When a student arrives late, the teacher should stop him

using L[1] by gesturing and giving the necessary words, e.g. 'I'm sorry I'm late', two or three times, until he can say it, too. Then the teacher can reply 'Good, but don't be late again. Sit down.' or something else that includes some praise.

How to persuade your students to speak English

By the end of a year, students should have quite a good idea of how to communicate using English, as well as a far better understanding of spoken English. The teacher may need to explain this in the mother tongue to a class that is against the idea. He could also add that they will probably also do better in their exams and that they will be able to speak a little to any English speaking people they happen to meet.

It will be some time before the class responds naturally in English. Don't worry. Every time they say something relevant to the lesson in L[1], say it slowly in English and make them repeat it. Praise them, tell them how clever they are and after a few weeks some students will try things out for themselves.

Discuss

In class, in small groups of 3 or 4, discuss the following questions. Take turns, within your groups, at being the 'chairman' who asks the question and who must make sure that everyone has a chance to speak.

(a) **What advantages are there in using English as the main language of communication in the classroom? Discuss them.**

(b) **What difficulties might you face, using only English,**
    (i) **with children or teenage learners?**
    (ii) **with adult learners?**
    Make a list.

(c) **How can you overcome these difficulties? (Add to the list you made in 2.) Think back to *your* teaching and/or learning experience.**

(d) **What is said in this Introductory Unit about correcting students' errors in oral English? Do you agree?**

(e) **Can you remember how you felt when you first began learning English? How did your first teacher teach you? What activities did he use in class? How did he correct you?**

After your group discussions, choose a 'reporter' from your group, and report your findings to your tutor and the whole class.

In pairs, discuss the basic aims of this course, as explained in Section 2 of the Introduction to this course, on page v.

After finishing this Introductory Unit, you should proceed to Unit 1, then Unit 13, before you try any other Units.

Part One

The language of the classroom: social, personal, organisational

Do you know how to use Part One?

Read the Introduction, Section 6

Begin by doing Unit 1, even if it is easy for you

Enjoy yourself!

Unit 1 The beginning of the lesson

The aims of this Unit are **1** to help teachers to exploit opportunities for conversation in English at the beginning of the lesson **2** to help teachers to get their students to relax and accept English as a viable means of communication in the classroom
You will need a set of role play* cards enough for one per teacher
See Introduction, page xii and also Unit 13 'The First Lessons in English '

 ### ⓐ Preliminary discussion

Discuss in pairs first, then as a class.

1 Do you teach children, teenagers or adults? Do you think you should talk to teenagers and adults in the same way as you talk to children in the classroom?

2 What do you usually do when you enter the classroom to begin an English lesson?

3 How long do your students¹ usually take to settle down and 'tune in'* to English? Why?

4 What do you usually say at the beginning of an English lesson? And what do you expect your students to say?

 5 How can a short, informal chat at the beginning of the lesson help your students to do well in English?

6 What could you talk about in English during the first few minutes to give students some practice in genuine communication in English?

¹ By 'students', I mean both pupils, i.e. school children, and adult learners.

(b) Dialogue practice

1 Dialogues

Listen to the dialogues on tape without looking at your scripts and find out what the teacher is talking about in each case.

Then listen again, this time repeating the teacher's part. Speak as fluently* as you can, noticing where the stress comes in each group of words. Be careful not to stress too many words when speaking clearly for beginners. If you do, it will not sound natural, and later on, your class will have difficulties understanding normal English.

(a) At school

Miss White, the teacher, has just entered the room.

T:[1] Good afternoon, everybody.
Ss: Good afternoon, Miss White.
T: Well, how are you all, today?
Ss: Fine, thank you, and you?
T: Very well, thank you. And what about *you*, Marian? How are you?
M: I'm well, thank you, Miss White.
T: Good.

TEACHING HINT The teacher asked Marian, individually, after she had asked the whole class how they were. Why do you think she did this?

(b) At college

The teacher has just greeted his class and is now trying to get them to chat in English.

T: I went to the cinema last night. Did any of *you* go? . . . No? . . . Well, what did you do, . . . er . . . Mr Zand?
Mr Z: . . . er . . . I . . . er . . . television.
T: Oh, you watched television, did you? Which programme?
Mr Z: . . . cowboys . . . American film.
T: A Western? With cowboys? Who else watched that?
Ss: Yes, I did. And me. Very good film.
T: I'm glad it was good. Right, I want you to ask your neighbour what *he* did after college yesterday evening. You can say, 'What did you do. . . .' In twos, come on, 'What did. . . .'

TEACHING HINT Why does the teacher name the student he wants to answer the question AFTER he has asked it? And why do you think he asks his students to ask their neighbours a question?

2 Language activity

Directing students' attention

At certain times during your lessons, for example at the start of a different activity or a new stage in the lesson, you will need to call all your students to attention and make sure they are listening. Native speaker teachers commonly use words like, 'OK', 'Right', 'Now', 'Alright'. These words are sometimes called 'marker' words because they mark places in classroom dialogue when something new is going to happen. (For more expressions of this type, see Part One, Unit 5,

[1] T = Teacher, Ss = Students, S = Student; other letters, like M here, stand for a name already mentioned in the dialogue.

Section **c**, **12**.) There is no need to *say* 'Pay attention'. It is not important which of those words you use; more important is the way you say it. It is the tone of your voice and your intonation that commands the students' attention.

Listen to these words on the tape and repeat them. Notice whether they have a falling or rising intonation. Mark each word ↘ if falling, and ↗ if rising. One word is the odd one out. Which one? Why?

Alright ... Fine ... Now ... OK ... Right ... Now then ... Right everyone.

Now listen to the extract on the tape and pick out all the 'marker' words.

ⓒ Classroom language

You will need to select and adapt the language suggested in these Sections throughout this book to suit your own students, bearing in mind their age, interests, backgrounds, everyday life and so on.

The language you use at the beginning of the lesson and the topics of conversation will also depend on what day of the week it is, the time of day and whether or not anything particularly interesting has happened recently. For example, on the last day of the week, you might get your students to talk about their plans for the weekend; if it is the last class of the day, you could get them to tell you about their most interesting lesson of the day.

Bearing all this in mind, read through the classroom language suggested below. The teacher's language is on the left, in tables, and in brackets (...) on the right are some sample student responses. Ignore anything which is not appropriate to your teaching situation; add your own suggestions wherever you can. See how many different sentences you can make from each table. Remember to say them in a natural way.

Then work in pairs, one of you being the teacher, the other taking the students' roles, and try to develop some of the topics of conversation which you think are suitable for your classes. See if you can keep a conversation going for one minute (or maybe two). Remember, your aim in class is to show your students that English can be used for communication purposes and that it is not just another textbook subject to be studied and not used.

Greetings

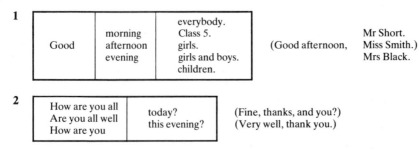

1

| Good | morning
afternoon
evening | everybody.
Class 5.
girls.
girls and boys.
children. | (Good afternoon, | Mr Short.
Miss Smith.)
Mrs Black. |

2

| How are you all
Are you all well
How are you | today?
this evening? | (Fine, thanks, and you?)
(Very well, thank you.) |

Beginning a chat

3

| Well, | did you have a good
did you enjoy the
did anyone do anything interesting during the | weekend?
holiday? |

4

What did you do Tell me what you did	last night? yesterday after school? at the weekend? in the holidays?

5

Can Could	you tell us	more about that?		
		what the	football programme party	was like?

6

Oh, you've got a new	shirt dress	on.	It's very nice.	(Thank you.)
	hair style. book.			

Taking turns to speak

7

Just a minute Wait a second Not you again	Gustav, Kumah, Mr Zand,	**you've** just said something. let someone **else** have a turn. **you've** said a lot today.	Yes, Ali? Go on, Miss Adberg.

8

OK, can you	ask talk to	each other your friend your neighbour	about_____

Introducing yourself It's a good idea to do this if it is the first time you have met a class and they don't know you.

9

I'll just	introduce myself. tell you a bit about myself.

My name is_____, spelt_____

10

I	come from_____ live in_____ have been working in_____

11

And what about you?	
Can you introduce	yourselves? your neighbour to me?

See Part Two, Unit 13 for more about the first lesson with a new class.

 Test yourself

After you have practised the classroom language above check your learning by doing the exercise below. Possible answers can be found in the tables but try to do this without looking. You could either write the answers down or do this orally, in pairs, testing each other.

What could you say to your class if . . .

(a) it was the first time that you had met them
(b) one of your students had had her hair cut
(c) one of the boys had a smart new shirt on

(d) one or two students kept answering all the time, giving others no chance to speak

(e) you wanted to start an informal conversation about what students had done over the weekend

(f) a student told you he had played football, and you wanted to get him to talk more

(g) another student told you his family had had visitors at the weekend and you wanted to find out more about them, etc.

(h) you wanted your students to find out from each other what they had been doing during the holidays, so that they could tell you what their friends had done

(i) and what should your students say to you after you have said 'Good Morning Class 5'? Is 'Good Morning, Mrs' acceptable?

(d) Exploitation

1 Unexploited dialogue

Mr Short has just entered the classroom. It's the first lesson after the weekend. He misses a lot of chances to get his students talking. What are they?

T: Good morning.
Ss: Good morning.
T: How are you?
Ss: Very well, thank you.
T: Did you have a good weekend?
Ss: Yes.
T: Did you play football?
Ss: Yes.
T: Good.   Have you done your homework?
Ss: Yes.
T: OK, can you collect it, Kumah, while I take the register?

2 Possibilities for exploitation*

What did the students in Mr Short's class (see 1) actually say?
What could he have done to get them to talk more?
A few ideas he could have used are found in the 'balloons' below. Draw lines to link each 'balloon' to the part of the dialogue he could have expanded. One line is done for you.

T: Who did you play with?
S: My team.
T: Tell us how the game went.
S: _____

_____

T: What else did you do at the weekend? Yes, Tse?
S: I went to a party.
T: What was it like? Did you enjoy it?
S: Yes_____
T: Why?
S: _____

T: Did anyone travel anywhere at the weekend?
S: Yes. I_____ went to my village.
T: Oh, did you? What was the journey like?
S: _____
T: And what happened when you arrived there?
S: _____

3 Oral practice

In groups of 3 or 4.

Taking turns to be the 'teacher', practise expanding the dialogue in 1, using the ideas in the 'balloons', adapting them to suit the interests of your students. Use the English from Sections **b** and **c** in this Unit too. Each 'teacher' could take one 'balloon' to start with. See Appendix A for a list of teaching points that could be based on this part of the lesson.

4 Sample exploitation[1]

Listen to the class on the tape. It's the same class as the one you listened to earlier in this Unit, in Section **b, 2.** For details and background information about the teacher and students recorded for this tape, please refer to the Introduction, page ix.

What you hear in this extract is the very beginning of the lesson, as the students walk into the classroom and see the recording equipment in action. They are naturally a bit shy of being recorded and the teacher has to work hard to warm them up and put them at ease.

– Notice the way in which the teacher rephrases and repeats her questions.

– Why do you think she does not attempt to correct the student who tells the class about Mohammad being ill?

(If you're not sure about the answer to this question, read the Introductory Unit, which begins on page 1.)

5 A game to play

THE CONVERSATION GAME[2]

In groups of 3. One person says something to begin a conversation, e.g. 'I saw a dreadful accident this morning/last month'. (NB it's easier if you think of something that really happened.)

The other two people have to ask questions about it to keep the conversation going as long as possible, without any silences. The conversation doesn't have to stick to the first topic only; it can develop along any lines that occur naturally to the speakers. Time yourselves, and see which person's topic lasted the longest.

A COMPETITION version is fun to play. Each group begins at the same time with a similar topic set by one person who then becomes the referee for that particular round, e.g. 'I love going to ... for the weekend/holidays' OR 'Why don't we make some plans for the next school/class outing'.

The group that continues the longest without a pause of more than an agreed time, e.g. 5 or 10 seconds, is the winner.

ⓔ Role play

1 Activity

Beginning the lesson

Read and carry out the following instructions.

– Arrange your chairs to make separate groups of five or six people, each like a mini classroom. Use a spare chair as the teacher's desk if there aren't enough tables for each group.

– Give out the role play cards, face down. Do not look at each others'. Whoever gets the card which says 'teacher' acts the teacher's role first then passes it on at the end of his turn.

– The remaining people act the role of students, intermediate level, and should behave according to the characteristics on their cards.

– Begin your role play at the point where the teacher enters the classroom and greets the students. You, as teacher, should spend about two minutes getting them to chat in English.

– End your role play as you pick up the register* to call their names.

---

[1] The tapescript for this and future SAMPLE EXPLOITATION Sections are included in Appendix C for those of you with no facilities to use the tape.
[2] I am indebted to Donn Byrne for the inspiration for this game, which is based on his game called 'Conversation Gambits', in his book *Teaching Oral English*, Longman, 1976.

– Remember your aim at this stage in the lesson is to settle the class down and get a friendly conversation going that involves *all* the students. Do not worry if they make mistakes at this stage. Encourage them to speak and give them time to answer. You could also ask them to ask each other about what they did last night or after class, while you listen.

– While you are acting the role of students, if you think your teacher has made a mistake in English or used a form or expression that does not sound appropriate*, do not interrupt the lesson. Instead, note down what you thought was wrong and check it out, *after* the role play session, with your tutor. It is very important for the teacher to use appropriate and accurate English when he is teaching.

– Take turns playing the role of the teacher, changing all the role play cards and thinking of something different to say about yourselves each time.

2 Follow up and evaluation

(a) *In your groups*

Choose a chairman, preferably someone who did not get a turn as teacher. It is his (or her) job to see that everyone gets a chance to speak in the group discussion and to report back to the class as a whole.

Thinking back to your role play session, discuss which topics were the most successful in stimulating conversation amongst the 'students'. What type of questions did the teacher ask in order to get the conversation going? What differences would there be if you were teaching real students? Would you perhaps have to give them more time to think of what to say?

(b) *As a class*

Chairmen should make a brief report on the most successful techniques and topics used in their groups, for the benefit of other groups. Check out any queries you may have noted down about the use of English.

(c) *On your own*

Write down all the good ideas that you could use in the future, e.g. ideas for exploitation, types of questions that got students talking. Keep a record of all the language points that have been covered. If you do this for every Unit you will have a useful set of notes to refer to at a later date.

❶ Further reading

(See full Bibliography, p. 190.)
Helen Moorwood (ed) (1978) pp. 7–8.
Joiner and Westphal (eds) (1978) pp. 12–20.

Unit 2
Checking attendance

The aims of this Unit are **1** to encourage teachers to recognise and exploit opportunities for authentic communication in English that occur when checking attendance **2** to point out the dangers of over-simplifying the English they use when talking to learners and to give practice in rephrasing rather than merely repeating what has been misunderstood
You will need 1 a 'register' for each group of 5 or 6 teachers **2** role play cards giving details of absences etc.
See page 18, Section **e, 1,** for details of how to make them

 ### ⓐ Preliminary discussion

1 Which do your students usually find easier to do: speak English or understand English? Why?

2 (a) If a teacher speaks slowly and clearly to his class, it is probable that his pronunciation*, intonation and stress will be unnatural.   True/False?
  (b) Students who only hear English spoken slowly in the classroom will have difficulties in understanding English outside the classroom.   True/False?

 3 Some students who understand English quite well often do not try to speak English in class. What reasons can there be for this?

4 What kind of classroom atmosphere is best for encouraging quiet students to use English: formal* or informal*, friendly or strict? Why?

5 What could you say to your class to let them know you want to stop chatting and call the register?

6 What topics of conversation may occur naturally when you are taking the register at the beginning of the lesson?

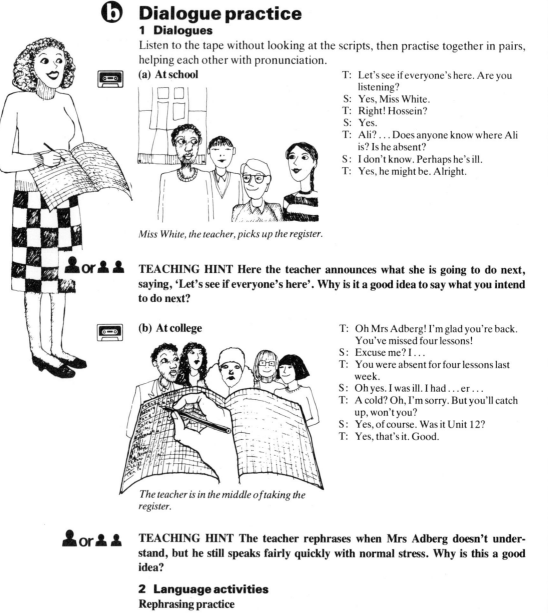

ⓑ Dialogue practice

1 Dialogues

Listen to the tape without looking at the scripts, then practise together in pairs, helping each other with pronunciation.

(a) At school

T: Let's see if everyone's here. Are you listening?
S: Yes, Miss White.
T: Right! Hossein?
S: Yes.
T: Ali? . . . Does anyone know where Ali is? Is he absent?
S: I don't know. Perhaps he's ill.
T: Yes, he might be. Alright.

Miss White, the teacher, picks up the register.

TEACHING HINT Here the teacher announces what she is going to do next, saying, 'Let's see if everyone's here'. Why is it a good idea to say what you intend to do next?

(b) At college

T: Oh Mrs Adberg! I'm glad you're back. You've missed four lessons!
S: Excuse me? I . . .
T: You were absent for four lessons last week.
S: Oh yes. I was ill. I had . . . er . . .
T: A cold? Oh, I'm sorry. But you'll catch up, won't you?
S: Yes, of course. Was it Unit 12?
T: Yes, that's it. Good.

The teacher is in the middle of taking the register.

TEACHING HINT The teacher rephrases when Mrs Adberg doesn't understand, but he still speaks fairly quickly with normal stress. Why is this a good idea?

2 Language activities

Rephrasing practice

(a) Complete these dialogues, rephrasing the questions to help the students to understand. Then compare with your neighbour and practise saying the dialogues together, taking parts.

T: Does anyone know where Paula is today?
S: Sorry?
T: _____

T: Well. There's nobody else away today, is there?
S: Sorry, what did you say?
T: _____

(b) Now make a list of all the ways you can think of of telling someone that you don't understand. Work with your neighbour. Which of these would you teach to your students? List them here, for future reference.

Useful phrases for students: e.g. Sorry? _____

_____

_____

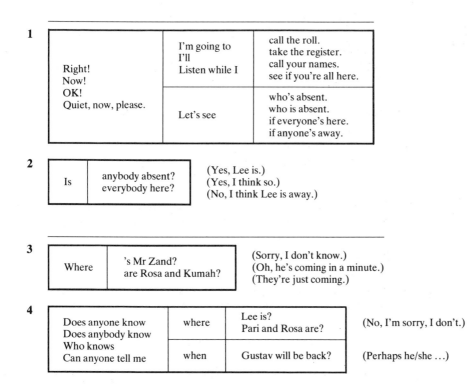

(c) Now listen to the tape and see what happens when one student did not understand something that another student had said. The teacher is getting them to practise talking about the future, using the present continuous form for planned events and the *'will'* form to express uncertainty.

ⓒ Classroom language

In Unit 1, each set of tables had a heading, e.g. INTRODUCING YOURSELF. In this Unit, there are spaces for *you* to write suitable headings, marked thus: _____ Begin by writing the headings.

From the substitution* tables below you can make a lot of different correct sentences by selecting one word or phrase from each section and reading across. How many different sentences can you make from each substitution table? Practise saying them out loud, as fluently and naturally as possible. Then say them again, slightly more clearly but without changing the stress and intonation and using gestures appropriate to a beginners' class. Be careful not to stress any forms that are normally weak, just because you are speaking to beginners.

1

Right! Now! OK! Quiet, now, please.	I'm going to I'll Listen while I	call the roll. take the register. call your names. see if you're all here.
	Let's see	who's absent. who is absent. if everyone's here. if anyone's away.

2

Is	anybody absent? everybody here?	(Yes, Lee is.) (Yes, I think so.) (No, I think Lee is away.)

3

Where	's Mr Zand? are Rosa and Kumah?	(Sorry, I don't know.) (Oh, he's coming in a minute.) (They're just coming.)

4

Does anyone know Does anybody know Who knows Can anyone tell me	where	Lee is? Pari and Rosa are?	(No, I'm sorry, I don't.)
	when	Gustav will be back?	(Perhaps he/she ...)

Now practise the items below in pairs. One person take the part of the teacher, the other take the student's part. Then change over. Notice that some are alternative forms which have the same meaning. Add to the language suggested here to make a natural sounding conversation. Rephrase wherever you can.

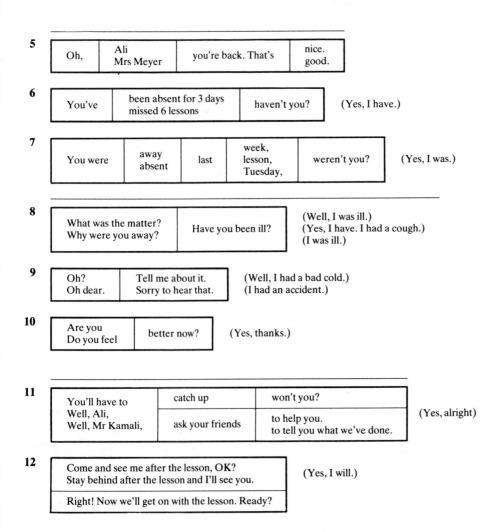

5

| Oh, | Ali
Mrs Meyer | you're back. That's | nice.
good. |

6

| You've | been absent for 3 days
missed 6 lessons | haven't you? | (Yes, I have.) |

7

| You were | away
absent | last | week,
lesson,
Tuesday, | weren't you? | (Yes, I was.) |

8

| What was the matter?
Why were you away? | Have you been ill? | (Well, I was ill.)
(Yes, I have. I had a cough.)
(I was ill.) |

9

| Oh?
Oh dear. | Tell me about it.
Sorry to hear that. | (Well, I had a bad cold.)
(I had an accident.) |

10

| Are you
Do you feel | better now? | (Yes, thanks.) |

11

| You'll have to
Well, Ali,
Well, Mr Kamali, | catch up | won't you? | (Yes, alright) |
| | ask your friends | to help you.
to tell you what we've done. | |

12

| Come and see me after the lesson, OK?
Stay behind after the lesson and I'll see you. | (Yes, I will.) |
| Right! Now we'll get on with the lesson. Ready? | |

 or **Test yourself**

Work on your own, writing what you would say, or work in pairs, orally. Possible responses can be found in the tables above. Where necessary, name the student you are talking to or about.

What can you say to your class if . . .
(a) two of your students are not present at the beginning of the lesson
(b) a student has returned to your class after four days' absence
(c) you are about to begin taking the register
(d) you think everybody is present but you are not sure
(e) a student has been absent for two weeks and has got behind in his work
(f) someone was away yesterday and you don't know why – he looks well today
(g) you wanted to know why a student has been away, and encourage him to talk about it

ⓓ Exploitation

1 Unexploited dialogue

Mr Short is taking the register. He misses a lot of chances to establish rapport* and to have a genuine conversation with his class. What are they?

T: Kumah?
S: Yes, present.
T: Pari? . . . Pari? Absent?
S: Yes.
T: Marian?
S: Yes.
T: Ali?
S: Here.
T: Gustav?
S: Yes.
T: Oh, Gustav, you're back, good.
   Rosa?
S: Present.
T: Lee? . . . Lee?
S: Yes.
T: Oh, I didn't recognise you, today.
   Hans?
S: Yes.
   etc. . . .

2 Possibilities for exploitation

Here, in the 'balloons', are some of the things he could have talked about. Draw lines to link the balloons with the part of the dialogue he could have expanded. Fill the gaps with something suitable.

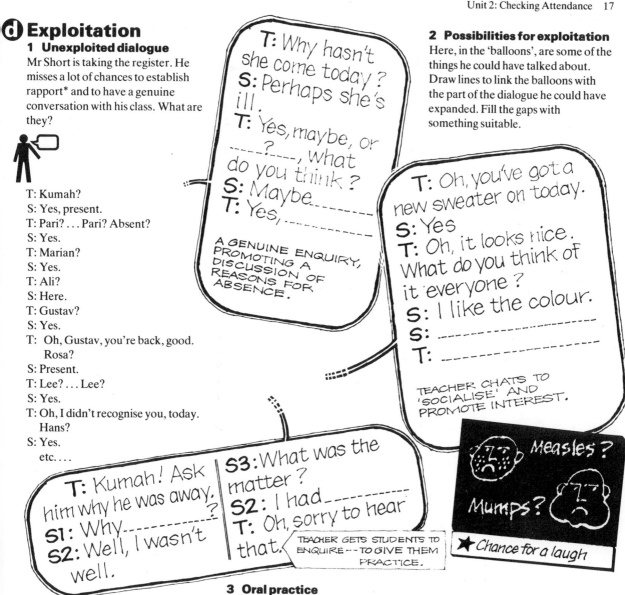

> T: Why hasn't she come today?
> S: Perhaps she's ill.
> T: Yes, maybe, or ___?___, what do you think?
> S: Maybe _____
> T: Yes, _____
>
> A GENUINE ENQUIRY, PROMOTING A DISCUSSION OF REASONS FOR ABSENCE.

> T: Oh, you've got a new sweater on today.
> S: Yes
> T: Oh, it looks nice. What do you think of it everyone?
> S: I like the colour.
> S: _____
> T: _____
>
> TEACHER CHATS TO 'SOCIALISE' AND PROMOTE INTEREST.

> T: Kumah! Ask him why he was away.
> S1: Why _____?
> S2: Well, I wasn't well.
> S3: What was the matter? _____
> S2: I had _____
> T: Oh, sorry to hear that.
>
> TEACHER GETS STUDENTS TO ENQUIRE -- TO GIVE THEM PRACTICE.

> Measles?
> Mumps?
> ★ Chance for a laugh

3 Oral practice

In groups of 3 or 4. Taking turns to be 'teacher', practise expanding the dialogue in a similar way to the ideas in the balloons. Add ideas of your own. When you have run out of ideas, look in Appendix A for other ways to exploit this classroom situation and practise those together, too.

4 Sample exploitation

Just listen to the example of an exploited dialogue on your tape. How does this teacher exploit the situation?

It's the same class that you heard earlier in this Unit, in the Language Activity section, when they were talking about their future plans, only this extract is from the beginning of the lesson. Listen two or three times and count the number of different tenses that the teacher uses, although the class has not in fact 'learnt' them all at this stage. They understand from the situation what is meant, and try to add comments of their own, for fun, and to experiment with the language they have learned recently, in this case, the present simple tense.

The teacher has just picked up the class register, after an introductory chat.

e **Role play**

1 Activity

Read and carry out the following instructions.

– *In groups of about 6.* Arrange your chairs to make separate groups. Put a chair, a table or a desk for the 'teacher' to put the register on.

– You need 10 role play cards. They will all have names on and some will have the number of times that particular student has been absent and the reason for his absence written on them. The register sheet should match the cards. One card will say 'Teacher'.

– Give out the cards face down, in each group.

– Read them to yourselves, and 'learn' your name and your role. The spare cards are the students who are absent.

– The 'teacher' will call and mark the register. Students should answer, 'Yes' or 'Here' or 'Present'.

– The teacher must find out why students have been away, and what has happened to the absentees, if he can. The teacher should try to develop a short conversation around each situation and try to elicit* replies or ideas from the class.

– When you are the 'teacher' use whatever language comes naturally to you and remember to rephrase where necessary. Bear in mind how you could exploit this situation to make a meaningful context for teaching something.

– The level of your class is late elementary.

– Begin your role play announcing that you are going to take the register. End when you have gone through all the names. This should take 5 minutes.

– When the first 'teacher' has finished, collect the role play cards and shuffle them. Redistribute them, making sure somebody different gets the 'teacher's' card each time.

– Remember to play your role and not to interrupt your teacher if you disagree with what he says or does. Make a note of it to discuss with him and your tutor later.

2 Follow up and evaluation

(a) *In your groups*

Choose a 'reporter' (preferably someone who did not get the chance to be a 'teacher'). His task will be to report back to the class as a whole on how your role play went. Help him to compile his report by discussing the following points: what did the teacher do? how did the students behave? what language was practised? which situations were exploited? what problems were there? how useful was it?

(b) *As a class*

'Reporters' take turns reporting on their role play to the class and problems can be discussed together.

Check on language points with your tutor.

(c) *On your own*

Write down all the good ideas that may come in useful later on. Keep a record of the language points that have been discussed. (See Unit 1, Section **e**, **2** (c).)

Unit 3 Physical conditions in the classroom

> **The aims** of this Unit are **1** to encourage teachers to use polite requests rather than imperative forms in the classroom and in general to use in the classroom the kind of English that is acceptable to the outside world **2** to create an awareness of the importance of intonation patterns and their significance
>
> **You will need 1** cue cards with specific details of weather or classroom conditions on them (1 per group, + 2). See page 24 **2** role play cards stating personality and ability level. See page xii.

ⓐ Preliminary discussion

1 In what ways does your climate affect your students? Consider season changes. Do you as a nation talk about the weather in the same way as the British do? What kind of things do *you* say about the weather?

2 How does your weather affect physical conditions in the classroom? What kind of adjustments do you sometimes have to make to doors, windows, heaters or cooling systems and lights, etc. to make your students as comfortable as possible? How do you talk about these things in English? What can you ask students to do?

3 If, on entering the classroom, you find it is too hot and stuffy (or cold and draughty), what do you say to your class?

4 Polite Requests are used more often than Imperative forms in social situations outside the classroom.   True/False?
Give some examples of situations in real life where Polite Requests are used rather than Imperative forms.

5 In a beginners' class, how could you help make the meaning of a Polite Request clear to your students without translating it for them? (See Part Two, Unit 13, Section **c**, 1–3, page 88.)

6 Imagine you are in a bus in Britain; the window in front of you is wide open but you can't reach it to close it yourself. What would you say to the person next to the window to ask him to close it, if he was:
  (a) a complete stranger to you and very smartly dressed?
  (b) a student from your college whom you don't really know?
  (c) a friend of yours?
  (d) a naughty child who had just opened the window to annoy you?

19

Dialogue practice

1 Dialogues

Listen to these dialogues on tape noticing which words carry most stress. Listen again, this time underlining the stressed words. See if you can say it with the tape, keeping the same rhythm. Now listen again, noticing the intonation patterns. Finally play the tape, stopping after each polite request to repeat it as fluently as possible, imitating the intonation pattern. Notice that it is sometimes the intonation and not the form which makes it polite.

(a) At school

The room is hot, stuffy and crowded.

T : Good afternoon, everyone. Quiet, now, please! It's terribly hot in here, isn't it?
Ss: Yes.
T: Well, look! Could you two open those windows please, and let some air in? Those windows. Yes. Could you open them?
S: Yes, of course.
T: Thanks. Now! Hossein, can you open that window over there? Thank you. . . .
S: That's alright.
T: That's much better. Everyone sit down now, could you? Quietly! Sit down. Good.

TEACHING HINT Why do you think the teacher uses a question tag ('isn't it,') when commenting on the heat? (It's not really a true question; the teacher knows the answer herself.)

(b) At college

The room is cold, crowded and dim.

T: Good evening, everyone. Don't you think it's cold in here? It's dark as well, isn't it?
S: It's always cold in here.
T: I'm afraid it is. Mr Lofti, would you mind turning that heater up please? Yes, up! And . . . er Mrs Meyer, will you check that heater next to you? Is it on? Miss Cheng, turn those lights on, would you? Thank you . . . OK. That's better.

TEACHING HINT The teacher asks the STUDENTS to do things, rather than do them himself. Do you think this is a good idea? Why? There are at least 3 reasons, maybe more.

2 Language activities

Intonation practice

(a) Listen to the tape. The teacher is asking different students to do things. You can tell from her intonation if she is asking politely or not. See if you can distinguish between the polite and not so polite requests. Repeat only the polite ones.

(b) The following comments do not function as true questions: they are statements of fact. The 'question' tags are said with a falling intonation to indicate that the speaker is sure of the truth of what he is saying; the tag serves to elicit agreement only.

Listen to the tape:

    It's very hot in here, isn't it?

    We've had a lot of rain today, haven't we?

    It's got stuffy in here, hasn't it? etc. See Section c.

    Then repeat.

3 Student language

Make a list here of things your students may need to tell you or ask you about being too hot or cold etc, e.g. Excuse me, I'm too cold.

_____

_____

_____

_____

© Classroom language

Revise Section **b**, **2** (b), before you begin this section.

Practise saying out loud sentences from the tables below. Speak as fluently as possible. Distinguish between statements of fact and true questions. (See Section **b**, **2** (b).) With 'or' questions, the intonation rises before the 'or', but falls at the end of the second question.

    Select the language appropriate to school children or adult learners. In some cases, it is suitable for both.

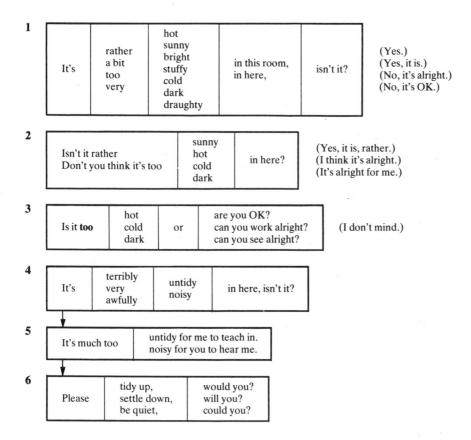

1

| It's | rather a bit too very | hot sunny bright stuffy cold dark draughty | in this room, in here, | isn't it? | (Yes.) (Yes, it is.) (No, it's alright.) (No, it's OK.) |

2

| Isn't it rather Don't you think it's too | sunny hot cold dark | in here? | (Yes, it is, rather.) (I think it's alright.) (It's alright for me.) |

3

| Is it **too** | hot cold dark | or | are you OK? can you work alright? can you see alright? | (I don't mind.) |

4

| It's | terribly very awfully | untidy noisy | in here, isn't it? |

5

| It's much too | untidy for me to teach in. noisy for you to hear me. |

6

| Please | tidy up, settle down, be quiet, | would you? will you? could you? |

7

Please	would could can will	you someone	turn switch put	the	light lights cooler air conditioner fan heater fire radiators	on? off?

(I will!)
(I'll do it!)
(I can!)

8

We need I think we need Don't we need I don't think we need We don't need	the	light lights cooler heater	on	? !

9

Will Could Can	you someone	turn switch put	it them	on off	please?
Would	you somebody	mind	turning switching putting		

(Alright.)
(I'll do it.)
(I will.)

10

Then So	we can we'll be able to we can	see better. keep warm. keep cool. get on.

11

Would Could	you	open close shut	a window the window nearest you the door the shutters	please?
		draw the curtains let the blinds down		

12

Would you mind if	we had I switched	the heating on? the heater off? the lights on?	
	we had	the door the windows	open?

(No, that's a good idea.)
(No, that'd be fine.)

13

Please	could you would you will you	go and	ask fetch get	someone somebody Mr_____	to fix to mend to see to	the	light? heater? cooler?

And if the conditions are perfect . . .

14

Oh!	Good. That's nice. Well done.	You've remembered to	tidy up open the windows	today!
		What a nice	warm cool tidy	classroom,	

Test yourself

What would you say to your pupils/teenage students/adult students if you wanted one of them to
(a) open the windows (give a reason)
(b) switch the lights on or off (say why)
(c) tidy up the room
(d) turn the fan (or the heater) on or off
(e) report that something needed repairing

What could you ask your students to do if you were teaching them how to use polite requests beginning with 'Would you mind ___ ing ...'?

What verbal response would you teach your students to give when carrying out the action requested?

Exploitation

1 Unexploited dialogue

Mr Short is about to begin a lesson with an intermediate class but the room is very noisy being next to a main road in the town. He could have used this situation to give his students a chance to speak. How?

T: Gosh! It's noisy in here!
S: Traffic ... outside ... bad!
T: Noisy, yes. OK Shut those windows, then.
S: Yes, Mr Short.
T: Right ...
S: Mr Short? It's too hot!
T: Let's have the door open a bit. You, will you open the door please?
S: Yes, alright.
T: Better? Right, let's get on now.

★ Chance for a laugh

GREETING IN U.K.

A: Hello, lovely day!
B: Yes, nicer than yesterday!
   Ooh, it was wet!
A: Yes, wasn't it?
   Well, hope it stays nice! Bye!
B: Bye!

2 Possibilities for exploitation

Here, in the 'balloons' are some ways he could have got his students to speak. Link each balloon with the part of the dialogue he could have involved them in.

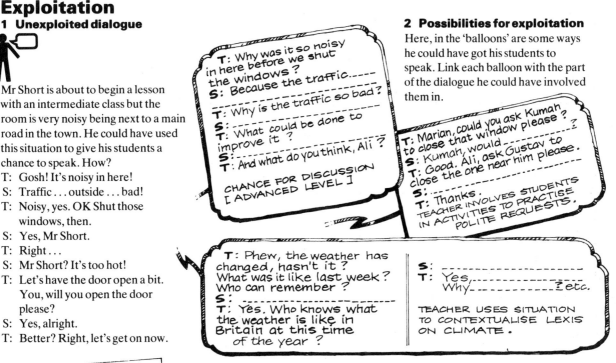

T: Why was it so noisy in here before we shut the windows?
S: Because the traffic......
T: Why is the traffic so bad?
S:
T: What could be done to improve it?
S:
T: And what do you think, Ali?
CHANCE FOR DISCUSSION [ADVANCED LEVEL]

T: Marian, could you ask Kumah to close that window please?
S: Kumah, would......
T: Good. Ali, ask Gustav to close the one near him please.
S:
T: Thanks.
TEACHER INVOLVES STUDENTS IN ACTIVITIES TO PRACTISE POLITE REQUESTS.

T: Phew, the weather has changed, hasn't it? What was it like last week? Who can remember?
S:
T: Yes. Who knows what the weather is like in Britain at this time of the year?

S:
T: Yes,
   Why ? etc.

TEACHER USES SITUATION TO CONTEXTUALISE LEXIS ON CLIMATE.

3 Oral practice

Take turns to be 'teacher', take one 'balloon' each and expand the dialogue in a similar way; add your own ideas or even change the theme if these ideas are unsuitable. Use gestures to encourage your 'students' to talk. More ideas for exploitation (topics for conversations, structures to practise, etc.) in Appendix A.

4 Sample exploitation

Before this extract, some of the students had been talking about a football match that had been cancelled because of the rain, the previous day. The teacher is beginning to draw the introductory chat to a close ready to start the lesson. Some of the students had not been interested in the football and were starting to get restless.

Listen carefully. What useful language items do you think the students might eventually 'pick up' from similar situations in following lessons? What points does the teacher actually get the students to practise here?

Role play

1 Activity

Making the students as comfortable as possible

 Split into two groups, one at each end of the room. For this role play session, you need to make your own role play cards which the 'teacher' will work from. The cards must be adapted from this example to suit the climate and conditions in your country.

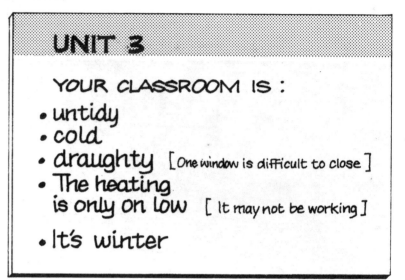

UNIT 3

YOUR CLASSROOM IS :
- untidy
- cold
- draughty [One window is difficult to close]
- The heating is only on low [It may not be working]
- It's winter

Obviously, if you work in tropical Africa, *this* card is not relevant. Make 3 different cards in each group, then exchange them – give them to the other group to use, and they will give you theirs.

- The 'teacher' selects a card without having seen it.
- Begin your role play as the teacher enters the classroom, calls the class to order, and sees to the things that need doing (referring to the card). Mime the actions.
- End when the conditions are as near to ideal as they can be, saying something like, 'OK that's fine, now. Thanks'.
- Then change over. A new 'teacher' with a fresh card.
- Remember to ask students politely to do things, rephrase wherever possible and use gesture to help them.
- The class should pretend to be at a fairly elementary level and may not always understand the first time.

2 Follow up and evaluation

(a) *In your groups*

 Choose a group secretary whose job it will be to make notes on the following points: which situation did you find the most relevant to your own teaching conditions? which topics of conversation produced the best discussion and/or most participation from the 'students'? which items on your syllabus do you think you could contextualise in this way?

What language problems, if any, cropped up?

(b) *As a class*

 Discuss each others' lists of points and clarify language points with your tutor.

Unit 4 Getting organised: seating, books, blackboard

The aims of this Unit are **1** to help teachers in the selection of socially appropriate forms to use when organising the room. Social appropriacy is often more vital to communication than grammatical accuracy, and it depends on comparative status of teacher and students, according to age, social position, etc. **2** to show teachers how to involve students actively in the organisation, using English purposefully and for genuine communication, as instructions are given and carried out, thus illustrating English *in use* and developing a spirit of co-operation between teacher and students

You will need 1 role play cards giving personality and ability (as Unit 3) **2** 3 or 4 board rubbers or extra dusters for cleaning the board

a Preliminary discussion

1 (a) How far is it possible for you to rearrange your classrooms? Can you make enough space for students to act out a dialogue or do their role play in front of the class, or to rearrange seating for group work?

(b) If your classrooms are overcrowded or have fixed desks, could you use the gangways for acting? or the corridor or playground?

2 It's sometimes possible to arrange the seating in a circle or semi-circle(s). What advantages do you think this arrangement has for language learning? (Put yourself in the students' position.)

3 (a) What organisational tasks do you and your students have to do before you can begin teaching? Could you ask your students to help you?

(b) Are there any tasks you could ask *children* to do but *not adults*? Why?

4 How can gesture and mime help your students to understand when you are rearranging things? Do you know of any gestures you use in your country that would not be understood by English native speakers?

5 If students can be involved in helping their teacher how can this help *them* to learn English? (See AIMS above. Give at least 2 reasons.)

6 Imagine yourself in a classroom. You want the seating arranged in a semi-circle. Your students are intermediate level. How would you ask if they were:

(a) children

(b) adults whom you knew well

(c) adults whom you hadn't taught before

(d) adults you knew but whose professional status was above your own, e.g. company directors?

ⓑ Dialogue practice

1 Dialogues

Notice the difference in register* between these two dialogues. The second is far more formal and more appropriate for adult students than the first, which is suitable for younger students in school. In the second dialogue, the teacher makes four requests, all equally polite, but using a different pattern each time. The fourth request, 'And-er-a table between the circles' does not need 'Could you put ...' in order to make it polite. It is sufficient to use a polite intonation pattern as this request is the fourth in a row. Even an imperative followed by 'please' can be polite if the intonation is polite, and the polite form is understood from an earlier request. Listen and repeat both dialogues.

 (a) At school

The teacher wants someone to clean the board.

T: Now. Please could someone clean the blackboard?
S1: Yes, I will!
S2: No, Me!
S3: Oh please, can I?
T: OK. Wait a minute. Put your hands down. Now let's see ... Now then, not you – you did it last time. Er ... it must be Lisa's turn. Alright, Lisa? Would *you* clean the board, please? Here's the cloth. Here you are ... Thank you, Lisa.

TEACHING HINT The teacher nominates Lisa and then repeats the request, using a polite form. Why does she repeat it, and why does she use a polite form to a child?

(b) At college

The teacher is getting ready to do some group work.

T: Could ... er ... could someone help me please? While I clean the board.
S1: I will.
T: Fine. Thank you. If you would just arrange these chairs in a circle, here; and could you perhaps make another circle over there...?
Ss: Like this?
T: That's lovely! And then, ... er ... a table between the two circles. ... That's fine. Thank you.

TEACHING HINT Why do you think the teacher cleans the board himself?

2 Language activities

Appropriacy and intonation: discrimination* exercise

Listen to these requests on tape. Distinguish between those suitable for (a) children or an informal group of adults, and (b) a more formal group of adults who you don't know very well or whose professional status is above your own. Remember, the intonation alone may tell you. Repeat those appropriate to *your* teaching situation.

1 Could you possibly move your chair this way a bit, please?

2 Would you clean the blackboard please, just the top half?

3 Would you mind moving back a bit, please?

4 Er . . . would you mind moving back a bit, please?

5 Please can you . . . er . . . arrange yourselves in groups of six?

6 Could you get into groups of six please now?

7 Now, you'll need your blue books for today's lesson, please.

8 Can you get your blue books out now please. Hurry up! Blue books!

(Listen also to the tape for Unit 6, Exploitation Section which is partially relevant here too.)

Gesture

Stand up and say some of these requests again, making suitable gestures to help clarify the meaning, as if for elementary students. Then choose a request from those above and make the appropriate gestures *without* saying the words. Can your friends guess which one you are doing? Quickly each have a turn at making your friends guess until you are all good at making clear gestures.

Ⓒ Classroom language

There are a lot of tables in this Unit. They can be divided into four main sets. Before you begin to practise them, scan through them all rapidly to see what they are about, then fill in the numbers that are missing from this short paragraph.

In this Unit, Tables 1 to ＿＿＿ concern the blackboard, while Tables ＿＿＿ to ＿＿＿ deal with the organisation of desks and chairs and tables. Tables ＿＿＿ to 14 are directions to students concerning their own books and papers and so on, and the final set of tables, ＿＿＿ to ＿＿＿, deal with the giving out of books and papers during the lesson.

Now write suitable headings above each set of tables, using the above paragraph to help you.

Taking one set of tables at a time, mark the language that is appropriate to your teaching situation, then practise it in pairs. Try not to *read* sentences directly from the tables; look at a table, select, silently, an appropriate sentence, memorise it, look up and say it from memory, as naturally as you can. Try to be critical of your neighbour's intonation; notice where the stress should fall and look out for weak forms that should be spoken more quickly. Remember, only practise items that you will use in your teaching situation; for example, if you only teach adults you may not need to ask them to clean the blackboard for you, in which case go on to the next set.

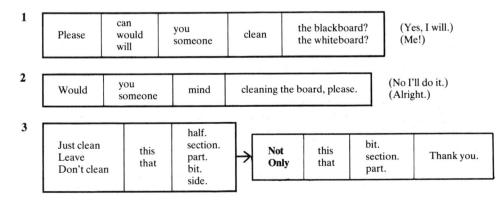

1

| Please | can would will | you someone | clean | the blackboard? the whiteboard? | (Yes, I will.) (Me!) |

2

| Would | you someone | mind | cleaning the board, please. | (No I'll do it.) (Alright.) |

3

| Just clean Leave Don't clean | this that | half. section. part. bit. side. | → | **Not Only** | this that | bit. section. part. | Thank you. |

4

Could you clean the	top bottom	left-hand right-hand	corner, please?

(Yes, of course.)
(Certainly, Mr Short.)
(This bit, here?)
(Here do you mean?)

5

Please could you	rub wipe	off the	words sentences drawings	on the	left right	at the	top? bottom?

6

Rub Clean	everything it all	off,	please.	Thanks. Thank you.
Leave this on				

7

Now! Would you mind	straightening the chairs moving up (along) a bit moving back a bit sitting in groups of 4 making a bigger space here	please?

(Yes, OK.)
(No, OK.)
(Yes, alright.)
(No, alright.)
(Alright.)

8

Will Could Would	you	all two both three	straighten your desks tidy your desks put all your books/files/papers straight put that rubbish in the bin move your desk this way make a gangway through here	please?

9

Could you Would you I want you to	move	your	chair(s) desk(s) table(s)	in up along back forward this way that way	please	?
	turn your chair round					

10

If you could . . . Could you possibly Please would you	arrange yourselves arrange your chairs	to make to form in	groups of	3? 4? 6? 8?

See Units 8 and 9.

11

Right! Now! Alright! OK.	You	just only	want need	your	English books blue books exercise books notebooks and pencils workbooks	out.

12

You'll need Could you get out Would you find	the	materials sheets worksheets polycopies handouts passages books	we you	didn't finish were using had began handed round gave out	last	lesson week time	please.

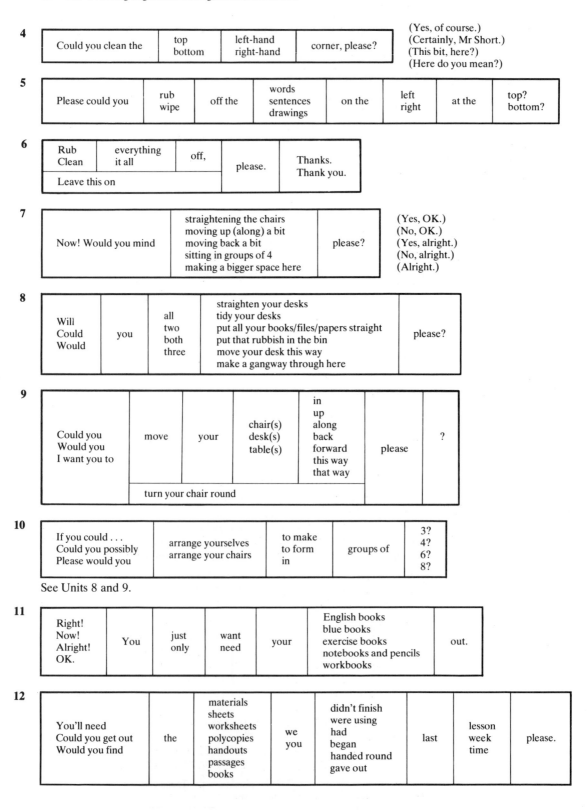

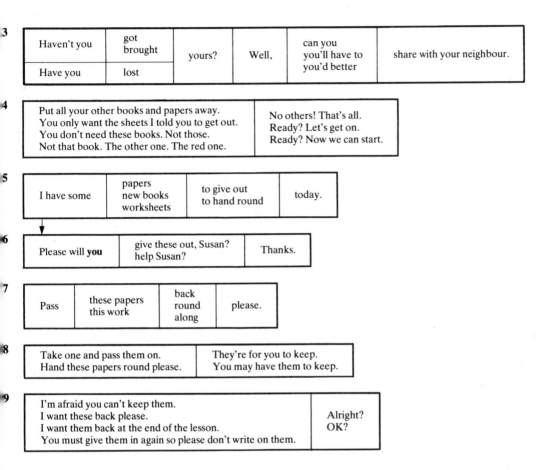

3

| Haven't you | got brought | yours? | Well, | can you you'll have to you'd better | share with your neighbour. |
| Have you | lost | | | | |

4

| Put all your other books and papers away. You only want the sheets I told you to get out. You don't need these books. Not those. Not that book. The other one. The red one. | No others! That's all. Ready? Let's get on. Ready? Now we can start. |

5

| I have some | papers new books worksheets | to give out to hand round | today. |

6

| Please will **you** | give these out, Susan? help Susan? | Thanks. |

7

| Pass | these papers this work | back round along | please. |

8

| Take one and pass them on. Hand these papers round please. | They're for you to keep. You may have them to keep. |

9

| I'm afraid you can't keep them. I want these back please. I want them back at the end of the lesson. You must give them in again so please don't write on them. | Alright? OK? |

 or **Test yourself**

Select only those situations from below which concern your teaching situation. As before, either work in pairs, testing each other orally, or work on your own, writing down appropriate responses before checking them in the tables.

What can you say if you want
(a) a child to clean the blackboard for you?
(b) a student to clean the writing off the blackboard, but leaving one particular picture on the board?
(c) the class to straighten their desks and generally tidy up?
(d) a class of teenage or adult students to arrange their desks, etc. to make a nice large space for some acting or role play in the classroom?
(e) your students in groups of six, as far as possible facing each other?
(f) your class to have only the one or two books or papers that they really need on their desks? (Say which ones)
(g) some students to share books because one or two students have forgotten to bring theirs?
(h) a student to give out some polycopies or worksheets?
(i) two or three students to pass round some reading passages that must be collected again at the end of the lesson?
(j) to tell your class what books or materials to bring with them for their next lesson with you?

ⓓ Exploitation

1 The Exploitation Section in this Unit is different from other Units. This is because when you are getting organised it is usually just before you start to teach something or start to do a different activity and you try to be as quick and efficient as possible. You do not want to stop to hold a conversation at this point in the lesson. When you are giving instructions to a class you generally use language as economically as you can, combining language with gestures and demonstration to aid communication. You expect your students to carry out your instructions without unnecessary talking. So this language, the language of instruction-giving, does not need to be exploited in the same way as the language of other Units.

You may well ask, 'So why use English at all for giving instructions; Why not revert to the mother-tongue? It will probably be quicker . . .' There are however two big advantages in using English here:

(a) It is an authentic use of English, used for a real purpose, thus illustrating the communicative value of English.

(b) The language used in the classroom when giving instructions is very similar to real life, basic everyday English. If teachers use English to organise the lesson, students will become familiar with many common expressions and will find later on that they can use them themselves after very little practice. Also their receptive skills will be developed as they listen.

2 Below are some situations in real life where similar language is commonly used. The social settings are varied; a different register of language will be needed for most of them.

 In groups, prepare to role play at least one of these situations so that you have direct experience of how the language you can use in the classroom relates to such situations in the outside world. Perform them in front of each other, or if you need larger numbers, combine groups.

Refer back to Section **c** before you begin. See also Appendix A.

Role play situations

1 Getting out of a crowded bus.
2 Getting on to a packed underground train.
3 Queuing to buy a ticket for the cinema or football, then finding your way to your seat in a dark cinema or crowded football stands.
4 Giving instructions to the painter and decorator who are to paint your house.
5 Asking a car mechanic to carry out the necessary repairs to your car.
6 Organising the members of a sports team (football, hockey, volley ball, etc.) into various positions on a pitch. (Starting position, position for a free kick, etc.)

NB 1, 2, 3, involve the use of fairly formal polite language, and 4, 5, 6, less formal, more directive.

ⓔ Role play

1 Activity

 There are three different situations in this Unit, all of which are useful for teachers at any level, teaching children and adults.

You could split up into 3 separate groups, one near the blackboard and the other two in different areas of the room, and each group begin with a different situation, moving on after a decided time. (Allow about 3 minutes per 'teacher' in each group.)

Situation (a) can be made into a game which may be more fun than acting it 'straight'. For the game, follow the instructions in brackets as well as the ordinary instructions.

Situation (b) needs quite a large group to be effective, at least 12, so you may need to combine for this one. Situation (c) can be a fairly small group.

(a) Cleaning the board

– Get the members of your group to draw and write in various sections of the board, so that the whole board is covered.

(The 'teacher' can ask members of the class to draw or write a particular thing. If the teacher asks politely and appropriately the student should do it. If the teacher makes a request in an inappropriate way the student should say nothing and remain seated. If he moves, he is out.)

– 'Teachers' take turns asking students one by one to wipe off particular items, one section or one item at a time. Do this quickly. Keep the pace* up.

(Again, as above, 'teachers' can try and catch students out by varying the type of request – polite or inappropriate. You could also insist on 100% accuracy as well. If the 'teacher' makes a mistake, the student should not move.)

(b) Arranging chairs or seating for groups of different numbers

– Decide on who is the 'teacher' and what size groups you will need for your lesson. (4 or 5)

– Using appropriate gestures and language the first 'teacher' should get the class to sit in the groups he requires, neatly, properly spaced, facing inward so they can talk easily. If desks are fixed, students will have to turn round to make a group.

– Change 'teachers'. The new teacher should make the class arrange their chairs back into orderly rows. Or, if the desks are fixed, he should get the class to turn round and sit facing the front in an orderly fashion.

– A third 'teacher' can then announce he is going to do some pair work, and organise the class accordingly. Students should be encouraged to face each other when speaking to each other. Another 'teacher' can arrange other different sized groups in a similar way. Remember that gestures help save time in this situation.

– 'Students' play roles according to their role cards. There are often one or two unco-operative students in each class, who take a long time to react, and other students who get impatient and start chatting. 'Teachers' must be aware of problem students.

(c) Getting the right books out

– Each 'teacher' can decide which items from among the books, papers, pens and notebooks he wants the students to have ready, and why. (He should decide in advance what activity his class will be doing.)

– The 'teacher' should begin by announcing what he is going to do, and then ask the students to get out the relevant books, papers, etc.

– Demonstration and gesture can help in this situation. Language can be of secondary importance. It should still be appropriate in form and tone, though.

– A few 'students' should pretend to have lost or forgotten the book or something that they need. The 'teacher' will have to get them to share, or, for example, borrow a pen from someone. Remember to make the students ask politely, e.g. 'Could I share with you, please?' or 'Can I borrow a pen, please?' and answer appropriately.

2 Follow up and evaluation

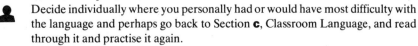

Decide individually where you personally had or would have most difficulty with the language and perhaps go back to Section **c**, Classroom Language, and read through it and practise it again.

Unit 5
Introducing different stages of the lesson

The aims of this Unit are **1** to enable teachers to introduce, and to define the aims of, new stages in a lesson for the benefit of their pupils **2** to discuss what use should be made of the mother-tongue while teaching English **3** to revise the language and ideas presented in Units 1–4

You will need copies of the English Textbooks that you will be using in school or college

---

ⓐ Preliminary discussion

1 Every lesson and every stage of a lesson should have a specific aim*. Look at Unit 13, Section **e**, Planning (e), page 92, for an example of how to express the aims of a lesson from the teacher's point of view. Why is it set down in two parts? Think back to a lesson you have recently taught or observed and tell your neighbour what the aims were. What had the students *learnt* by the end of it?

2 Do you think it is important that your students know what the aims of the lesson are? Why?

3 How can you make your students aware of the aims of your lesson? Discuss the various ways suggested below:

    (a) by giving a grammatical explanation in English

    (b) by giving a grammatical explanation in the native language

    (c) by giving a brief demonstration of the new form in use, perhaps using pictures or other aids

    (d) by referring back to something learnt before and comparing

4 Although using English as the main language of communication in the classroom has many advantages, there are some occasions where reverting briefly to the native language can help. Can you think of any times when using L^1 would be more efficient?

5 (a) Do you think that beginning a lesson with some revision is usually a good idea? Why?

    (b) Describe briefly some of the ways in which you can add variety to a lesson.

6 There are different stages within a lesson (e.g. revision, presentation of new items, practice and production of the newly learnt items by the students) and different activities within each stage (e.g. choral repetition, question and answer work, pair practice* etc.). How do you move from one stage or activity to the next, so that your students know what they are supposed to be doing? Discuss the ways suggested below:

    (a) by pausing and checking students have understood

    (b) by turning round to clean the blackboard

    (c) by explaining, e.g. 'Well done! Now I want you to. . . .'

    (d) by changing the focus of the lesson, e.g. from teacher to tape recorder, from blackboard to books

    (e) by a moment of silence

(b) Dialogue practice

1 Dialogues

First listen to the tape and repeat the teacher's part. Then try to remember the teacher's part and say it after you hear the student's response; then listen to the tape to see if you got it right ... and so on.

(a) At school

T: Who can remember what we practised last lesson? What pictures did we use? ... Yes?
S1: In a ... uhm ... shop.
T: Yes. Good. Anything else?
S2: A customer ... want to change her radio ...
T: Yes. That's it. She wanted to change her radio. Why?
S3: Didn't work ... well.
T: Because it didn't work well. Good. Now today we're going to revise that dialogue and learn something new. OK?

The teacher begins by revising a dialogue. She's about to stick the picture up.

TEACHING HINT Does the teacher actually correct the student's mistake here? Does she ask him to repeat it correctly? Why?

The second dialogue is basically a teacher's monologue. Mark suitable places for pauses (split it up into 'sense groups'). Then listen and repeat the teacher's part.

(b) At college

T: Right! Today, first, I want to go over the sports and hobbies learnt last lesson, remember? Then we're going to practise making suggestions and plans in English. You know, deciding what you're *going* to do *next weekend,* for example. Making plans. Arranging your programme. We'll do some oral work, and after that we could do some role play ... if we have time OK?
Ss: Yes.
T: Well. Can anyone remember the dialogue we did last lesson, er – the man who joined the sports club? We used these pictures, let's see how much you can remember. How about saying it together, looking at the pictures. Ready?

The teacher is drawing quick sketches of various sports as he speaks.

TEACHING HINT Where, in this last dialogue, could the teacher have usefully reverted to his mother-tongue briefly?

2 Language activity

Being a model

When you ask your students to repeat something you say, they are more likely to *remember* it if:

(a) they know what it means
(b) they have to listen very carefully
(c) they know you will only repeat it once
(d) they have a moment of silence to think about it and commit it to memory before repeating it themselves.

They are more likely to *recognise* it again if you say it in a natural way for them to repeat, than if you say it too slowly and carefully. Often when speaking clearly for repetition practice, sounds become distorted*, weak forms* get stressed wrongly and intonation patterns become 'sing-song' and unrecognisable.

– Listen to these sentences; put a X by the ones that sound unnatural.
1 They are going on holiday tomorrow.   4 Bye! I hope you'll feel better.
2 Have you got any cheap oranges?   5 Does Peter like playing volley-ball?
3 Jim? He's just come back from Spain.   6 It's ages since he's visited us.

– Then work in pairs. Each choose a short dialogue or passage from your textbooks, divide it into short repeatable chunks* that make sense and read it for your neighbour to repeat. He should have his book shut.

C Classroom language

In pairs, and referring to a specific lesson in your textbook, practise the language in Tables 1 to 4. Then read through the rest of the tables to get the gist* of what they are about, before practising them.

Beginning with revision

1

Right.	Who can Can anyone	remember tell me	what we	did practised doing talked about read about wrote about learnt used	last lesson? last time?

Remember?
Do you remember these pictures? Look.
Do you remember this? Listen. Who is speaking?

We did this last lesson, didn't we? Look! Listen!
We used these pictures, didn't we?
We practised a dialogue about_____, remember?

2

Let's	go over it again, revise it, do it once more,	shall we?

3

How about What about	doing it again quickly? revising it? having another practise? going over it again?	OK? Alright?

Talking about the lesson

4

First Then Later (on) In a few minutes In half an hour Half way through the lesson Near the end of the lesson At the end of the lesson When we've finished this Now, Right, now,	we're going to I want you to perhaps we'll if there's time, we'll if you've been good, we'll	practise this. learn a dialogue about_____ practise asking questions about_____ learn something new. make up a story. listen to a lecture. do some reading. do some writing. do some note taking. have some conversation practice. do some role play. play a game. sing a song. have a break for a moment or two. etc.

Defining aims (Intermediate and Advanced classes only; for Elementary, use L¹)

5

By the end of the lesson you'll	be able to have learnt how to	say what you and your friends like doing. talk about your likes and dislikes. give descriptions of people. use the present perfect for checking up. give people advice. warn people about things that may be dangerous. write a letter applying for a job. discuss plans for a holiday. etc.	► Table 7

6

By the end of the lesson you'll	have had some practice in	saying_____ talking_____ giving_____ using_____ giving_____ warning_____ etc., as Table **5**	► Table 7

and giving examples (These examples refer back to the tables above. Practise them together.)

7

Like As in For example Such as Look, like this	'I love playing football but I don't like swimming much.' 'Well, he's very tall and slim, with fair hair and so on.' 'If I were you, I'd buy the better quality one.' 'Have you finished that job yet?' 'Watch out! Mind that lorry!'

– First, from the tables above practise stating your plans to the class by selecting one or two sentences from each table and saying them out loud. Work in pairs and take turns. Remember, you may have to rephrase sometimes. Select the type of activities and the level of register that will be appropriate to the students you will be teaching.

– Now, working individually, fill out the tables below with 2 or 3 alternatives, basing your ideas on lessons *you* have taught or will be teaching, perhaps using your textbook to help you plan and think out your aims and teaching activities*. (Intermediate level)

8

First Later on Then	we're going to _____	_____ _____ _____ _____ _____

9

By the end of the lesson,	you'll	_____ _____ _____

10

For example, _____,	_____ _____ _____

Introducing a new stage in the lesson

11

| OK.
Well, everybody.
Now.
Now then.
Right.
Alright then.
OK?
Alright?
Ready? | Let's
Would you
We're going to
I want you to | | have a break/rest. You must be tired.
begin again, please.
listen carefully (and repeat when I do this).
do this exercise orally in pairs.
do a drill. Look, like this. |
| | It's time | we
you | had a break/rest.
did something different.
wrote something down.
did some writing/reading/pair practice etc. |

For terminating a stage in the lesson please refer to Unit 12.

Test yourself

This is a different kind of test from usual. You either need the textbook which you use to teach from, or two or three lesson plans which you can follow.

– Divide the lesson up into short stages*, each with a specific objective. Mark or number the beginning of each stage so that you can identify it quickly.

– Then, in pairs, taking turns to be the teacher, introduce each new stage of the lesson, using the language in the tables above. Begin by giving some idea of what the lesson is going to be about, (Table 4) then define your aims, (Tables 5 to 10) then introduce each new stage using the language in Table 11. You could also plan a revision activity which you could introduce using the language in Tables 1 to 3. Do not go further than the introduction of each stage; the language you will need while actually teaching will be covered in Part Two of this book.

(d) Exploitation

1 Revision

Review the EXPLOITATION Sections of Units 1, 2 and 3, noticing that the teachers exploited the language of those particular classroom situations by expanding and encouraging discussion specifically in order to:

(a) involve the students personally and relate the English they knew to the outside world

(b) give students a chance to practise their English in a meaningful context, using language they had previously learnt.

In Unit 4, which covered the language of organisation, the situation did not lend itself to exploitation in the same way. There is not time at this point in the lesson to stop and hold a conversation. We saw however that using English to organise things in the classroom can help students later on to recognise language they have not actually been taught, in similar situations outside the classroom. (See Unit 4, EXPLOITATION Section, Role Play situations.)

2 Other ways to exploit classroom language

In this Unit, as in Unit 4, the situation is not really suitable for expansion or for developing into a conversation. There is not time at this stage of the lesson to stop and chat. However there are other ways you can exploit the language of the classroom in this situation, namely:

(a) You can use language teaching activities to contextualise practice in the use of tenses and related work, e.g. to teach the use of 'ago' with the past simple: the teacher finds an exercise a student has written in his notebook and asks 'When did you write that exercise?' to elicit 'Four weeks ago.' Similarly, 'When did you read that story?' etc.

Read dialogue (a) in the balloons and see what the students are practising.

(b) You can familiarise students with language they have not yet learnt by deliberately bringing it into the language you use in class; e.g. a teacher following a functional* syllabus sees that next week he will have to teach 'suggestions'. So this week he uses a suggestion to introduce each new activity, thus: 'What about doing some reading now?' or 'Why don't we act that dialogue out?' or 'We could have a rest now, OK?' or 'Let's sing that song again'.

Read the dialogue in the balloon and guess what language item the teacher will be teaching soon.

3 Oral practice
Make up and practise two similar dialogues to those in **2**.

ⓔ Role play

1 Activity

Introducing your lesson to the class

In groups of 4, each take a different lesson or Unit from the English Language coursebook that you use, or will be using. Isolate a new teaching item. Then consider what might have been taught in the previous lesson; the previous lesson's teaching point will be your revision item. For both items, note down (a) exactly what forms the students learnt in the previous lesson, and what they will be learning next lesson (b) in what contexts or situations you have taught the old forms and will teach the new forms (c) a few activities you will use this lesson. (Define your aims as discussed in the Preliminary Discussion, 1.) Ask your tutor if you need help.

- Look back at the CLASSROOM LANGUAGE section, and the dialogues, and work out how to express your own aims and intentions to your class in a similar way, but using the teaching items from your coursebook instead of the items suggested here.

- You can use the pictures or aids that could have been used in the previous lesson, so that students can recall* the item you wish to revise.

- Plan to begin your role play from the time you walk into the classroom. You do not need to take the register as it seems everyone is present, so you begin with a little informal chat about something topical, then carry on to announce your plans for that lesson.

- Plan to end when you have stated your plans and aims in terms that the students will understand, and have just begun actually revising the previously taught item.

- When you have finished planning your role play, *rearrange* your groups so that, as far as possible, each person in each *new* group comes from a different group, and has therefore planned the introduction to a different lesson. (Regrouping here makes it a more varied and interesting activity as well as more useful. It also creates a genuine need for communication as members of other groups do not know what has been planned in every other group.)

- Each 'teacher' in turn should have about 3–4 minutes. ('Teachers' should tell their peer group at what level the class is supposed to act, and which point of the coursebook they have reached during the previous lesson, so that they can perform their roles as realistically as possible.)

- Remember to jot down any errors in English you hear, for checking out later.

2 Follow up and evaluation

 (a) Keeping to the same groups discuss how successful you were. How confident did your 'students' feel after you had introduced your lesson? Did they really understand what they would be learning during the course of your lesson?

(b) Jot down any useful ideas that you could use when teaching similar lessons in the future.

 (c) As a class, check out any language points which you were not sure of during the role play, or which caused difficulty.

Unit 6 Using visual aids

The aims of this Unit are **1** to train teachers how to use English effectively while setting up and referring to simple visual aids* **2** to show how simple visual aids can be used for language work that is teacher initiated but more student centred. Note: See Part Two, Unit 15 for a more detailed study of language specific to individual visual aids.
You will need 1 a large magazine picture or poster or wall chart, one per person, which you do not show to each other until the Exploitation Section **2** flash cards* with pictures **3** a selection of other visual aids you could use

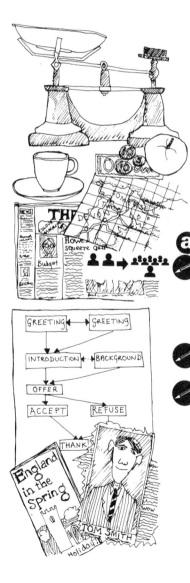

ⓐ Preliminary discussion

1 In what ways can visual aids be a help to teachers and learners of English? (Give at least four reasons and exemplify them.)

2 How could you use some of the following visual aids in your lessons? – wall charts or posters, maps and diagrams, flash cards, cue* cards, blackboard drawings, magazine pictures, information brochures or pamphlets, magnet board*, flannel board*, realia*, etc.

3 Which visual aids do you find most useful at the presentation stage* of a lesson, and how would you use them? Give examples.

4 How can flash cards, wall charts, and realia be used for student centred work; i.e. work where the teacher does not begin or lead the activity? This usually happens at the practice* and production stages of the lesson, after the presentation stage. (See Unit 17.)

5 How and where do you normally display large pictures, wall charts, and realia? If you ask a student to help you, what do you say?

6 How do you make sure that your students' attention is directed to the correct part of the picture you want them to look at?

7 In order to get them more involved, some teachers ask their *students* to prepare some of the aids needed in lessons. Could you do this with your students? (e.g. asking them to cut out magazine pictures to bring to class, or asking them to draw something on the board or help you mount* magazine pictures, etc.)?

ⓑ Dialogue practice

1 Dialogues

Listen to these dialogues on tape, then listen again, this time repeating the teacher's part, concentrating on fluency and intonation.

 (a) At school

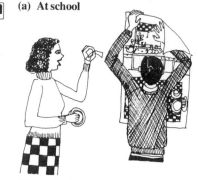

The teacher has brought a poster into class.

T: Could someone fix this picture up on the wall, please? Just there....
Ss: Me! I will! Could I?...
T: OK. Could you, please? Here's the sticky tape. Thanks.
S: Here?
T: Well, I think it needs to be a bit higher up. Can you reach?
S: Sorry, I...
T: Not really. Well never mind; ask someone taller to help you.... Go on! 'Would you...'
S: Ali? Will you help me please?
S2: Yes, of course.... Like this?
T: Lovely! Good, well done. That looks nice.

 TEACHING HINT Why does the picture need to be higher up? And why does the teacher ask this particular student to fix it up, even though she knows that she is too short to reach high enough?

 (b) At college

The teacher is holding some flash cards.

T: Now, we're going to do some pair work, using these flash cards. Could someone hand them out, please? Pass them round?
S: I will.
T: Thank you. You'll need *one* between *two* people. One card per pair, just *one* to start with.
S: ... Please, cards ... er ... finish.
T: Oh, you mean there aren't enough? There aren't enough? Well, there are some more on my desk. Could you get some more from my desk? Thanks.

 TEACHING HINT The teacher did not give the student enough flash cards on purpose. Why do you think he did this? Did he correct his student's mistake, his incorrect use of 'finish'? Why?

2 Language activities

(a) Reading from substitution tables

 When you use language from substitution tables, do you speak as fluently and naturally as you do normally? Or do you pause between the different parts of the tables? In other words, when saying phrases or sentences from tables, do you sound as if you are reading rather than speaking?

– Using the tables in the next Section, practise with your neighbour, who will tell you if the way you are speaking sounds like natural spoken English or if you are getting the stress and intonation wrong. Remember:
– Look at the table
– Select a sentence
– Then look up and say it as fluently and naturally as possible

(b) Rephrasing practice

See Unit 2, Section **b**, **2**, and then Unit 12, Section **b**, for a good game.
- Read through the second dialogue on this page and notice how many times the teacher rephrases what he says.
- Now look at the first dialogue on page 40. Imagine that this teacher has another lesson with less advanced children. She will use the same language but she will have to repeat and rephrase everything she says, at least once before they understand. Work out how she could do this and then practise with your neighbour, taking turns to be the teacher with a slow student.

© Classroom language

Practise in pairs, using pictures and other items mentioned to refer to. Make at least 6 sentences, all different, from each table. Table 6 should yield 10 or more.
NB Some tables contain both singular and plural nouns, so be careful to select suitable articles and pronouns.

Displaying visual aids

1

Could Would Will	someone you	go and fetch bring me find get out	the that a	wall chart(s) of the_____ set(s) of flash cards of food and drink magazine picture(s) of people flannel board(s) and figurines	?
Now, look. I've		got brought	these some	box(es) of_____ folder(s) of cue cards	

2

Has anybody seen We need	the	sellotape? sticky tape? blutac? drawing pins? scissors?	They're It's	to	stick this up with. fix this picture up with. cut these out with.
				for	sticking this up. fixing these up. cutting these out.

3

Please could you OK, I'll	put fix stick hang	it them	up here.	Is that	alright? straight? high enough?
				Can you **all** see it?	

4

Could you	give hand pass	these	magazine pictures flash cards cue cards	out please?	One Two Three	each. per pair. between 2.

Referring to visual aids

5

Take Have	a good look at the	poster. picture.	What Why Where How	do you think_____	_____? _____? _____?

6

Look at Tell me about What about	the	people buildings scenery surroundings _____ _____ section	on the left on the right in the middle in the centre at the top at the bottom	of the	poster. picture. diagram, etc.
			in the top right-hand corner. in the bottom left-hand corner.		

7

Now let's I'm going to	rub the picture off.
	take it down.

8

Can you remember	what	**was** happening?
I want you to tell me		happened? had happened earlier?

Clearing up

9

Would someone I'm going to	take	it them	down	now and put	it them	on my desk. away.
	collect the_____s in					back in the_____

 or

Test yourself

What would you say (and/or do) if you wanted

(a) someone to fetch three sets of cue-cards (say which ones and where from).

(b) a student to offer to fetch two sets of cue-cards.

(c) to ask a student to pin up a poster for you. Make him/her ask for the drawing pins.

(d) to ask a student to collect in, sort out and put away (say where) the different sets of cue-cards they had been using.

(e) someone to offer to collect in the cue-cards for you, and to ask where to put them.

(f) someone to find the sticky tape to fix up a picture for you.

(g) your students to collect magazine pictures from home or friends for your next lesson. Say what kind and size of picture.

(h) students to clear up and put away all the aids you had used in class.

(i) a student to fix up a wall chart before the beginning of the next lesson. Let the student ask which one and where to put it.

℮ Exploitation

1 Unexploited dialogue

Mr Short has brought a wall picture into class. His class sits in silence as he puts it up. He could have involved his students in many ways, but he didn't. Which ways?

T: Right. Quiet, please! I've got a wall chart to show you today.

Ss: ....

T: *(while he finds the sellotape)* er... Here it is. *(poster slips down)* Oh dear. *(applies more tape)* There. Now, look.

2 Possibilities for exploitation

Here in the 'balloons' are some ideas he could have used to involve his students and get them to use English purposefully. Draw lines to link each balloon with the relevant part of the monologue on the left.

T: [Holds rolled-up poster] Who can guess what this picture is of? Yes?
S: Shops?
T: No. Yes, Kumah?
S: People?
T: Yes. Where do you think they are?
S: --------------------

TEACHER PROVOKES STUDENTS' INTEREST WITH GUESSING GAME.

T: Right. Now I've got everything I need, where shall I put it up? Here?
SS: No.
T: Why?
SS: We can't see it.
T: Why?
SS: Too--- er--- down. Too low. Oh, you need it a bit higher, like this?
T: Not straight----- etc.
SS:

TEACHER INVOLVES HIS CLASS IN THE POSITIONING OF THE POSTER.

T: Now what do I need to fix this up on the wall?
S: Pins?
T: Drawing pins? I haven't got any. I've run out.
S: Sticky tape?
T: Yes — could you get it for me please?
S: Excuse me, where is it?
T: Oh, I keep it in that drawer.

TEACHER DELIBERATELY MAKES IT DIFFICULT, SO THE STUDENTS HAVE TO ASK FOR THINGS. TEACHER ALSO USES IDIOMATIC LANGUAGE HIS STUDENTS WILL ONLY UNDERSTAND FROM THIS SITUATION.

WHERE SHALL I PUT IT? HERE?

★ Chance for a laugh

3 Oral practice

In groups of 3 or 4.

(a) Find a picture your group have not seen before. Ask them to guess as accurately as possible the contents of the picture. If it is not too detailed you could ask them to draw a rough sketch from the information they receive from you. Of course they can ask you questions to find out further details, as they draw. Then they can compare their sketches with the original picture.

(b) Practise getting someone else to fix your picture up on the wall or board, using as much language as possible (refer back to the 'balloons'). Try to put your students in situations where they are obliged to talk, e.g. give them 2 pictures so they have to ask which one to fix up; hide the sticky tape or tell them the wrong place to find it so they have to ask again and explain.

(c) Make up a list of teachable language items that are often used in situations like the ones above. Which particular patterns did your group use a lot while they were carrying out **2** above? Then refer to Appendix A.

4 Sample exploitation

There are three short extracts here, on tape. In (a) the teacher is about to use a picture to present something new. In (b) it is at the end of that stage and the board is covered with pictures and writing, and very untidy; hence the use of the words 'clear up'. In (c) they're in another room which has a white board, not a blackboard. A student called Philip has just cleaned it.

Listen and try to identify what the teacher is aiming to practise in each case.

ℯ Role play

1 Activity
Setting up your visual aids

- Share out as many different visual aids as possible between your groups (of 6 to 8 people) so that each group has a selection of aids to use. Decide what language item you could teach using each aid.

- The aim of this activity is to give you practice in (a) using language effectively yourselves and (b) creating opportunities for your students to use language purposefully, while setting up the visual aids you will be using in the next part of the lesson.

- Begin by introducing this new stage in the lesson (see Unit 5) and plan to end your role play when you have asked one or two questions similar to those in Table 6 (Classroom Language Section) i.e. when everything is ready for you to begin to introduce the new teaching item. (See Part Two, Units 14, 15 and 16, for language more specific to individual aids and teaching items.)

- Time limit: set a limit which suits you, about 3 or 4 minutes per 'teacher' depending on the aids in use.

- Take turns being the 'teacher', try to use different visual aids each time or at least, if you have to use a similar aid to someone else, try to exploit it in a different way, with a different aim in mind.

- Remember the aim of this activity! See above.

2 Follow up and evaluation

(a) In your own groups, decide amongst yourselves which 'teachers' most successfully achieved the aim stated above. Discuss why.

(b) Split up and re-form into different groups so that each new group has at least one representative from each old group; he will then report on the most successful ideas produced by his old group.

NB Before this 'reporting' session begins, it would be useful to have all the visual aids used displayed on the walls around the room so that the 'reporters' will be able to refer to them while 'reporting'.

𝘧 Further reading

The best and clearest book on this subject is Andrew Wright (1976).

Sections in the following works give a brief summary of visual aids and some good ideas for preparing and use.
Donn Byrne (1976) pp. 37, 38, 56, 57, 60–67, 72–73, 84–91, 109–111, 116–120, 128–137.

John Haycraft (1978) pp. 97–109.

Helen Moorwood (ed) (1978) Section 6, pp. 75–89.

Unit 7 Tape recorders and other electrical equipment

The aims of this Unit are **1** to train teachers to use English effectively when handling electrical equipment in the classroom **2** to evaluate, from the linguistic point of view, the relative advantages and various uses of particular audio*/visual aids.

You will need **1** any audio or audio/visual aids that you may be able to use in the classroom (see list in 1 below) **2** materials to make cue cards for the role play activity (thick paper or card, scissors, felt tips)

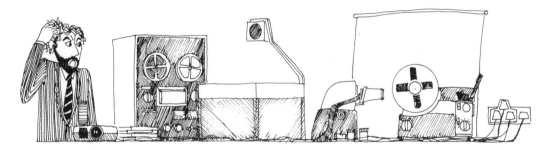

ⓐ Preliminary discussion

1 Which of the following pieces of equipment do you have access to in your school or college? tape recorder, overhead projector, slide projector, film projector, cine loop projector, video cassette player, audio lab. or listening centre. (If you feel you need to find out more about some of these audio or audio/visual aids please refer to the Further Reading Section at the end of this Unit.)

2 How do/could you use some of these in your lessons to help your students learn English?

3 The most basic piece of equipment is usually considered to be the tape recorder with suitable taped materials. How can students benefit from their teacher using tapes in the classroom?

4 If you intend to use a tape recorder in your classes, which of the visual aids mentioned in Unit 6 could you use with the taped material to make it more interesting and memorable?

5 What resources do you have in your country for borrowing records, tapes, films, slides and projectors for use in your schools or colleges? Are there any suitable materials for your students? How could you set about borrowing such things? What might your students gain from them?

6 One way of giving your classes more practice in listening and exposing them to English spoken in a meaningful situation is to talk about what you are doing when handling equipment in the classroom. What things could you say in English while setting up and preparing to use a tape recorder in your lesson?

(See also Unit 18 on Listening Skills.)

ⓑ Dialogue practice

1 Dialogues

Listen carefully to these two dialogues. Pay particular attention to the intonation patterns the teachers use. Notice whether they are rising or falling patterns. Then practise repeating the teacher's part after the tape until you can say it in exactly the same way.

(a) At school

The teacher is about to set up the tape recorder.

T: You're going to hear a dialogue on tape now. See these two people in the picture? Well, we're going to hear them talking about their party. Who can plug the tape recorder in for me?
S: I will.
T: Thanks. Now what do I have to do?
S: Switch it on.
T: Yes. I have to switch it on here. See? This knob. Right, I've put the cassette in, now let's see if I can find the right place on the tape.... Listen now and see if you can hear where Unit Ten begins....

TEACHING HINT How does the teacher keep the students interested and involved while she is setting the tape recorder up?

(b) At college

The teacher gets his class to tell him how to set up the overhead projector.

T: I want to discuss some of these pictures now so we'll need the O.H.P., the overhead projector. Can you tell me what I have to do first?
S: Electricity.
T: Well, do I have to switch it on first or plug it in?
S: Plug in.
T: Plug it in, good. Can you say that? Come on! You have to ... everyone!
S: You have to plug it in.
T: Good. Well, I've plugged it in. Now what?
S: er you have to switch it ...
T: switch it on, on. Everyone! You have....
Ss: You have to switch it on.
T: That's it. Now I'll adjust the mirrors.... Oh dear, the picture's upside down! How silly!

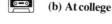

TEACHING HINT Why does the teacher ask an 'either/or' type question when a student produces the word 'electricity'?

2 Language activities

Forward and backward chaining* (for pronunciation practice)

A good way of helping a class achieve fluency is by breaking a sentence up into sections and getting them to repeat longer and longer parts of it.

With forward chaining you start from the beginning of the sentence and work forwards, whereas with backward chaining you start at the end and work backwards. Building up the sentence in this way means that you can keep to natural speed and normal stress patterns without the class finding it too difficult. An example follows.

This is a line from a dialogue between two people at a party. It is rather long and the class were having difficulty repeating it in one go:

/'I'm terribly sorry,/I'm afraid/I've broken/one of your/lovely/glasses.'/

First, practise it with your neighbour, completing each chain. Then make up some of your own and try them out on each other.

Forward chaining	Backward chaining
T: I'm terribly sorry	T: glasses
Ss: I'm terribly sorry	Ss: glasses
T: I'm terribly sorry, I'm afraid	T: lovely glasses
Ss: I'm terribly sorry, I'm afraid	Ss: lovely glasses
T: I'm terribly sorry, I'm afraid I've broken, etc.	T: one of your lovely glasses, etc.

C Classroom language

Read through these tables and work out exactly when you would need to use the language they contain, e.g. Table 3: after switching the tape recorder or projector on. Label them yourselves by writing a heading above each table. Then practise the language relevant to your teaching situation, in pairs.

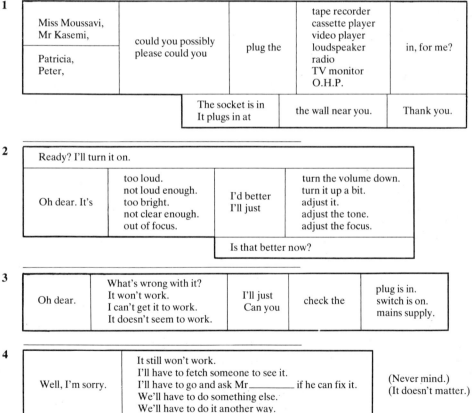

1

Miss Moussavi, Mr Kasemi, Patricia, Peter,	could you possibly please could you	plug the	tape recorder cassette player video player loudspeaker radio TV monitor O.H.P.	in, for me?
	The socket is in It plugs in at		the wall near you.	Thank you.

2

Ready? I'll turn it on.

Oh dear. It's	too loud. not loud enough. too bright. not clear enough. out of focus.	I'd better I'll just	turn the volume down. turn it up a bit. adjust it. adjust the tone. adjust the focus.
		Is that better now?	

3

Oh dear.	What's wrong with it? It won't work. I can't get it to work. It doesn't seem to work.	I'll just Can you	check the	plug is in. switch is on. mains supply.

4

Well, I'm sorry.	It still won't work. I'll have to fetch someone to see it. I'll have to go and ask Mr_____ if he can fix it. We'll have to do something else. We'll have to do it another way.	(Never mind.) (It doesn't matter.)

5

Oh. It's OK now? Good; that's better. Thank goodness! Now, wait a little	Let's I'll just	find the right get the correct find the	place on the tape. radio wavelength. picture.
	There we are. We can begin now.		

6

Did you	catch that? understand?	I'll go back and play it again. I'll let you hear it again before I ask you those questions. We'll go back and listen again. Ready?
That was a bit fast.		

7

OK. Alright.	We've finished with the O.H.P. now. We don't need the tape recorder anymore.	Could someone	unplug it take the plug out switch it off at the wall	please?

The following tables contain instructions for using a tape recorder. They apply to both individual listening work and group work in an audio laboratory.

8

First Then After that	you you have to	insert the tape and check it is rewound, back to the start. wind the tape on to the empty spool. set the counter to 000 at the beginning of the tape. press the PLAY switch/button/control and listen.

9

If you want to In order to	find a section further ahead, press STOP then FAST FORWARD then STOP and check the place. go back, press REWIND then STOP and check the place. adjust the volume, you turn this knob, the volume control.

10

At the end of the lesson	always remember to	rewind your tape back to the start. put it away in the correct box. replace the tape recorder and the tapes.

Test yourself

What can you say to your pupils or students if . . .

(a) you want someone to plug the tape recorder in for you? (say why you can't do it yourself)

(b) the piece of equipment you are using won't work?

(c) the students can't hear the tape very well?

(d) you have to find the right place on the tape?

(e) you have got the wrong place on the tape?

(f) after playing the tape through once your students haven't understood?

(g) you have finished using the O.H.P. or tape recorder?

(h) you want to keep talking as you set the tape recorder up, to give your students a bit of extra listening practice?

ⓓ Exploitation

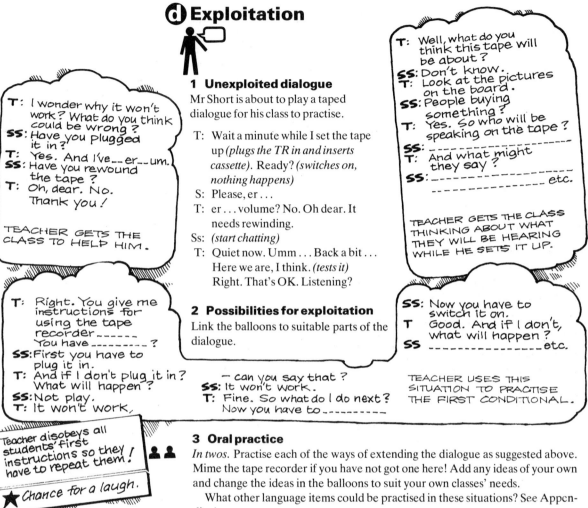

T: I wonder why it won't work? What do you think could be wrong?
SS: Have you plugged it in?
T: Yes. And I've__ er__ um.
SS: Have you rewound the tape?
T: Oh, dear. No. Thank you!

TEACHER GETS THE CLASS TO HELP HIM.

T: Right. You give me instructions for using the tape recorder_____ You have _____?
SS: First you have to plug it in.
T: And if I don't plug it in? What will happen?
SS: Not play.
T: It won't work.

Teacher disobeys all students' first instructions so they have to repeat them!

★ Chance for a laugh.

1 Unexploited dialogue

Mr Short is about to play a taped dialogue for his class to practise.

T: Wait a minute while I set the tape up *(plugs the TR in and inserts cassette)*. Ready? *(switches on, nothing happens)*
S: Please, er ...
T: er ... volume? No. Oh dear. It needs rewinding.
Ss: *(start chatting)*
T: Quiet now. Umm ... Back a bit ... Here we are, I think. *(tests it)* Right. That's OK. Listening?

2 Possibilities for exploitation

Link the balloons to suitable parts of the dialogue.

— can you say that?
SS: It won't work.
T: Fine. So what do I do next? Now you have to _____

T: Well, what do you think this tape will be about?
SS: Don't know.
T: Look at the pictures on the board.
SS: People buying something?
T: Yes. So who will be speaking on the tape?
SS: _____
T: And what might they say?
SS: _____ etc.

TEACHER GETS THE CLASS THINKING ABOUT WHAT THEY WILL BE HEARING WHILE HE SETS IT UP.

SS: Now you have to switch it on.
T Good. And if I don't, what will happen?
SS _____ etc.

TEACHER USES THIS SITUATION TO PRACTISE THE FIRST CONDITIONAL.

3 Oral practice

In twos. Practise each of the ways of extending the dialogue as suggested above. Mime the tape recorder if you have not got one here! Add any ideas of your own and change the ideas in the balloons to suit your own classes' needs.

What other language items could be practised in these situations? See Appendix A.

4 Sample exploitation

Using the tape recorder[1]

The teacher is going to play her class the tape of a song that she wants them to learn. However, first she asks them to give her instructions for setting it up. The class have done this before, very simply, and are familiar with words like switch, tape and recorder. They have just learnt the *'going to'* form to express intended action, but do not know the use of *'have to'* in the sense of *'must'*. Here the teacher uses the *'have to'* form as often as she can, naturally, in order to familiarise her students with it. They obviously understand from the context what it means and how it is used, so when they come to learn it later on they will pick it up easily.

(See Unit 5, Section **d**, 2 (b).)

– Listen and see how many examples of *'have to'* she uses, and how many different forms she introduces.
– She also uses two different ways of expressing the same idea, of necessity. Did you notice which?

[1] The tape recorder being used in this class was an open reel one, not a cassette, hence the need for the word 'spool'.

ⓔ Role play
1 Activity

If possible, assemble all the equipment that you may be able to use at some time or another in your lessons. If some pieces of equipment are unobtainable, try to get pictures of similar equipment from magazines or catalogues.

If you have a spare tape recorder with microphone, **record yourselves** doing these activities, then play them back during the Follow Up session, for evaluation.

– First practise in pairs with the equipment or the pictures, asking for information, and giving each other instructions for operating the controls: 'How do you make it louder?' 'What's that switch for?' etc. 'If you turn that knob, it'll adjust the volume' or 'Press that button to turn it on'.

– Next, make cue cards (¼ foolscap size) containing the following cue words. (Adapt if necessary to suit equipment and conditions in your country.)

tape recorder but traffic noise from open window. loud speaker not connected. wrong place on tape. (a)	*slide projector* but the first slides are in the wrong order, the room is too light, and the fan is noisy. (c)	*radio* but the tone and volume are wrong. needs tuning in. (e)
video cassette player it won't work. you have the wrong plugs in. wrong place on tape. (b)	*OHP* but light won't go on even after bulb has been checked. it needs moving to a more central position in the room. (d)	*TV/English language programme* need help tuning it in and adjusting the contrast. (f)

– Then in groups of 4 or 5, select a 'teacher' who takes one of the cue cards, and the appropriate picture. He needs to use whatever piece of equipment is on the cue card but he has to cope with the difficulties given. He can ask his class to help, if he needs to. He should keep talking while he sets it up, to keep the class from getting bored.

– Remember you need to mime setting up the tape or the slides; getting the right place on the tape or checking the slides are in order. Keep talking. Tell the class what you are doing and why.

– Begin your role play by announcing to the class what they are going to do today; plug in, switch on, set it up correctly, test it.

– End your role play after you have tested it, by announcing that it is ready and asking for their full attention.

Alternative or additional activity: a game to play
JUST A MINUTE

Take the same situation as that outlined in the above role play activity.

One person in each group acts as time-keeper, one person is the teacher, the rest of the group act as the class. The teacher must try to talk for one minute about what he or she is doing, i.e. setting up a piece of equipment for use in class, without pausing for more than 5 seconds, without repeating what he or she has said before (though rephrasing is permitted) and without speaking unnaturally slowly.

The time-keeper should state the time every 15 seconds and time any pauses to make sure they do not exceed 5 seconds, and say STOP after one minute.

The class should shout out TOO SLOW or REPETITION or PAUSE if they think a rule has been broken, and vote on it if it is not unanimous. For the purposes of this game, the teacher should not address any questions to the class at all.

You can also play this in pairs or threes. The teacher is allowed to ask questions but the students must answer immediately and no gaps may be left between speakers. Each group has a go while the others time them; the winners are the ones who continued the longest without a pause.

2 Follow up and evaluation

(a) Discuss in groups what 'teachers' found most difficult to do.
(b) Look in Appendix A to see what other possibilities for exploitation there are and discuss which of these would best suit your students' needs.
(c) Discuss also how you could integrate these ideas into your lesson.

 # Further reading

Donn Byrne (1976) pp. 137–140.

John Haycraft (1978) pp. 109–111; also some basic information on different types of Language Laboratories, pp. 111–116.

Finocchiaro, M and Bonomo, M (1973).

Helen Moorwood (ed) (1978) section 6 pp. 67–74.

Unit 8 Dividing the class up: choral individual and teams

The aims of this Unit are 1 to enable teachers to combine spoken language with gesture in order to give effective instructions to their classes when dividing them up 2 to show teachers how the normal classroom procedure (teacher asking, student responding) can be varied, to make the lesson interesting and motivating (e.g. a textbook exercise can be done in teams, competitively)
You will need character cards for role play activity

ⓐ Preliminary discussion

1 Calculate the following: if a teacher only asks individual students to respond or perform in English, (doing no choral, group or pair work) for how many minutes will the average student have spoken English

    (a) in each lesson? —————— Write your

    (b) in a week? —————— calculations here.

    (c) in a term? ——————

    (d) by the end of his English course? ——————

2 (a) What are the advantages of choral work?
    (b) What are the disadvantages of choral work?
    (c) Can you think of any ways to overcome these disadvantages? Which?

3 How can gesture help the teacher to organise choral responses?

4 What are the dangers of doing mainly choral work in class with little individual response or pair work or small group work?

5 How fair are you as a teacher? When asking individuals to respond or perform, do you ever ask one or two students more than once when others still have not had a turn? Do you look longer at one side of the class than the other?

6 (a) Describe a few activities which can be carried out with the class divided into halves or teams. What would you say to your class when dividing them up for these activities?
    (b) Children in Britain often enjoy team games and competitions in their foreign language classes, and adults do too, though obviously different types of games would be suitable for adult learners. What about children and adult learners in your country?

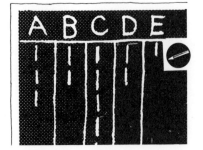

ⓑ Dialogue practice

1 Dialogue

In this Unit the one dialogue is suitable for both adult learners and children.

First, listen to this dialogue and imagine what gestures the teacher is using as she speaks to her class. Then listen again, repeating the teacher's part and making appropriate gestures yourselves. (Stand up to do this.) Finally, practise the dialogue in threes, standing up, taking turns to take the teacher's part. Remember that the gestures used by the teacher are as important as the language itself.

At school or college

T: Right, I now want you to repeat parts of the dialogue. All together, *(gesture)*, after me. Ready? 'Could you come on Monday?'

Ss: *(raggedly)* 'Could you come on Monday?'

T: Oh dear! That wasn't very good.... Let's do it again. All of you, but keep together, and quietly! 'Could you come on Monday?' *(gesture)*

Ss: 'Could you come on Monday?'

T: Better, good. Now again but quickly. Listen! 'Could you come on Monday?' *(gesture)*

Ss: 'Could you come on Monday?'

T: Good. OK, you, Kumah? Yes, by yourself....

S: er!...Could you come...er...on Monday?'

T: Fine. Now, Ali? Come on, on your own. 'Could...'

S: Umm. 'Could you come in Monday?'

T: On Monday, on. *(gesture)*

S: On Monday.

T: Good, now in halves. *(gesture)* I'll divide you down the middle, here. Now, you *(gesture)* can ask and you, this side, can answer. So you say 'Could you come on Monday?' and this side says, 'I'm sorry, I'm afraid I can't.' OK, this side, repeat the answer, 'I'm sorry, I'm afraid I can't'. *(gesture)* etc.

The teacher has presented a dialogue with the help of a picture, and discussed what it means. She has read it out to the class and now wants the students to practise the more difficult parts in chorus.

TEACHING HINT Why do you think the teacher asks two individuals to say the sentence after the class has repeated it well in chorus? Why does she ask Ali to say it after Kumah?

2 Language activities

Gesture

(a) Using gesture only (without speaking) select five of the following instructions and communicate them to your neighbour. See if he or she can guess which they are.

Be quiet and listen.	Everyone, listen and repeat.	No, stop.
All of you, together.	Come on, you as well. You!	Now in halves.
Not very good. Again!	In halves, you first, then you.	Again but quickly.

(b) How do you gesture 'No' in your country? In Britain and America we shake our heads to say 'No', and nod for 'Yes'. Are there any gestures that you know are different in English? Watch for them on films if you have the chance.

Forward and backward chaining (See Unit 7, Section **b**, **2**, for details)

Practise some more backchaining in groups of three or four, using the following sentences. Take care not to stress the weak forms.

They are/both/taller than me.
They ran/to school/as quickly/as they could.
If he hadn't been ill,/he wouldn't have/failed/his exam.

Ⓒ **Classroom language**

In pairs, take turns to read out the groups of phrases and sentences from the tables below as clearly and firmly as you can, working out what gestures would be suitable to accompany each sentence. Choose appropriate language for your students and keep it lively. Rephrase often, and use suitable gestures.

Choral response

1

I want I'd like	all of you you all everybody the whole class this half that half one of you just one person	to	answer this question. repeat this sentence. continue this sentence. correct my statements. read the next sentence.

Don't put your hands up. All together. Everybody! Listen! Ready? Listen and answer, quietly.

Everyone can try. Come on. Yes, you as well. And you. All together but quietly! A bit quieter please!

2

No! Oh dear	that wasn't	very clear! very good! all together! quiet enough!	Let's Shall we	do it try it	again. Ready?

Individual response

Now one at a time. Not all together. Listen before you answer.
Hands up before you answer!
Could you put your hands up before you answer, please?

Yes, a good answer. But a bit louder please. Again? ...

Now this time, don't put your hands up. I'll point.
Everybody can try, but one at a time. I'll ask *one* of you.
Don't shout out. Ready? Quiet. Listening?

You can take turns.
You can all have a go, ... have a turn, ... but one after the other.
One by one. Right?

Taking turns

In groups of four. Take turns to read out 3 or 4 sentences from each of the tables below. Remember to stress the important words. Normally, these will be words like: 'you', 'her', 'yours', 'hers', etc., or a name. As before, use suitable gestures.

3

It's	their your his her	go turn	first, second, third,	then now	it's **your**	go turn	and so on.

4

It's	Rosa you	first. next.	Now	you. Kumah.	Quickly!	That's it. Good.

5

Whose	go turn	was it? is it?	Not yours. It's hers/his.	You be quick! Come on!	(Mine.) (Hers.) (His.)

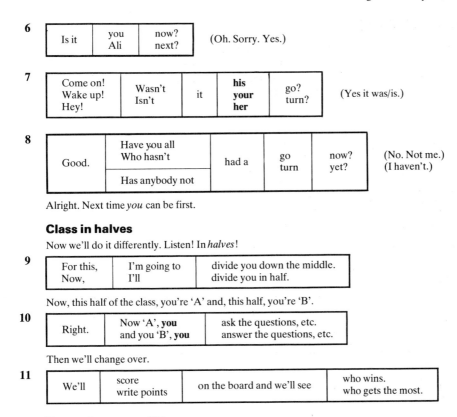

6

| Is it | you / Ali | now? / next? | (Oh. Sorry. Yes.) |

7

| Come on! / Wake up! / Hey! | Wasn't / Isn't | it | **his** / **your** / **her** | go? / turn? | (Yes it was/is.) |

8

| Good. | Have you all / Who hasn't | had a | go / turn | now? / yet? | (No. Not me.) / (I haven't.) |
| | Has anybody not | | | | |

Alright. Next time *you* can be first.

Class in halves

Now we'll do it differently. Listen! In *halves*!

9

| For this, / Now, | I'm going to / I'll | divide you down the middle. / divide you in half. |

Now, this half of the class, you're 'A' and, this half, you're 'B'.

10

| Right. | Now 'A', **you** / and you 'B', **you** | ask the questions, etc. / answer the questions, etc. |

Then we'll change over.

11

| We'll | score / write points | on the board and we'll see | who wins. / who gets the most. |

Teams for competitions

Now we can have a competition, with teams.
For this, we're going to have *teams*, going from front to back.
4 teams.
6 teams. Starting from *here*.
Each team! Please will you number off?
You're 1, you're 2 and so on. Number off, down the team.

Hands up, all number *ones*! Ready?
Now, we have 4, (5, 6) teams. A B C D E F etc.
I'll call a number; only that number can do it.
We need you in pairs within your teams.
Each team, pair off.
In pairs, number off.

12

| OK. Now | wait / listen | while I explain | how to play. / what we're going to do. |

See Units 15 and 17.

13

| Which team can | answer / do what I say / do it | first? / best? |

14

| Remember your numbers. We'll | keep the score. / see who gets the highest score. / have points. / see who gets the most points. / see which team wins. |

Test yourselves in groups of 5 or 6, taking turns to organise and play, in 2 teams, a competitive game, like GLUG, see page 132. The teams ask questions in turn until one team guesses.

Exploitation

1 Revision

 Review the EXPLOITATION Sections of Units 4, 5, and 6, paying particular attention to Unit 4. As you do so, decide which of those Units this Unit has more in common with, as regards possibilities for exploitation.

2 As in Units 4 and 5 the language in this Unit does not lend itself to exploitation because in this situation most teachers would want to get on with the practice of the language item being taught.

However using English in this situation is still very useful. The students get used to obeying instructions in English and much of this English is commonly used outside the classroom as well as inside. They will get used to reacting to English instructions and will not panic if they find themselves in similar situations later on in their lives.

3 Oral practice

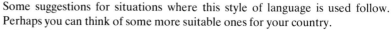 Some suggestions for situations where this style of language is used follow. Perhaps you can think of some more suitable ones for your country.

– In suitably sized groups, act out one or two of these situations in English; don't forget to speak English while organising yourselves!

(a) You are asked to organise a party for ten to twelve year old children whose common language is English. Think of some games they could play, or songs they could sing together and each of you organise the rest of your group to play or sing together, taking one game or song each.
(See Unit 17, Section **d**.)

(b) Imagine you are all waiting in a doctor's waiting room or a hospital Out-Patients Department. Nobody knows whose turn it is to see the doctor next so the nurse or receptionist comes in to tell everyone when their turn is. Some patients argue, because they think they arrived before others, but some patients have made appointments beforehand and so do not need to wait so long ... etc.

4 Student language needed

– Make a list of all major language items your students will need if they are to feel confident speaking English in the classroom while taking part in team games and competitions. Decide at what stage in their English programme you could introduce each item for active use.

– When you have made your list, look up the list suggested in Appendix A for this Unit and see if perhaps any of those items would also be useful for your students to know. Then have a look at Appendix B for other student language relevant.

5 A game to play

HOW MANY QUESTIONS – a team game.
In teams of 4 or 6, elect a secretary.

Your tutor will write an interesting sentence on the board, then say GO! On the word GO each team writes down as many questions (all different) as they can think of, based on that sentence. The winners are the team who produce the highest number of correct (and answerable) questions in the set time, OR the first team to write down 10 good questions. Only the 'secretary' is allowed to write; the rest of the team can dictate their questions, then take turns at being 'secretary'.

e Role play

1 Preparation for role play

Dialogue preparation for use in role play activity

- Each person should take a different Lesson or Unit from the textbook they will be using in their English classes and write a simple four or five line dialogue, in natural appropriate English, to practise one of the teaching points in that lesson.
- When you have written it, read it out loud so that you can judge how natural it sounds when spoken, then give it to your neighbour to check over and try out.
- At the end of the role play session, select all the dialogues that worked well and sounded natural. Try to get them typed up and copies distributed to everyone, so they can be used again and again in school or college classes.

2 Activity

Varying the patterns of response

In groups of 8 or 10.

- Find one of the four line dialogues that you have prepared yourself and had corrected. Find a suitable picture or wall chart to contextualise it, or draw a quick line drawing on a piece of card.

(a) First get the 'class' to listen and repeat the dialogue clearly in chorus, in halves and as individuals.

(b) Then ask some questions about the picture and the meaning of the dialogue, again asking the 'class' to respond together, or taking turns to answer individually.

- Use relevant gestures to help the 'class' know what they should do.
- Keep the pace up, as fast as possible until they get tired.
- Each 'teacher' should use a different dialogue and picture.
- Allow 5 minutes only per 'teacher'.
- Role play cards can be used; some 'students' should pretend to be rather slow, others sleepy, some too noisy and others too forward and talkative.
- Read 3 below *before* you begin so you know what to look for when someone else is teaching.

3 Evaluation

In your groups, discuss whether each 'teacher' gave equal attention to all the 'students' in the class. Did any 'teacher' have a tendency to look more at one side of the class than the other? Did all 'teachers' vary their positions occasionally, perhaps to give some extra help to one student or group of students?

In which areas, if any, did you have difficulties with language? Check these out with your tutor.

f Further reading

Donn Byrne (1976) pp. 32–34.

Unit 9 Dividing the class up: pairs and groups

The aims of this Unit are **1** to enable teachers to use English as economically as possible while organising group and pair work **2** to establish the value and uses of group and pair work.
You will need magazine pictures showing two people talking. Other pictures showing objects or things the people could be talking about (e.g. a watch, a car, football, clothes etc. *or* any other visual aids suitable for the role play)

ⓐ Preliminary discussion

1 (a) To do pair work, students are paired off into twos, and each pair practises at the same time as the other pairs. The teacher usually walks round the class and listens to as many of the pairs as she can. What advantages can oral pair work have over choral work or individual responses at the practice and production stages of the lesson?

(b) Listen to the example of pair work on the tape. Discuss what stage of the lesson this could be at, practice or production. What's the teacher doing?

2 (a) Which of these activities could you usefully get your students to do in pairs? Say why.
to practise a set dialogue from a set of cues on the blackboard
to practise a substitution dialogue
writing their own dialogues, using a model or substitution table
structural practice, using a 'question and answer' technique
exercises from the textbook, orally
writing a description of someone they both know

(b) At what stage in the lesson would you use them? And for what purpose?

3 How can a teacher use group work to practise (a) oral skills? (b) written skills? Consider the different types of activity for groups that you could use with (a) elementary; (b) intermediate; (c) advanced classes.

4 What kind of visual aids could you use to provide a stimulus for your groups or pairs? Give examples, e.g. 'When getting students to practise giving descriptions of places, you could use magazine pictures of places.' . . . etc.

5 What can the teacher be doing while the class is doing pair work? What could the teacher say to encourage the students as they work in pairs?

ⓑ Dialogue practice

1 Dialogues

Listen to the dialogues in turn and repeat the teacher's part, paying particular attention to the use of stress and the rhythm. (See Unit 3, Section **b**, instructions for the Dialogue Practice.)

 (a) At school

This classroom has desks that cannot be moved. The class has not done any group work before.

T: Now, to do this, I want you in groups. In sixes, please, groups of six. So, look, you three turn round, so you can talk to the three behind you.

Ss: Please, er . . . what . . . ?

T: Look, turn round, so you can see Kumah, Ali and Gustav.

Ss: OK.

T: Good. That's right. Now everyone else the same! All of you make groups like this one. You, six; you, six, and you over there, together. Turn right round. That's it, well done.

Ss: Please, not six . . . only four.

T: Oh, there are only four of you, I see. Well, four is fine, it doesn't matter.

▲or▲ ▲ TEACHING HINT The class obviously does not understand very well. How does the teacher help them to understand what she wants them to do?

 **(b) At college**

The class is not yet used to pair work. They have just practised a dialogue between Jim and Peter in chorus.

T: Well now, I'd like you to practise that dialogue in pairs, so that you all get lots of practice in speaking English. In pairs, then, please. Come on! You two together, you two, you two and so on.

S: Excuse me, . . . I . . .

T: Oh dear, you're on your own. You haven't anyone to work with, eh? Right, why don't you turn your chair round to make a three with the two behind you?

Ss: Come with us.

T: Thank you. Take turns at practising then I'll come and hear you myself, OK?

(To the class) Right, one of you is Jim, the other is Peter, then change over. Off you go, then. All pairs together, and I'll come round to listen.

▲or▲ ▲ TEACHING HINT Why does the teacher put the odd student with a pair to make three rather than practising with him himself?

2 Language activities

(a) Voice projection*

– It is not easy to speak loudly and clearly to a large or noisy class without distorting the sounds of the language and the natural intonation patterns. This activity is to give you practice in projecting your voice while still retaining natural stress and intonation patterns.

▲▲ – In twos; stand opposite your partner on the other side of the room. First, read the teacher's part of one of the above dialogues to your partner, loudly but as naturally as possible. Your partner should listen critically and tell you where your pronunciation differs from that of the tape. Then change over.

   – Next, select an exercise from a school or college textbook and dictate it to your partner to do orally, again standing across the room from your partner.

(b) Gesture

Discuss which gestures would be most effective for getting your class (a) to form pairs or groups (b) to stop pair practice (c) to hear individual pairs perform while the rest of the class listens quietly to them.

Ⓒ Classroom language

Study the language in the groups of tables below. When do you think a teacher would use such phrases and sentences? Think of a suitable label or heading for each group of tables and write it beside the table.

   Then practise the language that is relevant to your teaching situation, speaking out loud to your neighbour, as fluently as you can.

   Finally, TEST YOURSELVES, by organising each other into pairs, groups of 3 or 4, etc.

1

I want you in We're going to work in Can you get into	pairs groups	please.	In twos, with your neighbour. In fours. In groups of four.

2

Turn round Move forward	and	face look at	your neighbour. the person next to you.
Can you face		the people	behind you. in front of you.

3

Oh. Oh dear.	You	are	by yourself on your own the odd one out	aren't you?
		haven't anyone to work with, have you?		

4

Look, you Why don't you	move up and make a three. turn round and join in with them.

5

What about How about Would you mind	joining in with them? going to sit there, next to him? moving along a bit and working with them?

6

In your	pairs groups	I'd like you to would you you're going to	practise that dialogue. try out some questions and answers about yourselves. write a short paragraph about . . .

7

All those Those of you Students	on the left, on the right, on this side,	you	are	Jim. Peter.	You take	Jim's Peter's	part. role.
				group leader. You lead the discussion.			
				ask the questions. give the answers. etc.			

8

When you've finished Then	change over, swap round,	so that you	take the other part. each get a turn.

OK. Stop now!	That was good. Not bad! Well done!	Silence! Quiet please! That's enough!	Let's hear	what some of you have done. this pair. this group. how you have been getting on.

See also Unit 8, Section **c**, for language for team games.

ⓓ Exploitation

Workshop: exploiting your English Language textbooks

 Instead of exploiting the language of the classroom, this Unit gives you an opportunity to examine the materials in your school or college and to consider how they can be used to give your students more chances to use their English communicatively, working in pairs or small groups.

Most coursebooks contain reading passages, pictures, dialogues, exercises and written assignments. Some of these may be useful to promote valuable pair or group work which may not be suggested in the books themselves.

For this workshop, you should split up into twos or threes, each group taking a different lesson or unit of your coursebooks, preferably at different levels. Work through the materials, discussing how parts of them could be used for pair or group work in your classes. Look at the following suggestions which you may be able to adapt.

Exploiting a picture: pairs; students ask each other questions about the picture. E.g. Elementary level: 'Ask your partner three questions beginning 'What does...' about the people in the picture'.

Intermediate: 'Ask your neighbour five questions about what the people in the picture have just done or are going to do next.'

Advanced: 'Make up a possible conversation between the people in the picture' or 'Get your partner to describe one of the people without telling you which one it is, so that you can guess which person is being described', etc. See Units 15 and 17.

Exploiting a reading passage: pairs (or groups); each pair make up questions on a specific part of the passage for another pair to answer. This can also be done in teams, with points for good questions and answers. See Unit 19.

Exploiting written assignments: groups; topics can be discussed in groups prior to a class discussion. Essays can be written in groups as a joint task; sentences discussed and then dictated, with group members taking turns to be the 'secretary' and writing them down. This lessens the marking load for the teacher and helps weaker students. See Unit 21.

Exploiting exercises: pairs; exercises can sometimes be done orally in pairs before the teacher goes through them in class. This ensures that all students are working and getting some oral practice while doing the exercise first in pairs. See Units 15 and 20.

There are many more ways of exploiting textbook materials, too. When you have discussed the possibilities for pair and group work in your lesson or unit, write down your ideas so that members of the other groups can benefit from them.

Demonstration

 Each workshop group should select one of their ideas from their workshop, and demonstrate it, or part of it, to the rest of the class, using them as 'students'. Remember to tell them what level they are supposed to be, so they can act accordingly.

Also arrange a session where you can all report back to each other, to exchange other ideas and discuss how to put them into practice in the classroom.

Role play

1 Activity
Setting up pair work
In groups of 5 or 6.

- Using the magazine pictures suggested at the beginning of the Unit, or any other picture in which there are at least two people talking, imagine what these people are talking about, then write a very simple and natural four or five line dialogue to go with the picture.
- Plan the presentation and practice stages of the dialogue, thinking particularly about the pattern of teacher◄►student and student◄►student interaction, using pair work alternating with choral and individual work, for variety. Decide on what cues to give to aid their memory.
- Look back at the CLASSROOM LANGUAGE Sections of this Unit and Unit 8, and decide which language you will need to use in order to carry out the organisation of the practice stages.
- Decide in your groups in which order you will 'teach' this to the other groups, so that the materials can be passed on from the first to the second 'teacher'. Then split up and re-form groups, so that as far as possible you will be 'teaching' members of other groups.
- Fix a time limit and begin 'teaching' remembering to be as dynamic as possible, and using clear instructions with plenty of gesture to help your 'students' understand what you expect them to do.

2 Follow up and evaluation
Take a friendly vote to elect the 'best organised teacher' in your teaching groups. Then discuss why you thought so.

Then, as a class, discuss how you could introduce pair and group work to a class that has never done any before, and who are perhaps anxious about the idea.

3 Play a game
THE CONVERSATION GAME. See Unit 1, Section **d**, **5**, page 11.
GIVE ME ANOTHER ONE. See Unit 15, Section **d**, page 112.

Further reading

On pair work see Donn Byrne (1976) Chapter 7.

On group work see Donn Byrne (1976) Chapter 8, pp. 80–96.

Disick, R in Joiner and Westphal (1978) pp. 136–143.

Unit 10 Interruptions: late comers, things lost

The aim of this Unit is to show how interruptions in lessons can be used for communicative language practice, often with the questioning done by the students.
You will need character cards as in Unit 1, but with some additions; see Section **e**, **1**

ⓐ Preliminary discussion

1 Lessons rarely proceed from beginning to end smoothly without any interruptions at all. What interruptions may possibly occur during your English lessons?

2 What do you usually do in each case? How far does your action depend on what is actually happening in the class at that moment?

3 What things are your students always supposed to bring to class or provide for themselves? Do they usually? What do you say to them if they don't?

4 Unless you are in the middle of a complex activity like a substitution drill which may break down if interrupted, interruptions can form a useful basis for some genuine communicative language use. If one student walks in late, the rest of the class want to know why; they could ask him in English. How, for example, could the following situations be used as the basis of conversations? One student has not brought his textbook, another has not sharpened his pencil and one tells you he didn't have time to do the homework that you are just about to test them on.

5 (a) What reasons are your students likely to have for being late?
(b) What topics of conversation may arise naturally out of a student arriving late?
(c) Is punctuality in your country considered as important as it is in the Western world?

6 How would you express your displeasure to (a) a child who was always late, with a different excuse each time? (b) an adult who was often late but had never said why?

63

ⓑ Dialogue practice

1 Dialogues

Listen to both dialogues on tape; notice the difference in social register between them and the way in which the teachers use different tones of voice. Then select the dialogue which is relevant to your teaching situation and practise repeating it after the tape before practising it with your neighbour.

(a) At school

T: Hello, Rosa. You're a bit late today.
R: Yes, Miss White, I'm sorry.
T: Well, where have you been?
R: ...er...I forgot my book and I... go...
T: You went back for it?
R: Yes.
T: You shouldn't have gone back for it. You could have borrowed one, or shared. Anyway, Rosa, sit down now. Let's get on.

This is the first time Rosa has been late.

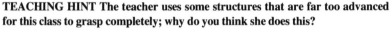

TEACHING HINT The teacher uses some structures that are far too advanced for this class to grasp completely; why do you think she does this?

(b) At college

T: Good afternoon, Mr Kasemi, er... what...?
Mr K: Good afternoon, Mr Ramsden, I'm sorry I'm late today.
T: Did you miss the bus or was the traffic heavy today?
Mr K: No,...er...actually I started out late.
T: Well, never mind. Please take a seat. And would somebody explain to Mr Kasemi what we've been doing today?...
S: I will.
T: Yes? Go on...

Mr Kasemi walks in late.

TEACHING HINT Why does the teacher use an 'either/or' question here, rather than simply saying, 'Did you miss the bus?'

2 Language activities

(a) Repeat the first dialogue above, substituting Lisa for Rosa. Lisa is often late because she is always forgetting things. Change your tone of voice to show your disapproval. Practise with your neighbour.

(b) Make up three 'either/or' questions enquiring about reasons for lateness relevant to your students' lives. Ask your neighbour the questions; he or she should apologise and give a suitable reason for being late.

(c) What language will your students need in order to apologise politely in English? Make a list of expressions your students ought to know by the end of their first year and by the end of their intermediate stage, for example, 'I'm sorry I'm late but I missed the bus', (end of 1st year). Write them here:

_____

_____

_____

_____

© Classroom language

Read the phrases and practise making sentences from the substitution tables below. First select language suitable for children or younger students. Then select the language that is appropriate to adult students. You are more likely to reprimand late comers in school than adult learners. Remember how to show your attitude, for example, your disapproval or concern, by the *tone* of your voice.

You will speak more strictly to a student who is often late than to someone who is rarely late. Practise in pairs, adding your own ideas, to make a natural conversation.

Lateness

Hello, Gustav, you're late today. (Yes, I'm sorry, I had to . . .)
Good morning, Mr Adjimi. You're rather late . . .
What happened? Is anything wrong? (Oh, no, I . . .)

Where have you been? (Well, I went to . . .)
What have you been doing?

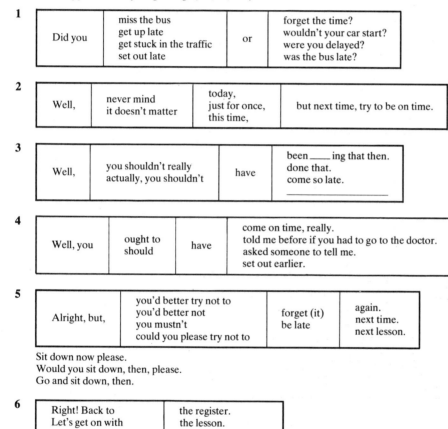

1

| Did you | miss the bus
get up late
get stuck in the traffic
set out late | or | forget the time?
wouldn't your car start?
were you delayed?
was the bus late? |

2

| Well, | never mind
it doesn't matter | today,
just for once,
this time, | but next time, try to be on time. |

3

| Well, | you shouldn't really
actually, you shouldn't | have | been _____ ing that then.
done that.
come so late.
_____ |

4

| Well, you | ought to
should | have | come on time, really.
told me before if you had to go to the doctor.
asked someone to tell me.
set out earlier. |

5

| Alright, but, | you'd better try not to
you'd better not
you mustn't
could you please try not to | forget (it)
be late | again.
next time.
next lesson. |

Sit down now please.
Would you sit down, then, please.
Go and sit down, then.

6

| Right! Back to
Let's get on with
Let's get back to
Right, we'll go on with | the register.
the lesson.
what we were doing.
our work. |

Lost, forgotten

(See Appendix B for Student Language, MAKING APOLOGIES.)

7

Look,	whose	pen book bag work test homework paper pencil	is this?	(Mine.) (His.) (Hers.) (John's.) (I'm sorry, I don't know.) (I think it's John's.)
	whose is this		?	

8

Has anyone Who has Who's	found lost	some homework? a book? a pen? a bag?	(I have.) (I haven't.) (Me.) (Not me.)

9

Who	do these does this	belong to?	(Me.) (Not me.) (Her.) (Him.)

10

Have you	forgotten your homework? left your pen at home? left your book behind?	(Yes, I have.) (I'm afraid I have.)

11

Has	anyone anyone else	forgotten their homework? left their pen behind? left their book at home?

12

Where's your	pen? book? exercise book?	(I've forgotten it.) (I'm sorry.) (I left it at home.) (I lost it.)

13

Oh well, Never mind, Well, OK,	you'll have to could you	bring it next time. borrow one. do without. do that work again. try and find it. share books. share with Jane.

14

Come and see me	after the lesson. at_____o'clock. later on.	I'll deal with that then. I'll help you then.

Test yourself

In each case give one answer suitable for adult learners and one suitable for school children.

What would you say if . . .

(a) someone was very late for the first time?

(b) three or four students walked in ten minutes late without apologising?

(c) a latecomer apologised very politely?

(d) you wanted to continue the lesson after an interruption?

(e) you thought quite a few students had forgotten their homework?

(f) Hossein had left his book at home for the third time?

(g) Rosa said she didn't have anything to write with?

(h) someone said he had a problem with his homework?

(i) you found a pen and a piece of homework on your desk as you came in?

(j) somebody handed in to you an un-named exercise book?

(k) somebody told you he had lost his homework?

ⓓ Exploitation

1 Unexploited dialogue

Mr Short is about to begin a new activity when Chee walks in late. What opportunities does he miss for some authentic and purposeful communication in English?

T: Now, let's see . . . Oh, hello, Chee.

Ch: Good morning, Mr Short.

T: You're late, Chee.

Ch: I know, I'm sorry.

T: OK. Don't be late again.

Ch: No, Mr Short. *(sits down)*

T: Right, as I was saying, I want you to write . . .

S: Excuse me, my pencil's broken, and I've lost my pen, Mr Short.

T: Well, borrow mine. Here you are. Right, back to work!

2 Possibilities for exploitation

Here are some ways in which Mr Short could have taken advantage of this situation.

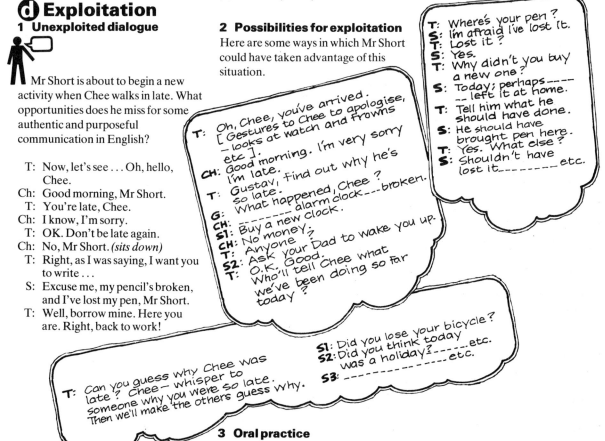

T: Oh, Chee, you've arrived. [Gestures to Chee to apologise, looks at watch and frowns etc].

CH: Good morning. I'm very sorry I'm late.

T: Gustav, find out why he's so late.

What happened, Chee?

G: ———— alarm clock——broken.

CH: Buy a new clock.

S1: No money.

CH: Anyone?

T: Ask your Dad to wake you up.

S2: O.K. Good.

T: Who'll tell Chee what we've been doing so far today?

T: Where's your pen?

S: I'm afraid I've lost it.

T: Lost it?

S: Yes.

T: Why didn't you buy a new one?

S: Today; perhaps——— left it at home.

T: Tell him what he should have done.

S: He should have brought pen here.

T: Yes. What else?

S: Shouldn't have lost it———— etc.

T: Can you guess why Chee was late? Chee— whisper to someone why you were so late. Then we'll make the others guess why.

S1: Did you lose your bicycle?

S2: Did you think today was a holiday?———etc.

S3: —————————etc.

3 Oral practice

In groups of 3 or 4.

(a) Take one 'balloon' each and practise expanding the dialogue along the lines suggested, adapting the idea to suit your own students if necessary.

(b) There are many ways of exploiting this situation for contextualising structural teaching, too. Look back at the classroom language section and see which structures arise naturally. Are there any others which you could bring in to a situation such as this? After you have made your own list, check in Appendix A, then practise in your groups bringing in and eliciting any structures which your students would find useful.

4 Sample exploitation

Listen to the tape and find out why Abdullah was late for college this morning. Then listen to the tape again and see if you can tell at which point all the students get really interested, and why. Also, why do they laugh at the end?

Are there any words the teacher uses that may have been new to some of the students? Do you think they understood them in the end? Which words are they?

If the teacher had wanted to, she might have further exploited this situation for practice in the first conditional or other tenses; how might she have done this?

ⓔ Role play

1 Activity
Dealing with interruptions

- Select your teacher and your latecomer. Decide whether he always comes late, or rarely. (This will affect what tone of voice you use and what you say to him.)
- Decide also whether you are teaching adults or school students and remember to use appropriate language.
- Remember when 'teaching' to speak at a fairly natural speed and rephrase whenever necessary.
- As 'teacher' you will have to guide and help the student who is late to make an appropriate apology, give a plausible excuse or explain the reason he was late. You must acknowledge the apology, accept the excuse and give a word of warning or reprimand if necessary. Exploit the situation as far as you can for developing a chat. Involve the whole class by asking why he was late and what he should have done, for example.
- As 'students' remember to act as if you do not understand everything all the time. For example, you can look puzzled or worried, whisper to your neighbour as if you had not understood or put your hand up if you have a query.
- Begin by teaching some new vocabulary from a picture, when the late comer arrives. After he is settled down, ask the class to write the new words in their books, which is when the other interruptions occur.
- You can use the same role play cards as you had for Unit 1. Add two or three saying LOST YOUR BOOK, FORGOTTEN YOUR PEN, etc.
- End when you have finally got the class to write and learn the three items of vocabulary you set out to teach.
- Take turns being the 'teacher' and the late arrival; change the 'level' of your class and use different excuses each time.
- Make a note of which structures or language items occur most often in this situation.
- Jot down any errors you notice for checking out later.

2 Follow up and evaluation

(a) In your groups assess which interruptions produced most language use. What did the students actually say themselves? What did they manage to understand? Did 'students' feel the teacher's language was appropriate to their 'age' and 'level'?

  What changes would you make if you had to cope with similar situations in your own classes?

(b) Report back to the whole class on which interruption proved most useful, in terms of language used.

  Make a more comprehensive list of structural items which could be based on or practised in these situations, for further reference.

  Check out any queries you may have about the accuracy and appropriacy of the language used in the role play activity.

Unit 11
Control and discipline

The aims of this Unit are **1** to teach the language needed to control classes in such a way as to promote effective learning **2** to revise the language taught in earlier Units by means of a WORKSHOP on lesson planning, based on the language items contained in Appendix A and previous EXPLOITATION Sections
You will need 1 materials for making new role play cards. See Section **e 2** a wall chart suitable for question and answer work **3** your school or college English Language textbooks

---

ⓐ Preliminary discussion

Discuss the points relevant to *your* teaching situation.

1 In what ways is teaching English to adults different from teaching English to children? Consider the following points: discipline, motivation, types of activities and materials used, length of concentration spans, the role and status of the teacher.

2 Is discipline ever a problem in the school or college you teach in? Do you anticipate any problems as a result of teaching English in English? If so, what do you think are (or will be) the reasons for it? Any of the following? – lack of motivation, lack of confidence, previous learning habits, importance of the written examination, or relative importance of English compared to other subjects on the timetable? Can you think of any other possible reasons?

3 In adult education, discipline is rarely a problem. However, adults have often acquired learning habits from their previous learning experience which may prevent them from performing well in English. Which, if any, of these learning habits do your students show?

(a) wanting to write down things when they should be listening or practising

(b) subvocalising* when reading English silently

(c) requesting or giving translations for every new item or difficult sentence, instead of responding directly in English

(d) copying down everything you write on the blackboard, whether or not it is useful

(e) learning dialogues and word lists by heart

(f) trying to say something in English that they have not already studied and perhaps get wrong.

4 Which of the learning habits listed in 3 above would you attempt to eradicate and how?

5 If you are in Secondary Education and are teaching further up the school, taking over classes previously taught by another teacher, you may find that Discussion Points 3 and 4 above apply to your situation, too. If so, you may find it useful to discuss them with your tutor.

ⓑ **Dialogue practice**
1 **Dialogues**

Listen to whichever dialogue is most relevant to your teaching situation. Notice especially the tone of voice used; the teacher is being firm but pleasant. Repeat the teacher's part only, then practise the dialogue in pairs, helping each other with pronunciation, referring back to the tape if you are in doubt about the accuracy of your pronunciation.

(a) At school

The class is just settling down after an interruption. They were doing a textbook exercise.

T: OK, everyone. Quiet now please! No more talking! Rosa, stop chatting now. And you, Kumah. Let's see, number 3. Whose turn is it?
S: It's my turn.
T: Gustav, sorry, just a moment! Chee and Ali, would you mind not behaving like that. Sit down. Yes, Gustav, number 3, please.
G: 'Joan has been in London . . . er'
S: 'in London for sev . . .!'
T: Hans, please don't interrupt while Gustav is speaking. Listen and see if he is right, OK?

TEACHING HINT Why does the teacher stop Hans answering for Gustav, do you think?

(b) At college

The teacher is presenting a new item orally while students listen.

T: Mr Adjimi, please don't write while I am showing you how to say this. Just listen!
Mr A: I'm sorry.
T: That's OK. Ready? Listening? *(The teacher reads a short dialogue, and students practise it.)* *(Later)*
T: You can work in pairs, speaking, then writing the dialogue. But without chatting in your own language, please. Start now.
S: Is this right?
T: Oh, not that one, that's the wrong one. Hang on. From the pictures at the *bottom* of the page, the second set. The one we've just practised!
S: This one?
T: Yes. *(kindly)* You'd better listen next time, hadn't you? Then you'll get it right.

TEACHING HINT Why do you think the teacher lets the students work in twos to write up the dialogue they have practised orally?

2 **Language activity**
Tone of voice

When controlling your class, often the *way* you say something is more important than *what* you say. Students understand from the teacher's tone of voice if they have done something wrong, for example.

Imagine you were teaching a class of adolescents, around 15 to 18 years old. Practise saying each of the warnings below in three different ways, as if:

(a) at the beginning of an activity; a general announcement to the whole class, (pleasantly)

(b) students take longer settling down than you expected; (this time more firmly but still pleasantly)

(c) some students continue to be disruptive; (very firm, addressing those particular students)

There is an example of the first one on tape; practise that one first.

– Could you stop talking and settle down, now, please?

– Would you keep your voices down during pair practice, please?

– I'm not going to begin until everyone is quiet, really quiet.

– Stop turning round and disturbing other people, please.

– No writing while I explain this, OK? Pens down, please.

C **Classroom language**

You will need to select language appropriate to the age of your students, for example most of the expressions in Table 1 are really only suitable for children. Remember that you can modify your language by changing the tone of your voice, for example to make it more polite, or very firm.

Study the language in the tables, ignoring that which is not suitable for your classes, then practise in twos, helping each other with pronunciation difficulties.

This time the tables have no headings, the language in them is self-explanatory.

1

No, don't!	That's silly.
Don't do that!	Settle down.
Stop that!	Come on, let's get on.
Stop doing that!	Now listen.
That's enough!	Now get on with your work.
You mustn't do that!	Let's start again.
Be quiet!	Whose turn is it now?

2

Now then, No, Ali, No, . . .,	that's not the way to	behave in class. learn English properly. do pair practice, etc.

3

No **No more** **Stop** Would you mind **not** Please will you **stop** **Without** You shouldn't be There'll be trouble if you go on I'll report you to Mr X if you go on	playing around! talking! chatting! making a noise! being silly/stupid! shouting! disturbing the others! interrupting the others! behaving like that! speaking Farsi/Spanish/Chinese! whispering! copying! Do it on your own! passing notes! turning round! Face me! dreaming! Wake up!	Get on, Calm down, Listen, Be quiet, Settle down,	please.

4

No	talking writing	while	I'm talking. I'm writing on the blackboard. I'm explaining this.
Don't	talk write		we're doing this. the others are still working.
	move your lips while you're reading.		

5

	talk start answer write it down read it write it	until unless	I tell you to. I've finished. I let you. you've understood. I ask you to. I've said it all. everyone's ready. everyone's finished.
Don't You mustn't You'd better not			
You needn't	translate	unless	I ask you to.

6

Wait a minute!	Not No, not	**this** **that**	book. picture. page. card. exercise. dialogue. one.	**This**	book. page. one.	This one. Here. Look.
			way.	**This**	way.	Like this.

7

You've	brought done got	the wrong	book, page, exercise, one,	haven't you?	What did I ask you to do? Who can remember what I said?
You're	reading doing			aren't you?	
	doing it the wrong way,				

8

Could you	do it	how the way	I told you to? I asked you to?
	read write	the bit the exercise	

9

You'd better	be careful be quiet listen next time try harder watch out	hadn't you?

10

If you don't	pay attention, listen properly, concentrate,	it'll go in **one** ear and out the **other**!

11

If you	do that again forget it again don't do your homework once more don't work harder keep on wasting time	I'll I'll have to I'll definitely I'll simply	send you to Mr X. set you extra work. tell the Headmaster. write to your parents. punish you. tell your parents.

Test yourself

Say the answers to these out loud in a suitable tone of voice. What would you say in these circumstances?

(a) Gustav turns round for the third time to chat to the person behind.

(b) Rosa has started the wrong exercise.

(c) Hossein keeps falling asleep.

(d) Ali and his friend are being silly.

(e) Mr Adjimi begins to write while you are presenting something new.

(f) His friend keeps whispering to him.

(g) Mrs Moussavi is writing a whole paragraph rather than the first sentence.

(h) Miss Kasemi is copying whole sentences instead of writing notes.

(i) Some children are not working well and repeatedly interrupt the others.

(j) Chee never finds the right page and even now is looking at the wrong picture.

(k) Some students are reading silently but moving their lips as they read.

(l) Mr Lee keeps giving translations instead of answering in English.

(m)The whole class has worked very well indeed throughout the lesson.

ⓓ Exploitation

Revision workshop

This Section revises work covered in whichever of the previous Units you may have studied, mainly from the EXPLOITATION Sections.

The aim of the workshop is to give practice in exploiting classroom situations for the presentation and practice of the language items contained in Appendix A.

By the end of this workshop, each group should have planned in detail the initial presentation of one language point, and some practice stages.

– Select items from Appendix A that you will have to teach at some time in the future.

– Split up into groups of two or three, each group taking a different item. Define what exactly the aims of your lesson will be. See Unit 13, Section **e**, **1** (e).

– Write six more examples of the teaching item, choosing ideas that can be demonstrated in the classroom and that your students will find interesting. Practise modelling the examples to each other, speaking as naturally as you can. Practise getting each other to repeat them, after you.

– Write a two line exchange that involves students in doing something as well as speaking, e.g. 'Would you close the window, please?' 'Yes, of course'.
(This would be suitable if you were teaching polite requests.) Your students can practise this in pairs, miming the actions.
See also Unit 14, Section **d**, **1** (a).

– Think of other elicitation procedures you could use to make your students produce the new item. See FOCUS page, Unit 15. These may include picture cues, word cues on the blackboard, mime cues from the teacher, or question and answer work, in which case try the questions out on each other before you write them down, to make sure they sound natural. You should end up with at least six cues or questions to elicit the new item.

– Next, think of some situations in real life where such items may well occur naturally. Write a longer dialogue which will include the new item and illustrate its use in a different situation. Try each exchange out on each other to make sure it sounds like normal spoken English before you write it down. Then practise modelling both parts for the others in your group to repeat. Use a blackboard sketch of the characters to refer to when getting the others to repeat. Write down some comprehension questions to test whether your students can understand what they are to repeat; you would use these questions at the presentation stage. Test them on each other, first.

– Lastly think of a situation similar to the one in the last dialogue, as near as possible to a real-life situation, that the class could perform as a role play activity, during the production stage of the lesson. Practise describing the situation and the characters involved to each other, so that you will be able to set it up efficiently when you come to do it in the classroom. See also Unit 17, Section **c**, Tables 1–6.

– Look in your textbooks to see if there is a suitable written exercise to give as reinforcement of the oral work they have done in class. If there isn't anything suitable, make one up; just five or six items will be enough.

– When you have written this lesson plan out, ask your tutor to check the English for accuracy and appropriacy. Then pass your lesson plans round for other groups to examine and copy down.

– If possible, either peer teach each lesson or try it out next time you have a class at a suitable level. Amend the plan if necessary afterwards. You could use one part of this plan in the Role Play in Section **e**.

e Role play

1 Activity

Discipline and control in your class

First decide whether you will be 'teaching' children or adults. Prepare two or three cue cards each for use during the role play instead of the character cards previously used. Use the ideas below that seem suitable. Cards should have one side blank.

Stand up and walk around

Stay silent, be lazy

Keep staring out of the window

Chat to your neighbour (L')

Interrupt other students

Do the opposite of what you're told

Try to translate everything

Answer the wrong question

Write as much of the lesson down as you can.

Say nothing, do nothing

Take someone's ruler

Answer out of turn

Prepare the same number of blank cards; these cue 'normal' behaviour.

Divide into groups of eight or ten people; share out both types of cards equally between the groups. Shuffle the cards and distribute them at the beginning of each 'teacher's' turn.

Teachers should either do some oral question and answer work based on a picture, or set a written task, a simple one, which can be continued by subsequent teachers. You could use one part of the lesson you planned in Section **d**.

Teachers should attempt to teach for three or four minutes, dealing with problems as they arise.

'Students' should respond to the 'teacher' after one, two or maximum three warnings.

Change over cue cards for each new turn. Enjoy yourselves!

2 Follow up and evaluation

Discuss in your groups:

(a) Did any teacher allow any student to get away with doing what he shouldn't? (Often the quiet or lazy ones are not noticed.)

(b) Was the language and tone suitable for the age and level of the class?

(c) What caused the most difficulty?

(d) In what circumstances might it be useful to revert to the mother-tongue in similar situations?

(e) Could you use cue cards in a similar way in your own classes to teach patterns like 'You'd better (not)' 'Would you mind not'?

Check out any language points with your tutor.

Unit 12 Ending the lesson or a stage in the lesson

> **The aims** of this Unit are **1** to teach the language one would normally use when finishing a stage in a lesson, or when ending the lesson itself, setting homework, etc. **2** to show how the few minutes just before the end of the lesson can be used in a practical way to promote communicative language use which will involve the students
> **You will need 1** the textbooks you use in school or college **2** role play cards

Preliminary discussion

1 (a) A lesson is normally made up of different stages each comprising different activities. How do you let your class know when one activity is over? (Refer back to Unit 5.)

(b) At the end of an activity, would you just say 'Stop', or would you perhaps give a reason for stopping at that particular moment, or offer some praise or encouragement? What exactly could you say if you wanted your class to stop (i) writing an exercise from their textbook? (ii) practising a dialogue in pairs? (iii) asking and answering questions about a wall chart?

2 What often needs to be done after you've finished teaching near the end of the lesson? Make a list of the usual tasks a teacher must do then. Also, do you think it is important how students feel at the end of a lesson, as they leave the classroom? Why? So what else might you do?

3 (a) Could you ask your students to help you do some of these tasks at the end of the lesson? How would you ask them in English?

(b) If you stepped back and asked some of your students to take over, how much of the organisation could they do, or be taught to do, in English? How could this be useful experience for them?

4 What kind of queries or comments might your students need to make to you at the end of the lesson?

5 Do you think a quick review of what the students have achieved during the lesson might be useful? Why? Perhaps a preview of the next lesson might be motivating. What do you think?

6 Sometimes a lesson goes faster than you have planned, and you have five or ten minutes left at the end. What can you do to use this time productively and amusingly? Do any of you know any good games that you can play quickly in English with your students? If so, describe them briefly, stating the language items needed by the students in order to play successfully. (See also Unit 17, Section **d**.)

ⓑ Dialogue practice

1 Dialogues

Practise each dialogue but be careful! The first teacher corrects two student mistakes in a very discouraging way. When *you* take the teacher's role here, try to sound more *encouraging*.

 (a) At school

The teacher has five minutes before the end of the lesson. The class is writing.

T: Well, everyone. Finish the sentence you are writing, then put your pens down. It's time to clear up. . . . Come on! Finish now. OK?
S: I no finish.
T: You haven't finished?
S: I haven't finished.
T: Well, never mind. You've tried hard. Right. Could you leave your exercise books open at the page you are on, and pass them up?
S: Can I collect them for you?
T: Yes, thank you, and could you put them on my desk? Well done everybody; most of you have worked very well, today. Do you remember what you have to do for homework? I told you earlier . . . yes?
S: Read page 57 and learn four lines of dialogue.
T: Of the dialogue. Is she right? Anyone?
Ss: Yes.
T: Now, while you're packing your books up, tell me what plans you've got for the weekend . . .

or **TEACHING HINT Why does the teacher ask the students themselves what they have to do for homework?**

(b) At college

The teacher decides to finish this stage of the lesson earlier than planned because it has not gone very well.

T: OK, everyone, we'll do another two questions and then stop and have a break before going on to something else. Er, question 5, anyone?
Ss: . . . . . .
(later)
T: Good, well done, that was a bit difficult, wasn't it? We'll stop there, anyway, and you can have a two minute break. Don't worry, we'll come back to that another time when we're not so tired. Have a break now.
(later)
T: Alright, everybody? Let's have a game now. Look . . .

or **TEACHING HINT Why do you think the teacher gives prior warning to the students that they will have to stop that activity soon? And why does he decide to play a game at this point, do you think?**

2 Language activities

A game to play

REPHRASING CHAMPIONSHIPS (an excellent revision game for teachers)
In 2 equal sized groups. Sit or stand in a circle. Your tutor should sit between you as he is the judge or arbitrator.

The aim of this game is to see how many different ways there are for teachers to say the same thing, keeping as close as possible to the original meaning, but using different levels of register, structural complexity, etc.

Example: The first player says, 'Would you open your books at page 15 please?' The player next to him can say: 'Would you find page 15, please in your books?' The next player could say 'Would you mind opening your books? You want page 15' and so on, around the circle until somebody repeats one that has already been said. Then continue with the next sentence. The group leader makes a note of how many different ways they have found for each sentence. The winner is the group who has found (and can say) the most ways. No hesitations are allowed beyond a count of 5 (or 10). If the next player has not by then responded, that group must write down the number of ways found so far and proceed to the next sentence.

Begin with the sentence given in the example, for a practice run through, then follow on with these:

1 How about having another look at the picture of the seaside?
2 Could everybody please repeat this sentence after me?
3 Everybody should try question number 3. Now!
4 Whose turn is it now? John's?
5 Has anybody not had a turn now?
6 Would you mind being quiet now please?
7 Today I plan to do some work on Listening Comprehension with you.
8 Just clean the lower section of the board, on the right please. Thanks.
9 Hands up before you answer please!
10 Who can remember what we talked about in yesterday's lesson?

c Classroom language

The classroom language in this Unit covers a wide variety of organisational tasks that may not all be relevant to your teaching situation. For example, you would probably not ask an adult student to clean the board for you.

Select the tables which apply to your teaching situation and in general you will find that the language itself is appropriate to the age of your students. Think of specific tasks to refer to and fill the blanks appropriately.

Work through the relevant tables, one task at a time, and practise the language with your neighbour. For example, you could practise setting each other homework, different types of assignments, for two or three minutes, before proceding to the next set of tables. Use your textbooks to refer to.

Remember to add anything of your own to make the language sound natural in use; for example, in order to direct students' attention you may have to add a 'Right' or a 'Now then' at the beginning of the exchange (see Unit one, Section **b**, Language Activity.)

Try to read fluently from the tables; it's better if you can memorise a sentence, look up and say it to your partner. Help each other with pronunciation.

Ending a teaching sequence

1

Last few One or two more		questions minutes					
Just Can you	finish complete		the	line dialogue sentence task	you're	on now practising writing reading doing	and then we'll stop.

2

I think Right!	we'll stop	there. doing this now now.	You've done enough of that. You've had enough practice at that. We'll have a short break and a rest.	
			It's time you	had a change now. finished that now.

3

You've all Most of you have	done	that	quite well. very nicely. better than last time.	Well done. But you could perhaps still do better.

4

So let's	begin go on to	some	oral work. reading. writing. listening.

(See Unit 5.)

Setting homework (Elementary level)

5

At home, Tonight,	not now,	do learn write practise read revise	the work we've done in class. this dialogue. the exercise on page 9.

6

Write it	in your notebooks out neatly on paper	and	give it in I'll go over it	tomorrow morning. next lesson.

Setting homework (Intermediate level)

7

For homework At home Before next lesson	I want you to	finish this piece of work. continue with these exercises, up to 8. do exercises 2 to 5, including 5. go over what we've just learnt. learn 6 lines of the dialogue on page 9. learn how to spell these words. read pages 67 to 74 and answer the questions.

8

It must be done by Can you give it in I'll test you on it	next lesson. next time I see you. tomorrow morning at 8.30. some time this week. Tuesday, latest.

(See Appendix B for Student Language, QUERIES ABOUT TASKS SET.)

Ending the lesson (Elementary level)

Good, well done.   Give back my papers/books.
Pack your books up.   Are your desks tidy?
Put them away.   Right. You may go.
Collect the work, please. Goodbye.

Collecting things

9

I want I'd like	to	collect take in	your	last lot of homework work papers books	now please.

Make sure your names are on your work, won't you?

10

Please will you	give it/them in?	
	pass it/them up to	the end of the row? the front?
	collect it/them,	Ali?

Give it in now, please.   Pile your books up here. Make 2/3/4 piles.
Pass your work up, now please.   Thank you, everyone. Well done.
Put your work on my desk as you leave.

(See Appendix B Student Language, MAKING APOLOGIES.)

Tidying up

11

Could you Will you	collect the books we've been using, see all the library books are returned, put everything back in its right place,	Ali, everyone, Rosa,	please?

12

Before you all leave,	could you would you	make sure see that check that	the desks are straight. those books are put away. you've not forgotten anything. the board is clean. all the library books are there.

13

Chee, Lisa, Kumah,	it's your job today to isn't it your turn to	clean the board. collect the readers in. make sure it's all tidy for the next class.

(See Units 6 and 7 for putting visual aids and other equipment away.)

Announcements

14

I have	something to tell you some announcements to make	before you go.	Could you listen, please?

15

Will you please remember Don't forget	to bring the money for＿＿＿ next lesson. there's a club meeting on＿＿＿ there's an English film called＿＿＿ about＿＿＿ on＿＿＿

Review

16

So today we have	practised＿＿＿ read about＿＿＿ written＿＿＿	and you've learnt how to＿＿＿

17

Next lesson we'll	go on to＿＿＿ revise＿＿＿	＿＿＿ and do＿＿＿

A game or a chat?

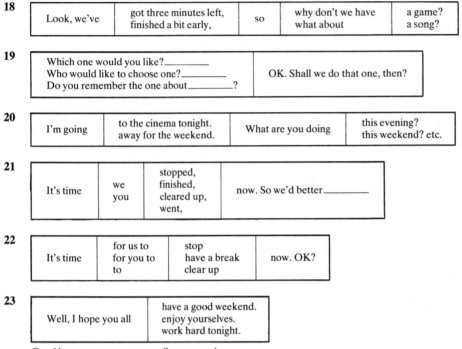

18

| Look, we've | got three minutes left, finished a bit early, | so | why don't we have what about | a game? a song? |

19

| Which one would you like?_____ Who would like to choose one?_____ Do you remember the one about_____? | OK. Shall we do that one, then? |

20

| I'm going | to the cinema tonight. away for the weekend. | What are you doing | this evening? this weekend? etc. |

21

| It's time | we you | stopped, finished, cleared up, went, | now. So we'd better_____ |

22

| It's time | for us to for you to to | stop have a break clear up | now. OK? |

23

| Well, I hope you all | have a good weekend. enjoy yourselves. work hard tonight. |

Good bye, everyone, see you all tomorrow!

 Test yourself

What can you say if you want
(a) to draw the present activity to a close? (give a reason, and praise)
(b) to tell the class to take a short break? (be encouraging)
(c) to set two lots of homework? (specify what is to be done, for when)
(d) the children to tidy up at the end of the day? (specify several tasks)
(e) to make an announcement about a class outing?
(f) to sum up the lesson you have just finished and say what will happen in the next lesson?
(g) to fill in the last two minutes of a lesson?
(h) your students to leave their work on your desk as they leave?
(i) to draw the lesson to an end? (Begin, 'Well, it's time we/you. ...')
(j) to give the class permission to leave, and say Goodbye ...?

ⓓ Exploitation

1 Unexploited dialogue

The teacher here is very businesslike but gives the class no opportunities to speak at all. What could he have done to allow his students to say something in English?

T: Finished?
Ss: ...er yes.
Ss: No.
T: Never mind. Pack your things up now. Books away! Lee? Collect these sheets up, please.
L: Yes, sir.
T: OK. Straighten those desks. Come on! Now, remember your homework. Right, you can go. Good bye everyone.
Ss: Good bye.
T: Have a good weekend.

2 Possibilities for exploitation

Link the 'balloons' opposite to the part of the dialogue on the left which could have been expanded and exploited.

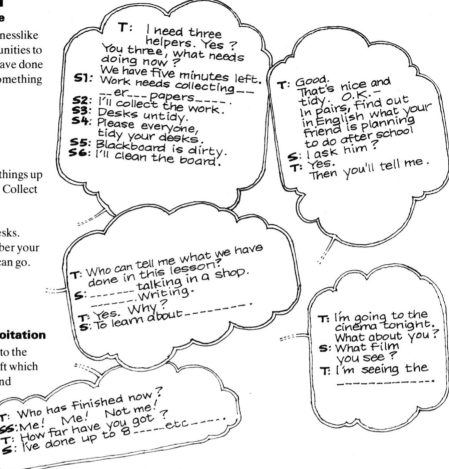

T: I need three helpers. Yes? You three, what needs doing now?
S1: We have five minutes left. Work needs collecting -- er--- papers-----
S2: I'll collect the work.
S3: Desks untidy.
S4: Please everyone, tidy your desks.
S5: Blackboard is dirty.
S6: I'll clean the board.

T: Good. That's nice and tidy. O.K.- In pairs, find out in English what your friend is planning to do after school
S: I ask him?
T: Yes. Then you'll tell me.

T: Who can tell me what we have done in this lesson?
S: ------- talking in a shop.
------- Writing.
T: Yes. Why?
S: To learn about--------.

T: I'm going to the cinema tonight. What about you?
S: What film you see?
T: I'm seeing the -----------.

T: Who has finished now?
Ss: Me! Me! Not me!
T: How far have you got?
S: I've done up to 8 -----etc-----.

3 Oral practice

In groups of 4 to 6.

(a) Take one 'balloon' each, change or adapt the idea to suit your own students, then practise exploiting the original dialogue along those lines, trying to get your fellow students talking for as long as possible.

(b) What language items could be practised in a meaningful way at the end of a lesson? For example, the pattern in Table 21 is often used in this situation. Write down as many as you can think of then check in Appendix A.

4 Sample exploitation

The teacher has asked her students to find out what their neighbour's plans for the weekend are, so on the tape you will hear the last minute of their work in pairs. In this case it fits in particularly well, because the teacher wants to revise the *'going to'* form for future plans before teaching them the use of the present continuous form for expressing planned future action and contrasting this with the use of *'will'* for uncertain or unplanned future events.

The pair work runs over the time available, however, and the students realise it may be too late to get to the college coffee bar before it closes.

How does the teacher exploit this situation to introduce some examples of the use of *'will'* for unplanned future?

See also Unit 5, Section **d**.

ⓔ Role play

1 Activity

At the end of the lesson

In groups of 8 to 10, if possible.

- Time limit: 5 minutes per teacher.
- Each 'teacher' should decide what has been happening in the lesson and what homework, if any, should be set. Collect together the books or papers required for that lesson. These should be given out at the beginning of each new session with a different 'teacher'.
- Give out the character card for the 'students' to act.
- Begin the role play at the point where most 'students' have just finished a written exercise. You want to stop them a bit early so that you get a chance to chat for five minutes or so about their plans for the coming weekend.
- Expand upon the ideas in the 'balloons' on the EXPLOITATION page, if suitable, or use your own ideas.
- Try to withdraw, so that by the end the students are just chatting among themselves. Do not interrupt or correct their English at this stage. The atmosphere must be relaxed and pleasant to induce the students to forget their shyness and use their English communicatively.
- End when you dismiss your class when the bell rings or when it is time.
- Read the points raised below before you begin.

2 Follow up and evaluation

(a) Which of the teachers in your group established the most relaxed and informal atmosphere? How was this achieved?

(b) Who managed to get the best and most natural conversation going? Why?

(c) Which errors, if any, consistently cropped up among the 'students'? Which do you think might crop up in a real class of schoolchildren or remedial adults, during a similar informal chat at the end of the lesson? How would you attempt to eradicate them?

3 A game to play

STOP[1] – another version of 'Hangman'.

The game can be played as a class game using the blackboard, or in groups using paper (if played in groups, give each group leader a different word to prevent groups overhearing each other). One person in the class thinks of a word and writes the number of letters in the word on the blackboard.

e.g. — — — — — — *(typist)*

Everyone else in the class must guess the word by calling out letters one by one, e.g. *F?* If there is an *F* in the word (in this case there isn't) the person at the blackboard puts the letter in the correct place in the word. If there isn't, he writes the letter at the side of the blackboard and crosses it out. At the same time he draws the first line of the sign STOP. (It can be completed in 13 lines and letters.) Every time a wrong letter is suggested, a line is added to the drawing. When the STOP sign is complete, the group has to stop playing. The aim of the game is to guess the word before the drawing is complete.

[1] From *Starting Strategies,* Teacher's Book by Ingrid Freebairn, Longman 1978.

Part Two

Teaching techniques and the language of instruction

How is Part Two different from Part One? Review pages viii to x of the Introduction; they tell you what Part Two is all about.

Aims and Objectives? Look at pages v–vi of the Introduction, then keep these aims in mind.

You will need (for every Unit) **1** your school or college textbooks **2** any other English teaching materials you have, e.g. pictures, visual aids, etc. **3** a good up-to-date grammar book.

13 FOCUS on the first lessons in English

My teacher speaks English all the time in class, slowly and very clearly, I understand her alright but the thing is, I can't understand anyone else.

We never talk English in class. It's too difficult. I can read O.K. but I'll never learn to speak. Suppose I'll have to go to England......

My teacher makes us speak English most of the time. If we can't understand she mimes or acts – its fun. Sometimes she tells us in our language but usually we manage O.K.

Well. My teacher speaks English most of the time too. She speaks very fast. At first we didn't understand, but now we can; even people talking English and on the radio too.

DO YOU have problems when you speak English in the classroom? If so, READ the INTRODUCTORY UNIT, page 1

WAYS to help your students understand. However, <u>one</u> of them is not always a good idea. Which one? (a) (b) (c) (d) (e) (f) or (g)

(a) using gesture while giving instructions and explaining
(b) demonstrating, miming, acting
(c) speaking very slowly and clearly all the time
(d) speaking, simply but with natural stress and intonation
(e) repeating and paraphrasing, giving students time to think it out for themselves sometimes
(f) giving lots of examples and using visual aids where possible
(g) establishing routines in class for various activities, e.g. pair work, so that students know what to do without being told

It often helps if you can CREATE an ENGLISH ATMOSPHERE in your classroom(s)

Set up an ENGLISH NOTICE BOARD

Display anything to do with English language and culture: information leaflets, bus tickets, timetables, maps. British Rail map, street map of London. Post cards of Britain. Menus, English recipes, pictures of pop stars, words of pop songs.
Film reviews. BBC World Service programmes. Labels of British or American products (tinned foods etc.). Pictures of fashion, sports – football, cars. Letters from pen friends. English stamps, coins.

WRITE OFF FOR TOURIST POSTERS!

ASK PEOPLE TO BRING SOUVENIRS FROM BRITAIN OR U.S.A. FOR **AN EXHIBITION!**

made in england

Set up a class library of English magazines, comics, easy reading books.

AT ELEMENTARY LEVEL, DISPLAY FLASH CARDS AND PICTURES AND YOUR STUDENTS' WORK.

START A 'PEN FRIENDS' CLUB!

Dear.............
Best Wishes
John.

and REMEMBER to CHANGE all DISPLAYS regularly so there is always something new and interesting

Unit 13 The first lessons in English

The aims of this Unit are **1** to show teachers how to control their language and help students of all levels to understand during their first few lessons entirely in English **2** to bring out the difference between teaching for passive control*, i.e. understanding, and active control* of English, i.e. speaking and using English productively **3** to examine the use of Questions in the ELT classroom, and give practice in handling them in different circumstances.

ⓐ Preliminary discussion

1 If you are about to teach a new class for the first time, whatever their standard of English – complete beginner, late elementary, intermediate or more advanced, – it may help you to get on with them better and establish a good rapport if you explain in their mother-tongue *why* you want them to try and speak English all the time in the classroom in their English lessons. Discuss briefly what you would tell them at the beginning of their first lesson with you. Refer to the Introductory Unit if you need some ideas.

2 On the FOCUS page at the beginning of this Unit, there is a list of techniques that teachers sometimes use to help students understand more easily. One of them is NOT to be advised. Which one, and why not?

3 The first time you teach a new class it's a good idea to begin to establish a set of standards concerning class procedures and stick to them. Which of the following do you think most important? Again, one of them is NOT to be advised. Which one, and why?
　(a) Complete silence while the teacher is talking, especially when presenting something new.
　(b) Everybody must take part in choral work and keep together.
　(c) Everybody should keep their voices low, especially in choral and pair work.
　(d) No student should answer out of turn.
　(e) Students should not interrupt you if they don't understand.
　(f) Students should not write unless you ask them to.

4 Now go through the list in 3 above and think what you would say to your students in English if you had to remind them about the above procedures.

5 If it's your first lesson with a group of complete beginners, how many words would you expect them (a) to be able to understand? (b) to be able to say and use by the end of your first lesson with them?

6 Discuss the differences between starting a course with adult beginners and children beginners.

85

ⓑ **Lesson extracts**

Listen to these extracts and notice especially which words or syllables carry the main stress (mark them thus ') and which vowel sounds are weak forms, in unstressed positions. Then practise them. *(G) stands for gesture.*

Extract one
In school

The teacher wants to teach 'Introductions' since it is her first lesson with this class and is a suitable chance to do so meaningfully. She has a picture of a boy and a girl who figure in the coursebook.

T: Good morning, everyone.
Ss: *(mutter)*
T: Listen. *(Gestures denote Ss to speak)* Good morning, Miss White. OK? I'm Miss White. You say it . . . Good morning . . . *(G)*
Ss: Good morning, Miss White.
T: Good. Right, I want you to listen. *(G)* Listening? Good. I'm Miss White and this is Tom. This is Tom and this is Janet. Tom. Janet. Can you say their names? *(G)* Listen and repeat. Tom. *(G)*
Ss: Tom.
T: Yes, good. Janet. Janet. *(G)*
Ss: Janet. *(ragged)*
T: *(gestures 'all together')* Janet.
Ss: Janet.
T: Good. *(explains in L¹ she wants them to introduce their neighbours to her)* OK. Right. This is . . . can you say it? *(G)* This is . . . th . . . th . . .
Ss: This is This is
T: *(gestures to one student and looks at his neighbour, questioningly)* this is . . .?
S: This . . . is . . . Ali
T: Hello Ali. *(looks at another student, who is introduced, and so on)* Nice to meet you . . . etc.

TEACHING HINT 'This is' is one of the new teaching items being presented but at no time does the teacher stress these words. Why?

Pronunciation practice

(a) Long and short vowels
Look at these pairs. The vowel sounds in each pair are not the same. What's the difference? Which vowel sound is the shorter, the first or second in each pair?

this/these   is/ease   good/food

(b) Weak and strong forms
What about 'to' 'two' and 'too' in these phrases:
I want to fish/I want two fish/to me/to and fro/me too?

(c) Stress timing
How many stresses in each of these phrases? Listen to the tape then repeat them.
  (i) Hi!   Good morning,
      Morning!   Good morning, everyone.
and these?
  (ii) Listen, please.   Would you all mind listening please?
      Can you listen, please?   I wonder if you'd mind listening, please?
      Could you all listen, please?

Answers below.

c (i) one stress on 'mórn', (ii) two stresses 'Líst pléase,' (the same number of stresses in each of the sentences despite the difference in length).

Remember, then that English is what we call a stress-timed language, (as opposed to syllable*-timed, like Italian). All the syllables between the stressed syllables are spoken rapidly. It should take the same amount of time to say 'Lísten, pleáse' as it does to say 'Could you all lísten, pleáse?' and so on. Practise.

Extract two
In college

It's the first lesson with a group of adult remedial beginners.

T: Well, good evening, everyone. Nice to see you all here. Welcome! Right, well, let's introduce ourselves, shall we? I'm Mr Brown, Brown, look, I'll write it for you ... OK? Now, could you sit in twos, please, like these two? In twos? *(G)*

Right, I want you to introduce yourselves in twos. Listen, like this: 'I'm Fred Brown,' 'and I'm John Smith. Nice to meet you, Mr Brown' and so on. OK?

Ss: *(introduce themselves to each other)*
T: Very good, well done! Now, will you introduce your friend to me and the rest of the class? You say, 'Mr Brown, this is ... and so on ... You?
S: Mr Brown, this is Hossein Adjimi.
T: Good evening, Mr Adjimi, nice to meet you.
S: And this is Sadegh Mohammad
S: Nice to meet you ...
(later)
T: You can also say 'Pleased to meet you', Pleased to meet you ... Can you repeat that?
Ss: Pleased to meet you.
T: Again but all together this time. Pleased to meet you.
Ss: Pleased to meet you.
T: Good. Now introduce your friend to the people in front of you or behind you, *(G)*
(later)
T: Now we're going to find out a bit about each other, where we work, live, etc.

TEACHING HINT (a) Why do you think the teacher uses expressions that he knows his students will not understand completely? (b) How does he in fact get his meaning across to them?

Pronunciation points

(a) Stress

Which two words are stressed here?
'It's nice to meet you.'
(See Extract one for further practice on Stress.)

(b) Liaison

In connected speech we often join two or more words together. For example, the question beginning 'Do you know ...' often sounds like 'Jeno' or D'yeno' when spoken rapidly by native speakers. Sometimes, as in this example, the consonants change in sound, too. (The 'd' becomes a 'j'.)

'It's nice to meet you' could become ' 'Snice t'meechou', the 't' and the 'y' have joined to make a 'ch' sound. A native speaker would never finish saying the 't' of the 'meet' before he started the 'y' of the 'you'. In fact many native speakers would miss the 't' all together: 'mee ɪ you' with a glottal stop in place of the 't'. Listen to the examples on tape.

Practise making the liaison here:
don't you? won't you? can't she? pleased to meet you.

Ⓒ Classroom language
Gradual introduction of classroom language

1 By the end of their first lesson in English, students should be able to understand and respond to the following directions **accompanied by relevant gestures.** They do **not** need to be able to **say** them.

Absolute beginners	*Remedial beginners/later elementary or beginners after 4 or 5 lessons*
Stand up, please.	Will you stand up, please?
Sit down, please.	Would you sit down, please?
Quiet please, ssh!	i.e. the same as for absolute beginners but preceded by
Listen!	Would you
Look at me.	Could you
Look at this.	Can you
Listen and repeat.	Will you, etc. in order to make them more polite.
OK?	**NB**: the stress remains the same as
Can *you* say it?	in the Imperative form, see Section **b**.
Good.	
Thank you.	

2 In the second lesson you could add, again making liberal use of gesture,

In twos/in pairs.⎫
 Everybody.   ⎬You say it after me. Ready?
 Altogether.   ⎭
Well done.
Now, quicker! Good.
OK. Sit down again please.

3 After 3 or 4 lessons you should try using fewer gestures to see if the students are beginning to respond to the verbal directions. If they are not, then play a game like 'O'Grady says', explaining the rules in L[1]:

'There is a very important man called O'Grady. You must do only what **he** tells you to do. If **I** tell you to do something like this: 'Look at me', you **mustn't** do it. If I say **'O'Grady says** Look at me' you **must** do it. If you do it when O'Grady has **not** told you to, you are out of the game. The last person still in the game is the winner.'

By using in the game all the directions you want them to learn, they will learn more quickly.

4 Gradually bring in the use of the language tabled in the rest of this Section.
It is divided for convenience into (a) Presentation stage (class listens to model) (b) Controlled Practice stage (repetition) (c) Further Practice (students manipulate forms for themselves) (d) Production Stage (students choose what they want to say), and in each Section the language follows consecutively, in short steps.
For Practice using dialogues, please refer to Unit 14.

In pairs, take turns to read out the groups of phrases and sentences from the following tables as clearly and firmly as you can, working out what gestures would be suitable to accompany each sentence. Choose appropriate language for your students and keep it lively. Rephrase often, and use suitable gestures. Where there are gaps thus ——————————, add something that would be suitable for one of your own classes, referring to a specific lesson or language item.

(a) Presentation stage (using a picture or some kind of visual aid)

OK.	Look.
Right.	Look again carefully.
Now.	Listen.
Fine.	Listen again.

I'll say it again. Listen.
Then I'll repeat it once more.

Now this is	about what we did last lesson. The_____ something new. It's about_____	remember? OK?

Ready to listen? Right, listen! Are you all listening?	OK, then.	(*Teacher models or plays the tape*)

Alright. Let's see if you understand. (*Asks questions to check meaning.*)

(b) Practice stage, controlled

Repeat after me. All together,
Listen, first, then repeat. OK?

Good. Now **you** say it after me.
Listen then **you** say it.
Listen and repeat. Wait.
Everybody! Again!
Group 'A' or 'B' etc.

Good. Can you say it **quicker**? Like this.
Wait until I've said it. Listen . . .
Now you.
Not bad. Do it again. Listen! Now you.
That was much better/very good/excellent.
Can **you** say it by yourself? Try. Listen, and repeat, . . .
Can **you** say it too? Go on . . . Good.

Correcting pronunciation

Now	listen to this	sound_____. word_____. phrase_____. question_____.	Not_____.	Like this_____. You	try! say it!
	put it together. Listen_____.				
	say it quicker_____ and quicker_____.				

Don't forget	it's 'ə' not 'a' in 'and'. the 'th' in 'the' etc.

(See Part One, Unit 8, Section **b**, 2, Back chaining.)

(c) Further practice

Now look. Listen.	It's different. There's something different.	There's a_____ What's different?	Listen.

Yes! Good.	There are 2 people instead of one. He's asking a question, now. It's negative now. etc.

Right, listen again then **you** have a go.

That was	very good, well done. quite good, let's do it once more.

OK Right Now then	something new! Let's change this_____	Now	what is it? who can do it? what should we say?

Correction techniques (using a pleasant tone of voice, to be encouraging)

Er, no . . . Ali, you try?   Nearly!
Not quite, try again. . . .   That's it!
Better, but still not quite right. Anyone?   Good, that was a difficult one.

(For more Practice activities, see Units 14 and 15.)

(d) Production (simple tasks only. They may need to be explained in L¹.)

Now imagine that you were	this person. Mr X.	What might he say?

Can anyone make some more sentences about . . . using the same pattern?
What else could Mr X say?
What about you? If this happened to **you** what would **you** say in English? and so on.
depending on the structure and the situation or context.
(For more on Production activities, see Unit 17.)

Correction techniques

At this stage, when students are experimenting with the new language they have
just been taught and beginning to use it for themselves, it would be psycholog-
ically unsound to interrupt and correct them, unless they were completely stuck
or obviously in a hopeless muddle and feeling unhappy. Teachers should,
therefore, not correct, but merely make a note of common errors and plan to
deal with them at a later stage.

ⓓ Teaching skills
Practice in questions: problem forms, aims and purposes, grading

1 Problem forms

Questions with WHO often cause problems. WHO can refer either to the *subject*
of the sentence or the *object*.¹ Students often get more practice in making
questions about the *object,* beginning WHO DID or WHAT DOES etc., so they
tend to use the same form for questions referring to the *subject* and thus get it
wrong. Look at the table below.

	Subject	Verb	Object
Statement	The policeman	caught	the thief.
Question about subject	WHO	caught	the thief?
Question about object			WHO did
	the policeman	catch?	

Exercise

In pairs, take turns asking and answering questions about all the people in the
following sentences. Do this as rapidly as you can and correct each other if
necessary.

(a) The headmaster punished the boy.

(b) The doctor examined the two Scottish footballers.

(c) My sisters look after old Mrs Smith. (NB singular verb is more usual in
questions.)

(d) Mrs Tomkin is going to help those children in Class 5.

(e) The gangster was pointing his gun at the hero.

(f) The witness saw that the bank robbers were threatening the cashiers.

¹ Note that WHAT can also refer to both the subject and the object in the same way.
However it is much rarer and such uses normally occur in more specialised language, e.g.
scientific or economic English. *Example*: Freak rainstorms often cause floods. WHAT
often causes floods? (NB singular verb) WHAT DO freak rainstorms often cause?

See Unit 8, Section **d**, for a game with questions: 'HOW MANY QUESTIONS?'

2 Aims and purposes of questions: checking understanding

Often questions are used in order to check whether students have understood or not. There are different kinds of things that students need to understand, and there are also different levels of understanding, for example:

the main points in a reading or listening passage
specific details in a reading or listening passage
the attitude of the author or the characters in a text
the meaning of particular words or expressions
the reference value of words like *he* and *then*
the meaning of a particular structural item
the general situation in a dialogue.

Here is a short extract from a taped dialogue followed by questions for you to analyse.

Tom and Fred happen to meet George, a friend of Tom's, in the street
GEORGE: Tom! Hello! I haven't see you for ages!
TOM: Hello, George; George, this is Fred. He comes from Manchester, like me, and he's a teacher at the school where I work, in Watford.
GEORGE: Oh, hello, Fred. Nice to meet you. . . .

Now study the following questions and analyse exactly the purpose of each. It may help if you ask your neighbour to answer the questions, first.

E.g. The question 'Where does Fred come from?' checks that the students understand that 'He' refers to Fred.

Where does Fred come from?   Where does Tom work?
Where does Tom come from?   Does George know Fred well?
How many people are there together?   Does George meet Tom every day?
What is Fred's job?   Who will speak next, after George?

3 Grading

You can grade questions according to different criteria, for example, according to how general or specific they are, how easy or difficult the actual answers are to say, or how easy or difficult it is to find the answers in the text.

(a) How would you grade the questions on the dialogue above if you were going to use them in one of your classes? Number them in the order you would ask them, then discuss with your neighbour why you have ordered them in the way you have chosen.

(b) Which of those questions would you ask in order to check if your students had understood the basic situation in the dialogue? i.e. Tom and Fred are friends, but Fred does not know George, whom they happen to meet.

(c) Finally, in pairs, preferably standing 3 or 4 metres apart, practise asking each other the questions and giving short, natural sounding answers. Remember, the purpose of these questions is to check understanding, not to elicit longer responses of the type used for oral practice.

For more work on questions, see Section **d** in Units 14, 18 and 19.

e Peer teaching[1]

1 Planning

(a) Divide into groups of approximately 8 participants.

(b) Each group should then split into halves to prepare a short lesson to teach to the other half, as follows:

Group A a first lesson in English for complete beginners

Group B a first lesson in English for a later elementary class, who have not been taught in English before

(c) Base your lessons on the textbook you will be using, but remember to adapt the textbook to your students' needs, rather than following it word for word.

(d) *Revise:* Part One, Unit 1, GREETINGS; some of this language may come in useful here, especially with a late elementary class, Part One, Unit 5, Section **b**, **2**, Being a Model.

(e) Write the aims of the lessons like this example:

'By the end of the lesson most students should be able to

1 say and use the following: Good morning, I'm ... This is ... Nice to meet you, etc.

2 understand these items: Listen, look, Let's introduce ourselves etc. ...'

(f) Then write in note form a brief outline plan of the lesson. If you find it useful you could use columns like this to set out your lesson plan: (This one has been filled in according to Extract One.)

TIME	TEACHER ACTIVITY / NEW LANGUAGE	CLASSROOM LANGUAGE	STUDENT ACTIVITY / NEW LANGUAGE
11·00	Greet class Good morning Introduce self Introduce Janet/Tom (pictures)	You say it Listening? I want you to listen Can you say their names? Listen + repeat	Listen (return greeting) Repeat Good morning Mrs White Repeat Janet/Tom
11·05	Explain in L' "Introductions" Present "this is"		"This is" Introduce their friends
11·10			

Obviously you will fill yours in according to your own plan. Remember to give students plenty of opportunity to practise the new language before you ask them to do something too testing.

[1] If you are fortunate enough to have real 'guinea-pig' students at the levels mentioned in **1** (b), above, you could carry out this exercise for teaching practice instead of peer teaching.

2 Peer teaching

- Assemble the aids you will need (chalk, pictures, things, etc.)
- Set a time limit and decide which of you will teach each stage of the lesson to the other groups. Leave at least 20 or 30 minutes for the follow-up session, **3**, below.
- 'Students' should remember to act as if they know very little English or none at all at the beginning of the lesson.

3 Evaluation

(a) *'Teachers':* Was anything more difficult than you had thought?
Did you achieve the aims you wrote down?
How much easier (or more difficult) would it have been with real students?
Did you remember to check understanding and learning?

(b) *'Students':* What exactly did you 'learn' to say? to understand?
Did your 'teacher' give you enough practice?
Did he/she vary the pace at any time? Was there any need to do so?
Would anything in particular have been muddling to real beginners?

(c) What recommendations would you make to other teachers using this particular lesson plan at this level?

❶ Further reading

W M Rivers and M S Temperley (1978) pp. 58–59.

Donn Byrne (ed) (1980) pp. 86–88.

14 FOCUS on dialogues

PRESENTING A NEW STRUCTURE?
REVISING AN OLD ONE?

Which FORMS shall I teach?

How can I make the MEANING clear?

How can I teach my students when to USE it?

No problems! USE A DIALOGUE!

Oh dear!

Help!

But there aren't any simple dialogues in my textbook

WRITE ONE YOURSELF!

HOW?

EXAMPLE 1 DIALOGUE to present:

FORM Present continuous tense, affirmative and question forms.

MEANING Future time.

USE Planned future actions, as opposed to future 'I will' which shows **un**planned actions.

A   Are you coming to Tom's party next Friday?
B   No, I can't. I'm spending Saturday with my family. I'm leaving Friday evening.
A   Well, come round on Thursday, then.
B   OK I'll see you Thursday. I'll come about 7, if I finish work on time.
A   See you Thursday! Bye!

EXAMPLE 2 DIALOGUE to teach:

FORM Third conditional, affirmative + abbreviated forms, questions.

MEANING Past, **un**fulfilled actions.

USE to talk about things that could have happened in other circumstances, but did not, e.g. an accident which would have been avoided; or something you wished for but didn't get, as here:

A   You know that competition we did?
B   The one three months ago?
A   Yes. Well Sam Porter won. He got £400!
B   Cor! He's lucky! I wish I had won!
A   If I had won I would have bought that car. What would you have done?
B   I would've spent it on travelling. I'd have flown to London!

Tired of dialogues?
Presenting forms that are usually <u>written</u> not spoken?

Like this :

1   Analyse your teaching point.
    (a) What are the possible **meanings**?
    (b) Which circumstances is it **used** in?
    (c) What common **forms** are there?

2   Ask yourself: does a change in form lead to a change in use or meaning? e.g. 'I (sha)'ll do that next week'
    = statement about future.

    'Shall I do that next week?' = $\left.\begin{array}{l}\text{offering}\\\text{asking}\end{array}\right\}$ advice.

    'Shall we do that?' = a suggestion.

3   Decide which **forms, meaning** and **use** to include and choose an appropriate setting. Think of two people and what they might say.

4   Write a *short* diaglogue, including the **forms** of the item, giving clues to meaning and use.

Do I write the dialogue on the board first?

NO!
Draw a picture of the people talking
ACT it out for your students!
Make them listen to understand. Get them to learn each line and say them in pairs.

OTHER METHODS OF PRESENTATION include:

● **model sentences** illustrated by demonstration, pictures, diagrams, realia
● **contrastive examples** also with pictures ● **situations** from the classroom, from the students' own lives, from the real world ● using a **written** or **spoken text** as a base.

BUT REMEMBER – learning discrete sentences is **not** enough. Students must be shown **how the sentences can fit into a conversation** or **a written paragraph.** Students must also learn **when** and **how** to use these sentences appropriately in spoken or written English and **practise recognising and using them** in **real-life contexts.**

Oh, what then?

Well, write some cue words on the board and get them to do it all in pairs!

Unit 14 Dialogues for presentation and practice

The aims of this Unit are 1 to show how language items can be presented and practised using a dialogue 2 to teach the classroom language needed when using dialogues 3 to give practice in the writing of suitable dialogues, and in the use of questions for the purpose of elicitation of short and longer responses

ⓐ Preliminary discussion

1 Discuss some of the usual differences between spoken and written English. The sentences below might help you: read them through, writing beside each sentence the word '*written*' or '*spoken*' as appropriate. Then discuss them.

(a) You can use intonation and stress to show meaning and attitude.

(b) You use punctuation, and verbal expressions of attitude and mood.

(c) It is impossible to ask for things to be repeated or explained every time you have not understood.

(d) Paralinguistic and non-linguistic features can help communication.

(e) There is generally more organisation of ideas, the use of 'marker words' like 'first', 'finally' is more common, and there are few unfinished sentences.

(f) If you haven't understood, you can check back and go through it again.

2 Sometimes you find that dialogues written in textbooks seem rather unnatural and stilted when you try to read them out loud or act them out. Why is this?

3 (a) What experience do you have of using dialogues for English teaching? What has been the purpose of the dialogues as far as you can see?

(b) What is the purpose of the dialogues on the FOCUS page at the beginning of this Unit?

4 (a) Presenting or practising a new structure orally by means of a dialogue can make it more memorable for the students. Why?

(b) Pointing out to students the function of a particular language item in dialogue, (e.g. the function of 'Can I play the piano, please?' is to ask permission to play, not to question one's ability to play,) can also help students to learn how and when to use this language item for themselves. Why?
(This might be easier to explain quickly in their mother-tongue but see Tables 5–7 and 13 in Section c for some ideas.)

5 (a) How long, approximately, is the 'ideal' dialogue for your elementary/early intermediate/late intermediate students to practise? Why?

(b) What topics would interest your students especially?

(c) At what stage (if at all) would you write the dialogue on the board?

6 How can you move from the controlled practice of a set dialogue which a student merely repeats, to a situation where the students are able to create their own dialogue or interact in English, e.g. as in a role play situation?

Discuss with particular reference to the two dialogues on the FOCUS page.

ⓑ Lesson extracts

Listen to both extracts and see if you can identify what the teacher's immediate aims are, in each case. Then practise repeating, after the tape, paying particular attention to the intonation of questions and the pauses the teacher makes. Repeat only the teacher's part.

Extract One

In school

The teacher is drawing a picture of an ice cream man. She has just told her class they are going to learn a dialogue about buying ice cream. Now she is beginning the presentation stage of the dialogue below.

Children:	Mm! Ice creams!
Man:	Are you next?
Girl:	Yes.
Man:	What would *you* like?
Girl:	Can we have three ice creams please, like those?
Man:	Three? Here you are. 30 pence please.
Girl:	Thanks. Lovely!

T: OK. Now then. Look at what I'm drawing . . . What's this?
Ss: Man.
T: Yes, a man; and what's he got in here?
Ss: Ice creams.
T: Yes, is he eating the ice creams? Eating them?
S: No, buying.
T: Buying? Is he buying them or selling them?
Ss: Selling.
T: He's selling ice creams, isn't he? Who to? Look, here are some children. What are they going to do? What will they say? Yes, Lee?
L: Children . . . er . . . going to buy ice cream.
T: The children are going to buy ice creams, yes, so what will they say to the man? Pari?
P: Please, want ice cream.
T: Anyone else?
Ss: I want ice cream . . . some ice cream . . .
T: Well, perhaps. OK. Listen to this dialogue, now, and tell me how these children ask for their ice creams. OK? See what *they* say.
Ss: Sorry, don't understand.

T: I'm going to read you a dialogue between the ice cream man, that's him, and the children. So listen to how the children ask, when they want to buy some ice cream. What do they say?
Ss: OK.

At this point she reads the dialogue, pointing to the characters as they speak.

T: Well then, how did they ask? Anyone?
Ss: Can we have 3 ice creams, please. Like those.
T: Good, 'Can we have 3 ice creams, please, like those', and she points to the picture, doesn't she? Now, let's practise that in halves. You, this half, you're the ice cream man, and er . . . you, this side are the children, in fact, the girl who speaks. Listen first, then you repeat if it's the man, and you repeat if it's the girl. Ready?

She begins to read the dialogue, line by line; the class repeats badly.

T: *(later)* Oh, no! Come on! Better than that! Listen properly, then repeat nicely. OK?
T: *(later)* Much better. Right, on we go.

👤 or 👤👤   **TEACHING HINTS (a) The class seem to have no difficulty in understanding the words, 'like those'. How do you think the teacher made it clear? (b) What do you think the teacher will do next? (i.e. after the choral repetition). (c) She didn't correct everything the students got wrong at the beginning of the lesson, why not? At what stage do you think she will definitely correct them if they are wrong?**

Pronunciation points

Intonation of 'attention' words. (Revision)

When a teacher wants to call the class to attention, he uses a word like 'Now', or 'Right' to mark the start of the next step. These 'marker' words are always said with a falling intonation and are followed by a pause. Listen again to the dialogue above and underline all the words that act as 'marker' words to get the attention of the class.

See Unit 1, Section **b**, 2.

Extract Two

In college

The teacher has presented and practised this dialogue with the class, and is now going on to less controlled practice, to see if the class can make up a similar one for themselves.

At the theatre box office
A – *man selling tickets*
B – *a theatre goer*

A: Yes?
B: Could we have two tickets for this evening, please?
A: For tonight?
B: Yes.
A: I'm sorry, we've sold out of tickets for tonight.
B: Er, . . . sorry? I . . . er . . .
A: No tickets left for tonight.
B: What about tomorrow?
A: I'm afraid there are no tickets left for tomorrow either. Sorry about that. Next week only.

T: You did that well, good. To sum up, then, who can tell me what happened in that last dialogue?
Ss: Bought . . .
T: Who bought. . .?
S: The man bought some tickets, two tickets, for theatre.
T: for the theatre, yes. Right. But this time, it's different. Look. I'll change my drawing. It's the same people, same place, but look at their faces! Are they happy? or angry?
Ss: No.
T: No? Are they angry or happy? Which?
Ss: Ah. Angry.
T: Well why could they be angry? Mr Dalvi?
S: Perhaps the tickets er very expensive?
T: Maybe. What do *you* think? Mr Meyer?
S: Tickets finished.
T: Well, yes, but you can't say that in English; what *can* you say? Does anyone know? . . . No? Well, listen to this dialogue and see what they say, then you can practise the same kind of dialogue in pairs, afterwards. Listening?
    Teacher reads the dialogue again.
S: *(later)* Oh, he says, 'Sold out of tickets for . . .'
S: for tonight.
T: Yes, and does he say anything else?

Because the man doesn't understand the first time, does he? So he says the same thing another way. How?
S: No tickets . . . er . . . left for tonight.
T: Good. No tickets left for tonight. Can you all say that?
Ss: 'No tickets left for tonight'
T: And what about tomorrow? *(he shakes his head)*
Ss: No tickets left for tomorrow.
T: Good. But what else does he say, before that?
S: Sorry.
T: Yes, he apologises, doesn't he? And what would he say if he only had two tickets left, and you wanted three? Come on! . . . 'I've only got . . .'
S: I've only got two tickets left.
T: And if he only had very expensive ones left?
S: Sorry, I've only got expensive tickets left.
T: Good. Right, I want you to make up your own dialogues, now, in pairs, asking for tickets, the man selling them apologising, and offering some different ones . . . OK? I'll write one or two words on the board for you . . . Say it first, then change over parts, then when I've heard you, you can write one down.

TEACHING HINTS (a) How does the teacher make sure the students listen very carefully to the dialogue? (b) The teacher doesn't actually ask the class to repeat this dialogue, so why do you think he bothers to read it to the class? (c) How does the class know what they have got to do next? Do they know roughly how long the dialogue should be?

Ⓒ Classroom language

Please refer to Part One, Units 8 and 9, Section **c**, for the Classroom Language you will need when dividing the class up to do choral and pair work to practise the dialogues.

Find a picture and/or a dialogue in your textbook and practise the language below in that context, working in pairs, taking turns to be the teacher. Adapt the language to suit your needs.

Announcement

1

Well, now, OK,	we're going to I want you to	listen to practise learn	a short dialogue today.

Setting the scene

2

Look at	this picture. my drawing.		Well,	who do you think they are, these people?	
There are two people talking. I'll draw them here, look. This is_____ and this is_____				what do you think they're	doing? saying? discussing? thinking?
				why do you think they're_____?	

3

Now, these people	are good friends so they	speak informally to each other. don't need to be so formal.	
	don't know each other very well have never met before	so they are	more formal. very polite.

4

Now, this is_____'s	boss manager headmaster headmistress	so	he she you	must be very polite to	him. her.

Identifying the language

5

The people in this dialogue are going to Does anyone know what you say in English when you	introduce a friend to someone. give someone directions to a place. offer something to someone. make a suggestion.
Who knows how you can	give some advice to someone. etc.

(At an elementary stage you may need to use L¹ to explain this.)

6

For example, Let's take an example, I'll give you an example,	supposing if	a friend your boss a stranger	needs advice on something. hasn't met Mr_____ before. is about to forget something. wants to arrange something. needs information quickly.

		What could	he she you	ask say ? reply

↓

(After an informal student response) ↓

7

Yes, Fine,	if it is	an informal situation a friend someone you know well	you could say that, good.
But if it was	your boss a stranger a formal setting		then what would you say?

Listening and practising

(See also Unit 18 for questions to guide students' listening; Section **c**.)

8

Books shut, then. Close your books.	Ready to listen?	It's_____ who speaks first.

9

OK, so what	were they talking about? did_____ want to know? did_____ reply?

(For other types of questions see also Unit 13, Section **d**.)

10

I want you to listen again and this time,	tell me	who says '_____'	
		exactly	what_____ said. what phrase_____ used to_____. how_____ replied.
	repeat	_____'s part, altogether. taking turns, this side of the class be_____, and you,_____.	
	when I stop,	complete the sentence. you finish the sentence.	

11

| Now, before we practise that in pairs, shall | we | read it in your books? repeat it once more all together? | |
| | I write | it all some cue words | on the board? |

(For pair practice, see Unit 9.)

Changing the dialogue for freer production

12

If **you** were in that situation, If someone said '_____' to you,	then	what would you	reply say add	?
		how would you continue the conversation?		
Any suggestions? Let's have some ideas.				

13

	accept the offer/idea/suggestion or say 'No' and explain why.
Yes, you could	agree with the other person and say something else.
	show you were pleased/a bit anxious/annoyed and explain.
	hesitate and ask him to explain again.
	ask the reason.
	ask for further information.
	carry on the conversation with a personal opinion.

So how exactly would you say that in English?

14

Alright then,	we'll change the dialogue so that you _____ instead.
	you work in pairs and I'll come round and listen.

(For more ideas on Oral Production, see Part Two, Unit 17.)

ⓓ Teaching skills

NB Before beginning this Section, go back to Section **d** of the previous Unit, page 90, and revise it well. This Section builds on to and constantly refers back to that Section **d**.

1 Writing your own dialogues

(a) Mini-dialogues

Short three or four line dialogues are easy for students to learn by heart, and fun to practise in pairs.

e.g. To teach the use of 'I'd rather:'

		Substitute:	
A:	Shall we go to the cinema?	play football	go for a walk
B:	Mm. I'd rather go to a disco.	play volleyball	stay at home
A:	Alright then.		

– In pairs, taking a different structural item, write a similar mini-dialogue for your students to learn.

(b) Slightly longer dialogues are often useful for presentation of new language items, see the FOCUS page at the beginning of this Unit.

– Discuss the four stages suggested under the heading: 'Write one yourself'.
– In pairs, choose an item you will need to present to your students some time.
– Following the four stages given, write a natural sounding dialogue, which covers the points in 4.
– Get another pair to practise it.

2 Aims and purposes of questions: elicitation

(a) Questions eliciting short answers, e.g. 'Yes, he did.' etc.

The purpose of these questions is to give the class practice in producing short form answers. As a revision activity, these could be in different tenses.

– Refer back to the dialogue that you wrote in 1 above, or to the one between Tom and George on page 91, and write ten questions based on the dialogue which will elicit short form answers beginning 'Yes, he ...' or 'No, he ...'
– Ask your neighbour to check them.
– Do the same for the two dialogues on the FOCUS page at the beginning of this Unit.
– Practise asking your questions, five at a time, as quickly as possible, working in pairs or small groups. Try to keep the pace fast, but correct any mistakes that occur.

(b) Questions eliciting extended responses

Which of the following questions do you think would be suitable for getting the students to give a longer response? Refer to the same dialogue on page 91.

What do you know about Fred and Tom?

How do you know that George has not met Fred before?

What do you think they might all do next?

Why do you think Tom and Fred left Manchester to work in Watford?

What do you think George might say to his family when he gets home after meeting Tom and Fred?

Study the question forms used here in (b). In what ways are they different from the types of questions you have studied before in these two Units?

For other methods of elicitation refer to Unit 15, Section **d**.

3 Staging questions

In order to guide students towards a better understanding of a text or dialogue, you can often stage questions in such a way as to help them find the answer to a more difficult question by asking them a series of easy questions first. These could focus on the information required in the answer of the more difficult question. For example, questions 4, 6 and 8 guide the student towards the answer to question 11 below.

(a) Read the dialogue below. It is a taped dialogue, intended for intermediate students, to act as a stimulus for some question and answer work. (It is not suitable as a set dialogue for intermediate students to learn by heart, since it contains a lot of language that is suitable for passive use only, at this stage.)

A young woman stops a man outside the station

WOMAN:	Excuse me, could you tell me the way to Park Road, please?
MAN:	Sorry? er ... Where ...?
WOMAN:	er ... Park Road.
MAN:	Oh, I know, Park Road. Well, actually, it's quite a long way from here, you'd better get a bus. A number 12, you need. It stops just round the corner here. You get off at the Royalty Cinema, then ... (*fades out*)

The questions, which you will be writing to elicit the answers given below, are in three sets. Each set of questions has a different purpose. The sets are also staged; the first set of questions focuses on points that will help the students answer the second set. Without doing the first two stages, students would probably find the third stage very difficult to tackle.

 (b) Write questions to elicit the answers given below.

Quick questions to check general understanding of the situation:

1 _____?To Park Road.

2 _____?A man.

3 _____?No, she can't.

4 _____?By bus.

Questions to check understanding of specific details:

5 _____?No, it's quite a long way.

6 _____?A number 12.

7 _____?Round the corner.

8 _____?At the Royalty Cinema.

Questions to elicit longer answers for oral practice:

9 _____?
Perhaps she wants to visit someone who lives there.

10 _____?
Because he didn't hear the name of the road properly.

11 _____?
She has to get a number 12 and get off at the Royalty Cinema.

12 _____?
Because it is too far to walk there, and the bus is quicker.

13 _____?
Perhaps he is going to tell her how to get to Park Road from the Royalty Cinema.

⊖ Teaching practice

1 Planning

(a) Divide into groups of 4, if possible. Each group should choose a different dialogue of about four lines from the textbook, or adapt a dialogue. Refer to Section **d**, **1** (a) in this Unit. It should be suitable for one of your classes to practise and learn. Practise reading it out loud with pauses for repetition.

(b) Collect any visual aids or realia you may need, and practise drawing a quick sketch of the characters in the dialogue on the blackboard. You can refer to them when introducing the dialogue and when reading it out loud in parts.

(c) Decide what you will say to introduce the dialogue, before you read it to the class.

(d) Write some sets of graded questions to fulfill the following purposes:
  − a 'sign-post' question to make them listen with a purpose
  − some questions to check general understanding of the situation
  − some questions to check particular items that may cause problems.

(e) Decide how this dialogue could be changed slightly to give students a chance to use their own ideas, during pair work, see Section **d**, **1** (a).

(f) Write a brief outline of the lesson so that it can be divided into four stages, to allow each teacher to teach one stage. See the example below.
  (i) Introduce characters, set the scene. Sign-post question. First reading.
  (ii) General questions, including sign-post question. Second reading. Third reading with pauses for repetition, class in halves.
  (iii) More detailed questions to promote some short oral practice. Listen and repeat, faster, class in halves, then individuals, then in pairs. Check pair work.
  (iv) Hear some individual pairs practising, class listening. Suggest variation on the dialogue, and ask students for some ideas of what they could say in the new situation. Less controlled pair work, teacher wandering round to listen.

(g) For each stage, make out a detailed plan as in Unit 13, Section **e**, **1** (e) and (f).

2 Teaching practice

Decide on a time limit for each stage of the lesson.

- If peer teaching, use role play cards suggesting some common mistakes that could occur.

- Each group of 4 should combine with another group, so that they can be 'taught' a dialogue that they have not prepared themselves.

3 Evaluation

Take each 'Lesson' in turn and discuss the following:

(a) *'Teachers':* Did your questions fulfill the purpose you intended?

        Were they adequately staged and graded?

        Did the 'students' repeat well in the choral repetition?

        Did they keep together? Why?

        What mistakes did you correct, and at what stage?

        Did they enjoy doing the freer pair work at the end?

(b) *'Students':* Did they always know what they were supposed to be doing? Why?

        Did they find the dialogue easy to repeat?

        Did they find any of the questions particularly easy or hard?

        Did you feel the teacher corrected them at the right stages?

        Did you feel the dialogues were worth learning?

(c) *Everyone:* Which of the dialogues would be suitable for *your* classes?

🅕 Further reading

Look up DIALOGUES and QUESTIONS in the index of *Teaching Oral English* by Donn Byrne. Follow up the references given and make notes on any useful ideas.

Helen Moorwood (ed) (1978) Section 1.

W M Rivers and M S Temperley (1978) pp. 24–40.

15 FOCUS on oral practice

Spot the odd one out!
Which of the ten activities is linguistically unsound?

1 Substitution table

Fred He Jane She	has 's	got	a	big small new nice	ball. balloon. toy car. bicycle.

2 Discrimination exercise

Listen and answer either
'Yes I do' or 'Yes please'
as appropriate.

Do you like apples?
Would you like an apple?
Would you like a biscuit?
Do you like biscuits?
Do you like coffee?
Would you like some?
etc.

3 Substitution drill

'Ali goes to school every day'
– yesterday
– shopping
– Mrs Moustapha
– to town
– every day etc.

4 Conversation drill

You are B; tell A what he/she needs.

A Oh dear, it's raining. B You...

A The baby's thirsty. B She...

A He's very cold. B He...

5 Using picture cues

(a) Make true statements comparing the things in the pictures, e.g., Cars are more expensive than bicycles.

(b) Say which you would rather have as a present, tell your neighbour why.

(c) Describe one of the objects to your neighbour (without naming it), until he/she can guess which it is.

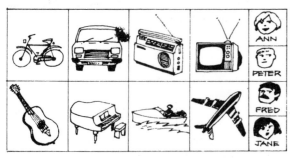

6 Guessing games (with cue cards) See Tables on p. 108

Teacher or student picks a card and the others must guess which it is by asking questions based on a model given. For example: (to practise the simple past)

T 'Guess what I did at six o'clock last night.'
S Did you visit your sister?
T No, I didn't
S Did you go to the cinema? etc.

7 Transformation drills

Change *'will'* to *'going to'*:

Peter will have a party tomorrow.
His mother will bake a cake.
His friends will give him presents.

8 Using wall charts

(a) Make sentences about the picture below following the pattern:
'I saw x _____ ing...'
E.g. We saw a girl waving at the people outside.
    I heard people shouting for help.

(b) When the boy telephones the fire brigade to tell them there is a fire, what questions will the fire brigade ask him?

(c) Make up a dialogue, in pairs, between the boy and the fire brigade.

Fire!

9 Imaginary situations

Your friend's parents have gone away for a few days, leaving your friend in charge of the house and family. You check that your friend has remembered to do everything (sweep the yard, tidy up, do the shopping, feed the chickens). You ask questions like, 'Have you swept the yard?' etc. In an office situation, a boss might check on the secretary in the same way.

HOW MANY ALTERNATIVE VERSIONS OF THIS?

10 Expanding

Expand the following

Fred / holidays / July.
Where / he / go?
How much / fare / cost?

Unit 15 Oral practice

The aims of this Unit are **1** to help teachers evaluate different types of oral practice activities from the linguistic point of view **2** to teach the language needed to handle a variety of oral practice activities in the classroom **3** to give practice in different elicitation techniques that can be used at the practice stage in the lesson

ⓐ Preliminary discussion

1 (a) List the types of activity suggested in your textbooks which can be used to give the student practice in speaking English.
(b) How far are these activities designed to help the student, and how far to test him?

2 Have you developed any useful techniques of your own to give your students practice in spoken English? What stage of the lesson do you use them, and why?

3 Activities based on an 'information gap'* between two speakers, e.g. guessing games, are often more motivating than drills or exercises. Why?

 4 Students will not perform well at the end of their course if they only have practice in forming new structures, sentence by sentence. They also need practice in recognising the meaning of the new item and in using it in appropriate situations. In short, they need practice in FORM, MEANING and USE.

(a) In pairs, study the selection of practice activities on the FOCUS page opposite and discuss exactly what they give students practice in: mark (F) if they only give practice in the form; that is if the students can still get them right without understanding the meaning or use. Mark (F and M) if they have to understand the meaning to get them right, and (M, F and U) if the activity helps students to realise when it is used. Do the same for your textbook activities.

(b) Which of these activities are mechanical and which are meaningful? Consider the TRANSFORMATION DRILL, number 7. Do any of the items or their transformations sound strange to you? Discuss why.

5 (a) What visual aids could you use to make some of the activities more interesting and meaningful? What about the ones in your textbooks?
(b) What kind of pictures could you have on the flash cards for 6?

6 Some of the activities on the FOCUS page opposite are very controlled while others are freer, and more suitable for the later stages of a lesson, leading up to free production. At what stages of a lesson would you use each activity? Which ones could lead into a useful writing exercise? (See Unit 20.)

105

ⓑ Lesson extract

This Unit contains only one lesson extract because it is equally suited to both adult learners and children. This extract could also be used as a starting point for the Teaching Practice in Section **e**.

Play the tape and practise repeating the teacher's part. Then underline in the text all the 'marker' words the teacher uses to make the class pay special attention, when something different is going to happen. Then play the tape again, repeating just the phrases with marker words in.

 In school or college

The teacher has presented the present perfect tense as it is used relating to past experiences which affect the present time.
She has practised the form in a controlled way, using a substitution table, and she now wants to get her class to practise using it in meaningful contexts, and relate it to language they have already learnt. In this case, the class have recently learnt how to describe places and use the question 'What's it like?' The teacher, at the start of this extract, has just put up a map of their own country and listed the main towns.

T: So, we're going to talk about places you've visited, towns you've been to, in the past, but that you can still remember and tell us about, now. OK. How can I ask you if you know a place, if you've been to a place? What is the question? Yes? Kumah?
S1: You have been ...?
T: Anyone else?
S2: Have you been to London?
T: Good. Well, Rosa, have *you* ever been to London?
S3: Er, no.
T: No, I haven't.
S: No, I haven't.
T: Good. Someone ask Gustav if he's been to Hamburg. Have you ever ...?
S: Have you ever been to Hamburg, Gustav?
T: Uha.

S: Yes, I haven't.
T: Haven't?
S: Oh. sorry, yes, I have.
T: Yes, I have, fine. Well, what's it like?
S: It's very big town and modern. Er shops ... er cars, ...
T: It's a very big town, yes. Good. Well, now, I want you to work in pairs and find out which of these towns you've been to, the towns we have listed on the board. So you'll have to ask each other 'Have you ever been to?' and then ask 'What's it like?' or 'What do you think of it?'
OK. In twos, you ask first, you, you; and the others answer, then change over. Go on, Have you ever ...
(Massed pair work; teacher wanders round)

T: Alright. Stop now, good. So now you all know where your friends have been? Yes? Good. Right, you can all write down two sentences about your friends, true sentences; remember the ones you read from the table? Like those, but true. You give me a true sentence about your friend, er, – Lee.
S: Ali has been to Bawku.
T: Is that true, Ali?
S: Yes, I've been there three times.
T: Three times? Very nice. So, all of you, quietly write two or three sentences about your friend, then you can read some of them out to the class.

👤 or 👤👤   **TEACHING HINTS (a) Why does the teacher ask Gustav what Hamburg is like? (b) Why does she use a map of their own country rather than a map of Britain or the USA? (c) Why does she get the class to practise in pairs even though some of them are making some mistakes? (d) Why does she ask them to do some writing after the pair practice?**

Ⓒ Classroom language

Select the language which relates to the type of practice activity you will be using in class. Adapt it where necessary to suit your own students. Then practise in pairs, referring to the activity you have decided to talk about, and giving one or two examples as models for your partner to follow, as you would in a class.

Substitution tables

1

How many	sentences different sentences	can you	say? say to your neighbour? write down? remember?	Listen, I'll do one_____. Like this_____. Nice and quickly.

2

Who will be the first	team group pair person one	to	read out learn say write	5 10 15	sentences? questions?

3 (With a table on the blackboard, you can gradually erase parts of it.)

Now I'm going to rub	some a few more	words off.	Can you still say a sentence?
Now	turn round, face the back, without looking at the board,		how many can you remember? say some to yourselves.

4 (With mixed tables where not all combinations produce correct sentences.)

Now, be careful,	this table is more difficult; only some sentences are correct.	
	this time you have to	make true sentences about the picture. answer my questions from the table.

Discrimination exercise

5 (referring to words on the blackboard)

Listen	and tell me which this refers to, this, (past tense) or this (present). then answer either like this,_____, or like this,_____ whichever is suitable.

6

I'm going to	read say	some	sentences questions	which are either	past or present. offers or queries. about one person or two people. a request or a command.

See Unit 18 for more on listening and oral work.

Substitution drill

7

We'll start with Look at Listen to	this sentence, '_____'	Can you repeat it?	All together. Faster! And again!

8

Now	say it with change it, say	'yesterday' instead of 'every day' (and remember the verb). 'shopping' instead of 'to school'.

9

Listen to Look at	the cue and use the cue word.
Listen, and I'll	do the first two for you so you understand. show you how I mean.

Conversation drill
(with pictures or word cues)

10

We're going to	practise using the verb do a conversation drill,	with	'need'.	Look at these cues. What are these things?

11

There are two people talking, A and B. A says something and B answers.	Listen_____ Like this_____

12

Now, I'll be A and you	are B. take B's part.	Listen to what A says and reply using one of the cues. So you make a sentence with 'need', OK?

Using picture cues

13

Look at these	people on the board.	They	want to do like doing are going to do have just done want to buy have just bought etc.	one of these things.
	names of the people in the picture.			

14

So,	can you I want you to	make a sentence ask a question	about each person;	like this '_____' using this pattern '_____' beginning '_____'

15

Now, in	twos, threes,	make up a short dialogue do some questions and answers,	like this,_____ for example_____ about yourselves.

Guessing games
(to practise question forms)

16

There are	3 5 8	people people doing things objects words expressing time	in this picture. on the board.	They all have numbers.
		different things in my bag. cards with pictures on.		

17

I'm going to One of you can	choose write	one	card number thing	and not tell anyone which it is.

18

Then the rest of you	can have to	ask questions to	find out guess	which one it is.

Shall I	show you? demonstrate?	Questions on this Keep to the same	pattern,_____ OK?

You	have to can only	ask questions with Yes or No answers,	like this,_____ for example_____

Right; so	I'll you	choose one, and all of you can guess.
If you guess correctly,	you	can choose next time. get the next go.

Using indirect questions

(to give students practice in asking questions and to promote pair practice)
The table refers to the Wall picture illustrated on page 104 at the bottom. Be careful to use the correct intonation for indirect questions (falling; listen to the question the teacher asks Gustav to ask, in the taped dialogue).

Now I want you to practise some questions. Ready?					
Someone Lee,	ask	Ali Rosa Tse		how	she/he thinks the fire started. the fire started.
				where the students were sitting.	
				what	the students outside did, on seeing the smoke. she/he thinks about the fire.
Ask		your	neighbour partner(s)	who	the fire brigade had to rescue and why. telephoned the fire brigade.
		each other		why the people in the building could not get out. how long it took to put the fire out. how much damage it caused. if anybody had to go to hospital.	

Correction techniques

(at the controlled practice stage, where accuracy is important)
See Part Two, Unit 13 for more on corrections.

Wait Excuse me Just a minute	'_____?'	Was that	correct? how I said it? alright?	Think! What was wrong?	
Er, not '_____' (gesture)				Listen Say it	again!
				What should it be?	

Yes,	well done. much better.	Let's all say that together. Can you say it again for us?	Listen, OK?

Teaching skills

Elicitation practice

See also Unit 14 Section **d**, **2** and **3** for the use of questions for elicitation purposes.

1 Conversation drill

 The purpose of using a two line dialogue for structure practice is to give students practice in using the new structure in a natural way in a meaningful situation. In the example on page 104, 4 CONVERSATION DRILL, the dialogue would consist of:

A: Oh dear, it's raining.   B: You need an umbrella!

which sounds like natural spoken English.

Supposing you wanted your students to practise the structure *'should have done'* using the following picture cues to produce sentences like:

 You should have gone to bed earlier.

 He should have driven more carefully.

 She should have bought some more bread.

 He should have tried it on before he bought it.

 What can you say that will make these sentences into natural sounding responses? **NB** 'What should he have done?' (pointing to the cue picture) would most naturally be answered, 'gone to bed earlier', rather than the full sentence.

Look at the following utterances. Only 4 of them would naturally elicit the full sentence. Write the most natural oral response in the space beside each one and find out which 4 utterances would make good elicitations.

(a) Should he have gone to bed earlier? _____

(b) Shouldn't he have tried the shirt on before he bought it? _____

(c) Oh dear. There's no bread left. _____

(d) Did he buy some more bread? _____

(e) I'm terribly tired this morning. _____

(f) What time should you have gone to bed? _____

(g) What should he have tried on in the shop? _____

(h) Hey. That new shirt doesn't fit, does it? _____

(i) Paul had a car crash on his way home last night. _____

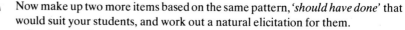 Now make up two more items based on the same pattern, *'should have done'* that would suit your students, and work out a natural elicitation for them.

Do the same for some other patterns that your students often need practice in.

2 Substitution tables

(a) Think of a pattern that your students often get wrong and need remedial practice in. In pairs, draw up a simple substitution table with a maximum of six items in the longest column. Make sure that all the possible sentences are correct English and sound natural. Try to use ideas that will interest your students.

(b) Then make up six to eight questions or statements that will naturally elicit a sentence from the table as a response.

You could also tell a very short story which could be summarised by a sentence from the table. For example, see the table on the FOCUS page at the beginning of this Unit; you could tell a story, thus: 'Fred's uncle gave Fred a toy car for his birthday. Fred was happy because it was a big one.' The students pick out the main points (it doesn't matter if they don't understand every word) and read out 'Fred's got a big toy car'.

(c) Practise in pairs, eliciting and reading out sentences from the table you have written.

(d) Make up a short four line dialogue containing one of the sentences from the table, or a similar one, that will illustrate how this structure can be used in an everyday situation. Try it out on your neighbour to make sure it sounds natural. See how long it takes him or her to learn it. Is it simple enough for your students to learn for homework?

(e) Finally make a copy of all the tables and dialogues produced by other pairs that have worked well. This way you will have a ready made set of tested practice materials that you can use again and again in class.

3 Discrimination exercise

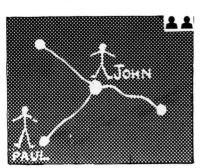

AIM: to teach the difference in meaning between *'been to'* and *'gone to'*.

(a) Draw a map on the board showing the relation between your town or village and two or three other main towns in your country.

Explain simply in English to your neighbour, the difference in meaning between 'Paul has gone to X' and 'Paul has been to X' using the map. Add some pin men with names, who all live in your town or village.

(b) Write out six items for a discrimination exercise that you could use to check your students understand the meaning. For example, 'Paul has been to X, where is he now?' Try them out on your neighbour.

(c) Think of a way to elicit the full sentence in a natural way.

4 True/False statements

(a) Look at the following sentences and say whether each refers to past, present or future time.

(a) If Cyril had won the lottery he would have bought a Mercedes.

(b) If Fred was rich enough he would buy a Mercedes.

(c) If Charlie gets a rise in salary he'll buy a Mercedes.

(b) True or false statements about sentences like these can help you diagnose whether the students have understood the meaning and implications of the structure. The students listen to your statements, which should either be true or false, and then tell you which they think it is, giving the corrected version if it was false.

For example: Sentence (a) above can be written on the board and the following statements made orally by the teacher:

'If Cyril had won the lottery he would have bought a Mercedes.'

True or False? Correct the false ones:

Cyril won the lottery.	He has bought a Mercedes.
Cyril tried to win the lottery.	He can't afford a Mercedes.
He didn't buy a Mercedes.	He didn't win the lottery. etc.
He wanted to buy a Mercedes.	

(c) Now write some true/false statements about sentences (b) and (c) above and try them out on your neighbours.

(d) Finally do the same for other structures that you will have to teach, each person taking a different teaching item, and trying the statements out on each other.

5 Indirect questions

(to elicit question forms)

See CLASSROOM LANGUAGE, Section **c**, Table 22.

Asking your students to ask the questions is an excellent way of making sure that they get sufficient practice in using question forms. Very often, it is only the teacher who asks the questions in the classroom. In real life, however, the student is just as likely to have to ask questions as he is to answer them, and unless he gets practice in asking questions in class, he will not be able to do so.

The form of indirect questions is not difficult for students to understand even early on in their English course. At later stages, however, students often have problems with the word order when they use indirect questions orally. If you use indirect question forms from the early stages, your students will get used to hearing them and are more likely to get them right later on. They will also have benefited from learning how to ask ordinary questions for themselves.

 Do either (a) or (b) or both.

(a) Find an exercise in your textbooks which consists of questions about a picture or a short reading passage.

Work in groups of four or five, taking turns to be the teacher who asks one student to ask another student each question. The questions in the book should be covered up so the 'students' cannot see them.

(b) Using a large wall picture, or poster or a clear magazine picture, work in small groups as above, asking each other to ask questions about the people or places in the picture. See Table 22 for examples of different types of indirect questions.

6 A game to play

 GIVE ME ANOTHER ONE!

Any number of players up to 8, in a circle.

Player A chooses a pattern sentence, e.g. 'Jim likes playing football'. He then gives another sentence on the same pattern in order to show which words can be changed, e.g. 'Jim likes watching television'. He then says, 'Give me another 6!' (or whatever number he thinks possible, up to 10). Each player in turn says one different sentence on the same pattern until the six are done. Then someone else chooses and the game continues.

You are OUT

– if you hesitate for longer than the agreed time (5 or 10 seconds)

– if you make a mistake and do not correct it yourself before the next player's turn

– if you give a sentence which is meaningless or unacceptable, e.g. 'Jim likes making' or 'Jim likes crying'!

You should decide on how to judge the game before you start; either have one referee for each round, or vote on whether a sentence is acceptable or not, or whatever system you like best. The game finishes when only one person is left in, and he or she is declared the winner.

(The person choosing can be challenged to say himself all the sentences he suggested, if it is agreed by everyone else that it is impossible. If he can't do it, he is out for the next round; if he can, he gets an extra life, i.e. he can stay in once even if he is OUT according to the rules above.)

ⓔ Teaching practice

1 Planning

The AIM of the teaching practice in this Unit is to examine and supplement, if necessary, the practice activities suggested in your textbooks and to practise teaching them.

(a) Work in pairs or small groups, each taking a different unit or lesson from the textbook used in your schools or colleges. Examine the lesson carefully; then select or think out about three different types of practice activity that you could use to give students practice in forming and using the teaching item in meaningful situations. Plan to maximise individual student practice time by including activities that could be done with massed pairs, all speaking at once.

(b) Prepare any necessary flash cards or plan blackboard sketches to help contextualise the language being practised, and to act as cues or prompts for pair work.

(c) Suggest the stage at which these activities might fit into a lesson, (e.g. immediately after the presentation stage, if they are controlled) and make sure you can explain exactly what the aims of each activity are.

2 Teaching practice

At least ONE activity should be introduced and carried out by each teacher.
- Begin by introducing the activity to the class or peer group.
- Remember to check the students understand what it is they are saying.
- Vary the pace if possible, and also vary the patterns of teacher/student interaction by using massed pair work as well as individual responses.

3 Evaluation

Discuss which activities you think would be most useful in your teaching situation.

If there are a number of practical suggestions that are not included in your textbook arrange for them to be typed up and circulated for the benefit of all teachers, with a note of the aim of each activity and a rough idea of how to make it work effectively in class.

4 Optional activity

Refer back to the set EXTRACT in Section **b** in this Unit.

Plan a longer lesson around the extract. It should include some other types of practice activities, e.g. a substitution table which would come before the recorded extract, and one or two less controlled types of practice to follow on after the extract.

Follow the steps set out above for PLANNING and TEACHING, then evaluate your performance in the light of 3 above.

ⓕ Further reading

On using questions Donn Byrne (1976) pp. 48–53.

On practice activities Donn Byrne (1976) pp. 32–43.

On visual aids at the practice stage Andrew Wright (1976) Chapter 2, pp. 14–21.

Helen Moorwood (ed) (1978) Section 2.

W M Rivers and M S Temperley (1978) Chapter 4.

16 FOCUS on vocabulary

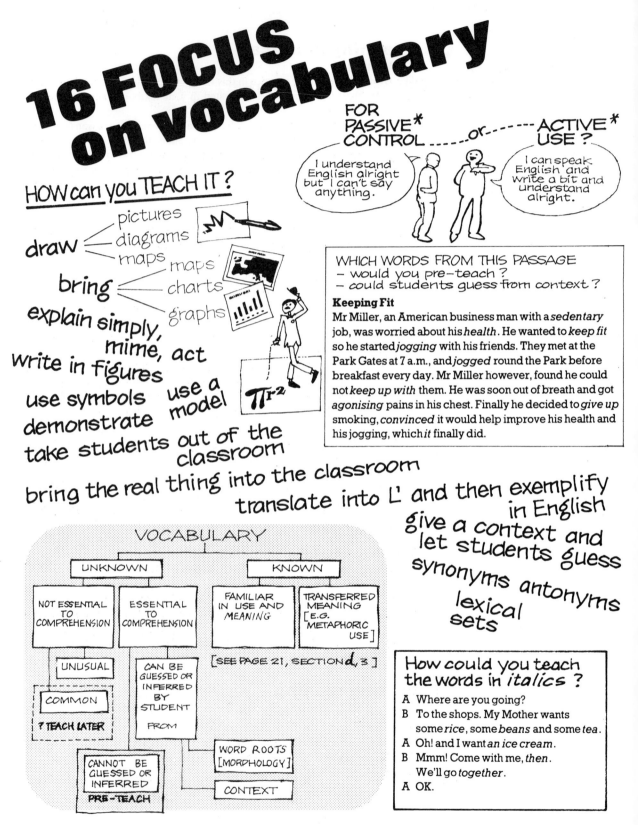

FOR PASSIVE* CONTROL - - - - or - - - - ACTIVE* USE?

I understand English alright but I can't say anything.

I can speak English and write a bit and understand alright.

HOW can you TEACH IT?

- draw
  - pictures
  - diagrams
  - maps
- bring
  - maps
  - charts
  - graphs
- explain simply, mime, act
- write in figures
- use symbols
- use a model
- demonstrate
- take students out of the classroom
- bring the real thing into the classroom
- translate into L' and then exemplify in English
- give a context and let students guess
- synonyms antonyms lexical sets

πr^2

WHICH WORDS FROM THIS PASSAGE
- would you pre-teach?
- could students guess from context?

Keeping Fit

Mr Miller, an American business man with a *sedentary* job, was worried about his *health*. He wanted to *keep fit* so he started *jogging* with his friends. They met at the Park Gates at 7 a.m., and *jogged* round the Park before breakfast every day. Mr Miller however, found he could not *keep up with* them. He was soon out of breath and got *agonising* pains in his chest. Finally he decided to *give up* smoking, *convinced* it would help improve his health and his jogging, which *it* finally did.

VOCABULARY

- UNKNOWN
  - NOT ESSENTIAL TO COMPREHENSION
    - UNUSUAL
    - COMMON
      - ? TEACH LATER
  - ESSENTIAL TO COMPREHENSION
    - CAN BE GUESSED OR INFERRED BY STUDENT FROM
    - CANNOT BE GUESSED OR INFERRED
      - PRE-TEACH
    - WORD ROOTS [MORPHOLOGY]
    - CONTEXT
- KNOWN
  - FAMILIAR IN USE AND MEANING
  - TRANSFERRED MEANING [E.G. METAPHORIC USE]

[SEE PAGE 21, SECTION *d*, 3]

How could you teach the words in *italics*?

A Where are you going?
B To the shops. My Mother wants some *rice*, some *beans* and some *tea*.
A Oh! and I want *an ice cream*.
B Mmm! Come with me, *then*.
   We'll go *together*.
A OK.

Unit 16
Teaching vocabulary

The aims of this Unit are **1** to make teachers aware of the variety of techniques that can be used to teach vocabulary for active or passive control
2 to give practice in the English necessary for presenting, eliciting and checking understanding of new vocabulary

ⓐ Preliminary discussion

1 What do we really mean by 'teaching' vocabulary? Distinguish between active and passive knowledge. Refer to the FOCUS page at the beginning of this Unit.

2 Broadly speaking, 'vocabulary' falls into two categories:
   (a) words with a specific meaning, e.g. pen, running, asleep
   (b) words with a value or a grammatical function, e.g. but, therefore, of
Discuss which categories the following words fall in: a stone, an idea, lazily, although, than, benefit, it (it's raining), hurry, dazzling, which, witch, or, the. Which category of words do you think is easier to teach successfully? Why?

3 When planning to do a reading or listening comprehension exercise in class, how do you decide which new words to pre-teach, before the passage is read or heard, which to leave until later, and which not to teach at all? Which words would you pre-teach from the passage 'Keeping Fit' on the FOCUS page? Would you pre-teach these words for active or passive control at the initial stage? Why?

4 (a) If you plan to present a new structure, would you introduce new vocabulary items at the same time? Why?
   (b) How many new words can your students learn effectively in one lesson?

5 Study the various techniques shown on the FOCUS page at the beginning of this Unit for teaching new vocabulary.
   (a) Are there any other techniques you find useful? Add those to the page.
   (b) How far is it helpful to set word lists for students to learn by heart?
   (c) Discuss in pairs or groups what technique or combination of techniques you would use to teach the following vocabulary items. Note them down beside each word.

a sponge ———	a hammer ———	a coat hanger ———
a lion ———	to creep ———	to shave ———
sad ———	a benefit ———	it's *worth* £5 ———
to increase ———	a valve ———	economic inflation ———
two million ———	therefore ———	carbon dioxide ———
a crankshaft ———	lazy ———	a reward ———

6 How useful is the question 'Do you understand?'? What about, 'Is there anything you don't understand?'? How can you check that a student (a) has really understood the meaning of a word? (b) can actually use the new word correctly and appropriately? Give examples.

115

Lesson extracts

Listen to both extracts and see which techniques the teachers use to present new vocabulary items to their classes. Then select the extract which is most suited to the level of students you are teaching, and practise repeating the teacher's part. Compare your pronunciation with the pronunciation of the teacher on the tape.

Extract One

In school

This is an elementary class. They have just learnt the verb 'want' and the teacher wants to teach them some names of food before introducing countables and uncountables next lesson. This lesson they will learn a short dialogue[1] with the new words in it. The teacher has a large bag with some smaller paper bags containing rice, tea, beans.

T: Look. What's in here? What's this? . . .
Ss: Don't know.
T: Well, it's rice. Rice. Look! Take some. It's rice. Can you say it?
S: Rice.
T: Good. And you? Rice!
S: Rice.
T: Good. What's this, Moussa?
S: Rice.
T: Good. Everybody! What's this?
Ss: Rice.
T: Good. Now. Something different. What's in here? Can you guess? It's black. You drink it! *(Mimes).*
S: L[1] *(tea).*
T: Yes. In English we say 'tea'.
Ss: Tea.
T: Again!
Ss: Tea.
T: Good. And these are? *(She shows them)*
Ss: L[1] *(beans)*
T: Beans. Beans. What are they?

Ss: Beans . . . Beans . . . Bea . . . bea . . .
T: Not bea, beans!
S: Beans.
T: Good. Now what's this?
S: Rice.
T: And these?
S: Beans.
T: Good. Now look at me. What am I eating? *(mimes)* Yes? . . . No one? Well – it's ice cream. Ice cream.
Ss: Ice cream.
T: An ice cream, yes. Is it hot or cold?
Ss: Cold. Very cold!
T: Who can draw an ice cream on the board? A picture of an ice cream?
S: Me!
T: OK. Here's the chalk. Now, what is he drawing?
Ss: Ice cream.
T: An ice cream, yes. Good. Thank you. Now, someone come and take some . . . er . . . rice. You! Yes. Good. What is that?
S: Rice.
T: Good. Now, someone give me some beans. . . .

Follow up
The teacher finishes checking their learning then goes on to present a dialogue to practise the new words.

 TEACHING HINT How does the teacher reinforce the students' understanding of the new words?

---

[1] See the dialogue on the FOCUS page at the beginning of this Unit.

Extract Two

In college

An intermediate class, interested in American culture. The teacher has found a short reading passage for them, which he hopes will promote some discussion in the second part of the lesson. See the FOCUS page at the beginning of this Unit, the passage entitled 'Keeping Fit'. The teacher is introducing it as the tape begins.

T: We're going to have a discussion today but first I want you to read a short passage, about an American businessman. He's a businessman, with an office job, and he wants to keep fit. Who knows what 'keep fit' means? Keep fit?

S: This jacket fits me.

T: Well, that was a good sentence but 'keeping fit' has a different meaning. Anyone? No?

S: er, sport? Something to do with sport?

T: Possibly, yes. Some people do exercises every morning, like this *(mimes)* to keep fit, to keep healthy, to keep your muscles in trim. If you are fit, you can run a long way. OK?

S: Yes.

T: Do you do exercises sometimes?

S: Yes. I do.

T: Why? . . . to . . . ?

S: To . . . er . . . keep fit.

T: Good. He wants to keep fit. Now. Some people in the USA go jogging every day. Jogging; who knows what jogging is? . . . No one? Well. It's running. Running slowly to keep fit. Who can write it on the board for me? You? Thank you. j..o..g..g..ing. Good. Now I'll give you out the passage. . . .

TEACHING HINTS (a) Why does the teacher explain 'keep fit' and 'jogging' but not 'sedentary' or 'agonising'? (b) Why does he want the word 'jogging' written on the board?

Ⓒ Classroom language

When teaching vocabulary, you normally start by doing one of two things: you either give the students the word and ask the meaning, or you explain the meaning or concept, and ask the word.

Finally you check that your students have understood.

The tables in this Section keep to this order and are followed by some suggestions for language your students may need.

In pairs, 'teach' each other the words in Section **a**, **5** (c), using the language from the tables. Fill in the blanks appropriately. Then select vocabulary from your textbooks to practise language from the remaining tables.

Teaching meaning

Announcing your intention

1

First, Before we begin,	I want to	check that make sure	you know	the meaning of a few words. what one or two words mean.

Making students guess the meaning

2

Who knows Does anyone know Can anyone tell me	what this word means: '_____'? when you would use the word, '_____'? where you would see hear the word, '_____'?

3

I'll give you	a clue. some help.	It's something to do with_____. You might hear a _____ saying it.
Let's see if you can guess.	I'll give you	a context: _____. an example: _____.

4

Not really. Nearly right! Not quite! Wait!	Listen to me and I'll Watch me and I'll	explain. give you (another) example. show you. draw one. act it.

Looking at the word in context

5

Now look at the	picture opposite.		What	does that tell you? does the word '_____' tell you? is the author talking about?
	sentence	before carefully. after. beginning '_____'.		
So what could this word	be about? refer to? mean?			

Looking at the word itself

Look. The word	ends in	'tion' 'ness'	so it must be a noun.
	begins with 'un' so it means 'not' something.		

Teaching a new word

Introducing the next stage

I want I'm going	to teach you	a few new some useful	words that we shall need	later on today. for a dialogue. for some role play.

Using something visual to explain the concept

Look! Listen! Watch!	Who knows Does anyone know	what	this is, we call this, this person is doing, we say when_____,	in English?
			this / does, shows,	

Explaining the concept

If Supposing Pretend	I you	had_____ were_____ lived in_____ felt_____	I'd you'd	have to – be – need – _____ –	What?

Describing appearance/use/function

It's	big and_____ made of_____	It's used for_____ing things, when they_____. People use it to_____.
You see it in_____s		You can_____it.

Beginning from a known word

You all know the	word_____. phrase_____. idea of_____.	OK. Well, what's	the opposite of it? another word for it? the general term for it?		
			the	verb noun	from it?

In this	context sentence	for example,_____.	It begins with	A B C
It is	similar to '_____'. something to do with '_____'.		Have a guess! What could it be?	

Teaching 'link' words and words with a grammatical function

13

In line 6, what does the word	'however' 'although' 'alternatively'	tell you about what follows?
	'them' 'which' 'this'	refer to?

(See also Part Two, Unit 18, Table 4, and Unit 19, Tables 21 and 22.)

Checking students' understanding

14

Find the Show me a Point to a	person	in the	room picture	who is_____.
	thing word phrase	in the picture which_____.		
		in the passage which	means the same as_____. describes a_____.	

Teaching appropriate use

15

'_____' is	a bit too rather very	formal. informal. colloquial. old fashioned.	You	only should	use	'_____'	if you're

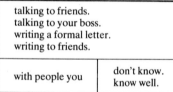

talking to friends. talking to your boss. writing a formal letter. writing to friends.	
with people you	don't know. know well.

Student language. See also Appendix B.
Saying they don't understand

16

Excuse me, Please, Mr_____,	what	does '_____' mean? is the meaning of '_____'?
	I don't understand '_____' in line 1.	

Asking questions, making guesses

17

Is it	something to do with_____? similar to_____? a kind of_____?
Does Could	_____ refer to_____?

ⓓ Teaching skills

1 Eliciting new vocabulary

(a) Select some of the words given in Section **a**, Preliminary Discussion, **5** (c). Put them into a suitable context, then 'teach' them to your neighbour as if you were presenting them to a class. Your aim is to teach these words for active control, so you will have to work out natural ways to elicit the new words from your 'student', and make him or her use it.

(b) Do the same for some vocabulary from your textbook that you would pre-teach for active control before beginning on a new unit.

2 Remedial vocabulary teaching

The list below contains pairs of words that are similar but not the same in meaning or use. Students often muddle these up. Add other pairs that *your* students often get mixed up because of similarities in meaning.

Think how you would explain in English the difference between some of these pairs. Think of examples, two or three for each word, contextualising them; finally, work out ways to check that students can distinguish the meaning of the words and can use them correctly.

lend	borrow
kill	die
surprise	shock
alone	lonely
to drop	to fall
in time	*on* time
It costs £10	It's worth £10
nightmare	dream
hard	hardly
————	————
————	————
————	————

3 Vocabulary selection (This exercise leads up to Teaching Practice in Section **e**)

In groups of three or four: each group should take a different unit of the course book and isolate, with reference to the flow chart on the FOCUS page.

(a) which lexis will need to be pre-taught for active use

(b) which lexis could be pre-taught for passive control, i.e. recognition purposes only

(c) which words are not important in themselves but may cause problems, or cause students to panic, and should, therefore, be rapidly pre-taught

(d) which words students should be encouraged to guess from context (e.g. 'agonising' in the passage 'Keeping Fit')

(e) the words you could help students guess at by asking carefully graded questions, directing them to the correct meaning

(f) the words which are uncommon or just too difficult to teach at this stage, that you might translate, if asked to explain them, but would not bother to teach.

4 Using a dictionary

(a) Each choose a different reading passage from your coursebooks and look up, in a dictionary that your students use, the words they are likely to look up themselves. Cross check to see if a suitable word or meaning is given in both halves of the dictionary. Ask yourselves whether your students can understand the passage better, having looked these words up in the dictionary.

Prepare explanations and further examples to help students learn the most important of these words. In each case write down two or three ways you could elicit this word, to make sure the student has understood its meaning and its use.

Keep your notes and pool them so you each have a complete record of lexis from reading passages.

(b) Look up the word 'time' in your dictionary. There should be at least six different uses of this one word, and maybe six different words in your language for it. Are there any single words in your language which have several different meanings, and which therefore may cause your students problems when trying to work out which English word to use?

(c) What, then, are the dangers of using a dictionary, and how could you teach your more advanced students to use a dictionary efficiently?

5 A game to play

ASK THE RIGHT QUESTION[1] – an elicitation game

You need a set of cards, between 30 and 50, which you can make quickly yourselves; each card has a word or phrase written on it. See the examples below. Put the cards face down on the table. In pairs, take turns picking a card (don't show it to your partner). You have to try to make your partner say what is on the card, by explaining, defining, asking questions and so on.

E.g. A: If you travel somewhere you need this.
    B: A ticket.
    A: No, it's something you carry, quite big.
    B: A bag.
    A: Nearly. What do you put your clothes in?
    B: A suitcase.
    A: That's right. (A then gives the card to B)

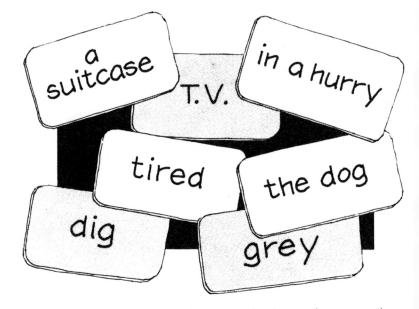

The game can be made more difficult by putting longer phrases, e.g. 'in a suitcase' or 'turn the TV off', or making them more specific, e.g. 'the suitcase' or 'the man who was walking'.

[1] I am indebted to E.L.T.I. (English Language Teaching Institute) British Council, London, for this game, which I have adapted slightly.

e Teaching practice

1 Planning

(a) Choose a short reading passage suitable for the students you will be teaching.

(b) Isolate the vocabulary you think will cause difficulties, and decide, applying the same criteria as in Section **d**, **3**, when and how you will teach or explain each word.

(c) Choose up to six or seven new words that need pre-teaching (i.e. before the students read the passage) and decide exactly how you will make clear the meaning, elicit the new word from the students, check their understanding of it. Think of ways to get them to use it for themselves if they need the word for active control, e.g. for subsequent discussion of the passage.

(d) Divide the words up between group members, and plan the order in which you will teach them; prepare any aids you will need. Think up a sign-post question for the reading passage.

2 Teaching practice

– If peer teaching, re-form groups, so you are teaching people who are new to the passage.

– Begin by announcing what you plan to do.

– Teach in turn, keeping the pace as lively as possible.

– If there is time, set the class to read the passage silently, helping them to guess the other unknown words from context. Give them a chance to ask you questions.

3 Evaluation

(a) On your own, write down from memory all the words that were 'taught'. Underline those you found the most memorable. Try to think why they were easier to remember.

(b) Discuss in your groups the results of (a) above. Did you all agree? Why? So which methods of teaching vocabulary do you think are the most effective?

(c) Could any of the meanings have been ambiguous to students? Could students actually *use* the new words they needed for active control? Was this checked?

(d) Discuss how vocabulary is tested in end of term or end of year exams. How far should you adapt or extend the techniques you used here for checking learning in order to help prepare students for the exam?

f Further reading

W M Rivers and M S Temperley (1978) pp. 251–258, and see Index.

17 FOCUS ON ACTIVITIES FOR ORAL PRODUCTION

ROLE PLAY and DRAMATISATIONS

Extending or continuing a set dialogue

Inventing a conversation for characters in a picture, e.g. two people leaving a cinema, or a tourist arriving at a hotel reception, or someone shopping.

Social events e.g. shopping, travel, party, interview

Dramatising a sequence, e.g. a family discussion about choice of job for teenage son, or discussion between witnesses of a car accident (using cue cards).

(See Tables 1–7, Section **c**)

EXPLANATION and DESCRIPTION

Interpretations of graphs, maps, diagrams, e.g. from geography or social science textbooks.

Mini-speeches on topics of interest. e.g. home town, hobbies, school rules, pop stars.

(See Tables 16 & 17, Section **c**)

Street directions, or directions for a journey.

Instructions for operating a machine, or how to drive a car or mend a fuse.

Describing a process. e.g. rice-growing, bottling factories, cocoa production.

DISCUSSION/CONVERSATION

Interpretations of pictures
e.g. the story behind a picture or speculations about the people in the picture.

'What can they be saying?'

Social issues
e.g. traffic, pollution, education, role of women, planning a new town or school. (Ideas from a reading text, book or newspaper.)

Personal experience
e.g. discussion of horoscopes, disasters; plans for future, holidays.

(See Tables 8–15, Section **c**)

Pictures for opinions e.g. fashion, pop stars, consumer goods.

GAMES and PROBLEM SOLVING

Guessing games (teams or whole class) Class has to guess, by asking questions that can be answered 'Yes' or 'No', what object, action, person or place one student is thinking of, or has a picture of, e.g.

'Twenty Questions' (object) 'Personalities' (famous person)
'Glug' (action) 'Hide and Seek' (place)

(See page 132 for details.   See Tables 18–19, Section **c**)

Elimination games (teams, groups or whole class)

'Just a minute' 'Conversation Gambits'
'My grandmother went to market' 'Simon Says'
'Don't answer "Yes" or "No"' (See page 132 for details)

Problems (pairs)
Each person in the pair has a picture or some information that the other needs, but cannot see. They must find out, by asking questions and explaining, enough information to solve the problem or complete the task set, e.g.

'Find the difference', with two nearly identical pictures or maps.
'Arrange a meeting', with two diaries with various engagements for the week.

(See Dialogue 2, and Tables 20–21, Section **c**)

STUDENT 'A'   STUDENT 'B'
'Find the differences'

Unit 17 Oral production

The aims of this Unit are **1** to make teachers aware of the importance of the production stage of the learning cycle **2** to give teachers ideas for language activities which will encourage students to speak English more freely and use the language they have learnt in meaningful situations **3** to teach the classroom language needed to direct production activities

ⓐ Preliminary discussion

1 By 'production' stage, we mean the stage or stages of the lesson where students are allowed to speak or write in English with less guidance from the teacher or textbook. This stage is one step nearer to real life situations where students will have to communicate without the help of a teacher. What opportunities do you or could you give to your students to produce language more freely in the classroom, (a) at sentence level? (b) more extended production, e.g. dialogues, role play or a simulation.* What about activities based on an Information Gap,* see page 105, Section **a**, 3.

2 It is important to choose topics that your students will like and situations that they will find worthwhile. What do your students like doing and talking about? In what kinds of situations may they need to use their English after finishing school or college?

3 Look at the suggestions for production activities on the FOCUS page at the beginning of this Unit. Discuss how you could adapt them to fulfil the needs of your students. See 2 above.

4 How will you explain to your students exactly what you want them to do? Take some of the most useful production activities on the FOCUS page and work out ways of introducing them to your class, explaining, demonstrating, modelling, acting etc., so they know what is expected of them and the reason why they are doing it.

5 (a) Discuss what steps you would need to set up the same activities. Remember you may well need a rehearsal stage before you leave them entirely on their own. What would you need to say in English to them at the beginning of each step?

(b) What should you do about mistakes that students make at the production stage? During the presentation and practice stages it is necessary to correct most mistakes to help students learn the correct form and use, but the main aim at the production stage is to encourage them to use what they have learnt and communicate in English even if it is not completely accurate. So how far do you think students should be interrupted and corrected at this stage?

6 Are there any other activities or materials you could adapt for use at the production stage of the lesson? Could you collect magazine pictures of people and places, or advertisements? Perhaps topical newspaper cuttings, or pictures, graphs, charts or diagrams from students' geography or social studies textbooks would make a good base for extended production activities, which can be done in groups.

(See Part One, Unit 9 for more on pair and group work. See also Part Two, Unit 19 for more on written production.)

Lesson extracts

First, read the notes above the extracts which describe the classroom settings and tell you what the students have just been learning. Then listen to both extracts and decide which one would be more suitable for your own students. Then listen to that one again, pausing so that you can repeat the teacher's part. Pay special attention to the intonation of question forms and of explanations.

Extract One
In school

Wall picture of a party on the board. Late elementary children. They have just learnt 'Let's'... and 'Shall we!...' which they have practised in controlled situations. They already know how to use 'I like' and 'I don't like' with names of food and drink.

The teacher has already got them into small groups to begin the production stage of the lesson.

As they talk about the party food and drink, she writes or draws it on the blackboard to help the children remember what to talk about later on.

T: Settle down in your groups, now. Quiet, please! OK. Look at this picture. What are these children doing? Anyone? Yes?

S: Party.

T: Yes, they're having a party, aren't they? Well, today we're going to talk about parties. What are they eating and drinking? Can you see?

Ss: Coca Cola, 7 Up, sweets, cake, biscuits ...

T: Yes, good. Why do you think they are having a party? Why? Yes?

S: New baby born.

T: Yes, perhaps there's a new baby in the family, ...

S: Birthday?

T: Perhaps it's someone's birthday, yes, any other ideas?

S: School finish.

T: Yes, you have parties at the end of term, good. So let's get together and plan the next school party, shall we? Just for this class, this form, OK? Let's say you can have six different things to eat or drink. Not more than six things. You could have some of these I've written here, or chocolate, crisps, nuts,

lollipops, jellies, whatever you like, but only six. So, I want you in your groups to decide which six things you want for our party. You can discuss it, like this: Let's have lemonade.

But I don't like lemonade. I like Coca Cola best.

Who else likes lemonade? No one? Coca Cola then.

Shall we have some chocolates? It's too hot. Chocolate might melt. and so on.

The group leader can make a shopping list, of six things, and we'll all look at them together. Off you go then. Group leaders, you start off: Ask your groups, 'What shall we have for the party?' *(Teacher walks round and listens, without correcting mistakes)*

(Three minutes later) Alright, everyone, let's compare lists. Kumah, what have you got?

S: Oranges, biscuits, sweet rice.

T: Why do you want sweet rice at the party?

S: I like it very much.

T: But you need plates for sweet rice.

S: We can bring plates from kitchen.

T: Do you agree with Kumah's idea? etc.

Follow up

After the class discussion, the teacher suggests they write an invitation to the Headmaster and his family to come to their party. So they plan the letter together and each group writes it out neatly. The best letter is selected to be sent. Then the class discusses who will do which preparations for the party. The next lesson they will do a role play activity, 'going shopping', to practise buying what they need, as if they were in Britain.

 TEACHING HINTS (a) Why does the teacher not correct her students' mistakes at this stage? (b) Why do you think she limits the students to six things only?

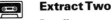

Extract Two

In college

```
April
2 Mon              9 Mon
See accountant
3 Tue Meeting      10 Tue
To Airport to meet
Mr Barrow
4 Wed              11 Wed
Mr Crawford 3.00
5 Thu              12 Thu
Meeting with Barrow
Dentist 2.30
6 Fri Visit factory 13 Fri
7 Sat Football!    14 Sat
8 Sun              15 Sun
```

Most students in this intermediate class are or will be in some kind of business, so the teacher has chosen a topic which they should find useful.

They have just learnt different ways of making suggestions. They have revised ways of apologising, and expressions of time and dates.

Earlier this lesson, in preparation for this activity, they have each prepared, on a sheet of paper, a one week page of a business engagement diary for the following week. They each filled in any seven of the ten possible half days with things like

> *Meeting at . . .*
> *See Accountant*
> *Visit factory*
> *Dentist 2.30*
> *Mr Crawford 3.00 etc.*

but without telling each other which times they left free. The teacher wants them to work in pairs, as if they were businessmen trying to find a time to meet when they were both free. They need to practise making arrangements to meet.

T: So, you all know what you have in your own diaries, but you don't know when your neighbours are free, do you?

S: Three times.

T: Yes, they have three free times next week, but you don't know *which* days. Right, you are going to have a telephone conversation to decide on a day and a time to meet a business colleague to talk about a new project. One of you can be Mr Russell, and you're going to telephone a Mr Schmidt in another company to arrange a time to meet. OK? Now, you are both free at different times, you will have to ask each other questions to find out the other person's programme for next week. You may only be able to find a lunch time convenient to you both. So, Mr Russell telephones Mr Schmidt. Look, I'll do it with one of you so you know what I mean. Mr Adjimi, you be Mr Schmidt and I'll be Mr Russell. Ready? Brrrr Brrrrr. You pick up the phone, Mr Adjimi. Hello, is that Mr Schmidt?

S: Yes.

T: Oh. This is John Russell here, of O.P. company.

S: Er, good morning.

T: Good morning, I was ringing to ask if we could meet some time to discuss the new project.

S: Oh, yes, when can you come?

T: Well, let's see, next week I'm free on Tuesday at 10 a.m.

S: Oh dear. No. Not . . .

T: *(quietly)* I'm sorry, I have to . . . .

S: I'm sorry, I have to go to a meeting on Tuesday.

T: Well, What about Thursday afternoon? Are you free then?

S: I'm sorry, I'm afraid I have appointment with the dentist.

T: Oh. *(quietly.)* What about . . .

S: What about Friday after lunch.

T: Friday? Let's see . . . Yes, that's fine. Why don't we have lunch together and talk afterwards, you know, do our business in the afternoon?

S: Where shall we meet then? At the Homa Restaurant?

T: The Homa? Yes, what time? Half past one?

S: Yes, that's fine.

T: Goodbye, then, see you next Friday, one thirty.

S: Goodbye.

T: Well done, Mr Adjimi, you did that very well. OK? everybody? Now, you do the same. All of you, together, in your pairs, looking at your diaries, find out when you are both free and arrange to meet, decide when and where and so on. Ready? Right, off you go, the phone is ringing, Mr Russell, you ask for Mr Schmidt.

Ss: *(All)* Hello . . . etc.

Follow up

After completing this first activity, students could change partners and arrange a second meeting with someone else. Or they could all exchange diaries and do a similar activity. The diaries could be saved and used again for a different class.

TEACHING HINTS (a) Why does the teacher speak quietly when prompting Mr Adjimi? **(b)** The student should have said 'an appointment' but the teacher does not correct him at this stage. Why?

ⓒ **Classroom language**

Before beginning this Section please revise Part One, Unit 6, Section **c**, and Part Two, Unit 15, Section **c**, Tables 13 to 21.

See also the FOCUS page at the beginning of this Unit; the tables follow the same sequence.

Select the language from the tables below which refers to the types of production activities you will be using. Find in your textbooks and from your teaching materials *specific examples* of dialogues, discussion points, pictures etc., to refer to when practising this language. Fill in the blanks and adapt where necessary.

Role play and dramatisations

Extending a set dialogue

1

You remember Let's go back to	the dialogue we	practised did	about_____	Who were the people in it? What were they doing?

2

Now	I want to let's	change it a bit. do it another way.	Instead of_____
		continue it.	After they_____

3

So what kinds of thing	could he ask might they say will you talk about	in this situation? at a party? in a job interview?

Setting the scene with a picture or a social situation

4

We're going to do some role play now. Listen while I tell you the situation. Look at the picture while I explain.	Imagine Supposing Let's pretend	you were_____
Now in groups of 2/3/4 think up what you can do.		

5

I want you to	invent think up plan	a	dialogue conversation	pretending **you** were these people; working in twos, taking parts.

6

What would you	need to ask probably say	if you were	this man/woman? in this situation?

7

We're going to use	cue role play	cards.	Each card tells you	who you are. what kind of person you are. which role you play.	
			On your card it says	what you	want to do. have to do.

Promoting discussion
Referring to a picture

Why do you think	this man the girl _____	look(s) happy/angry? is doing that? _____?

What	could might	have happened earlier? have been happening?		Why do you think that?
		happen	now?	
			in a few minutes?	

Now in	twos groups	prepare	a short story to discuss what you think	about the picture.

Encouraging replies

Come on.	You could say:	Perhaps he	was_____ will_____	OK? Yes?_____
		He	might have_____ could have_____	

Expressing opinions, simulations,* (using pictures or lists of items)

Look at these pictures of	cars. clothes. furniture. _____	Which do you	like best? prefer? think are best? like least?	Why?

Which What kind of_____ Which of these	would you	buy for	yourself? your parents? your friends?		Arrange them in order of preference/importance. Discuss your choice with your neighbour. Persuade another pair your choice is best.
		take with you	to school? on holiday? camping? _____?	
		use at	home? work?	

Social issues, developing ideas from reading passages, etc.

Now we've	read thought talked got some ideas	about the problems of	pollution traffic in towns, planning a new school, choosing a career, _____,	all together,

can you discuss in	twos groups	what **you** would do? how these might affect **you**?	Write down	four six	things ways

in order of importance.	And I'll come round and	see what you think. help you.

Explanation and description

15

In	pairs groups	I want you to could you can you work out how to	give someone else	directions from school to_____		
				a description of your	school _____	
				instructions to use a	_____	
			explain to someone	how	rice/maize _____	is grown.
					Coca Cola is bottled. to operate a_____ to drive a car.	
				what this	graph map diagram	shows.

Rehearsal for production activity

16

But first, let's	have a practice all together, so you know	what to do. how to play.
	go over some	words phrases	that might be useful.

Guessing games

17

Someone has to Each team must	think of write down draw	an object, a thing, or an animal, for 'Twenty Questions', an action or a verb, which we'll call 'Glug', a famous person, someone we all know, a job or a career, like doctor, for 'What's my line', a place you might hide_____ in, for 'Hide and Seek', a word, for 'Stop,
And don't show the others! Keep it a secret!		

and then	everyone else has the other teams have	to guess	what it is, what 'Glug' stands for, who it is, what job it is, where the_____ is,

by asking questions	which have Yes/No answers.		For example	_____ _____ _____
	beginning with	'do' 'does'. 'can' 'will'. 'did' 'have', etc.		

18

Whoever Whichever team	guesses first	has the next go. gets a point. thinks of the next thing.	OK?

(See Table 16.)

Problem solving (e.g. Find the differences)

We've got There are	pairs of sets of two	adverts maps pictures drawings diagrams house plans	which	are almost exactly the same. only have three things different.
Could you each draw* two simple				

*for another pair to use

You work in twos, with two similar pictures, but	don't let the other person see yours. don't show your_____ to the other person.
Ask each other questions to	find out what is different. discover what the differences are.
When you have found out	write down the differences, and call me. then pass the two pictures on to another pair.

(See Table 16.)
(See also Part One, Units 8 and 9, for ways of dividing the class up.)

ⓓ Teaching skills

1 Explaining rules of games

In an elementary class, or when introducing a complicated game for the first time, it might be best to use L¹. However, listening and following instructions in English for playing a game can be a meaningful and useful exercise for students.

The instructions for playing some of the language games mentioned on page 124 and in Tables 17–20 on page 130 are written briefly below. In order to explain orally to a class, you will need to expand and rephrase the written text, giving examples and demonstrating wherever possible.

Working in groups, each person should take a different game and work out how best to explain it to a class. Adapt the game if necessary to suit your students' backgrounds. Then practise explaining the games to each other as clearly as possible, playing one or two rounds of each game together, in your groups. Make a note of the difficulties that cropped up and discuss how to overcome them.

Finally, make notes in the right-hand columns of the language items that students will need in order to play each game. Remember that you may have to revise these before playing the game in class.

Game	Language needed	Game	Language needed	Game	Language needed
'JUST A MINUTE' Teacher writes 4 to 8 topics that the class has already talked about, e.g. 'tea' or 'football' or 'holidays' or 'my village', on small pieces of paper which are then folded up. One person or team is chosen to pick one topic, and must talk about it for a set time e.g., 15 or 30 seconds,	_____ _____ _____ _____ _____ _____	without hesitating or repeating anything. Points can be awarded for each 5 seconds of speech. Students or teams are out if they hesitate for over 3 seconds, or repeat the same thing. Mistakes in English need not matter, since the object of the game is to encourage fluency.	_____ _____ _____ _____ _____ _____	DON'T ANSWER 'YES' OR 'NO' One team asks members of the other team questions to try to make them answer 'Yes' or 'No'. The answering team can use other responses, e.g. 'Of course not' or 'I think so', or just 'I did' or 'It is', etc. The teacher times how long it is before a 'Yes' or 'No' is said. The team with the longest time wins.	_____ _____ _____ _____ _____ _____

Game	Language needed	Game	Language needed	Game	Language needed
'TWENTY QUESTIONS' One person or team thinks of an object or animal etc. The others can ask up to 20 questions with 'Yes' or 'No' answers, in order to guess what the object is. If they guess in less than 20, they have won. Questions like, 'Is it alive?', 'Is it made of wood?', 'Does it have 4 legs?', 'Is it bigger than a car?' etc. are possible.	_____ _____ _____ _____ _____ _____	kilo of tomatoes'. The next student repeats that, and adds something new, i.e. 'My Grandmother went to market and bought a kilo of tomatoes and a blue dress.' Student 3 repeats it and adds one item. If any student forgets something or gets it in the wrong order, he is out. This can be played individually or in teams; the members of the team can help each other out.	_____ _____ _____ _____ _____ _____ _____ _____	line of a conversation like 'I went to a party last night'. The aim of each team is to keep the conversation going by thinking of appropriate questions to ask every time there is a silence. If there is a silence of more than a set time, e.g. 5 or 10 seconds, the team is out. Again, the teacher needs to time each team's performance.	_____ _____ _____ _____ _____ _____ _____
'MY GRANDMOTHER WENT TO MARKET AND SHE BOUGHT . . .' This game practises weights, measures, the use of 'a' and 'some', etc. Student 1 begins 'My Grandmother went to market and she bought a	_____ _____ _____	**'CONVERSATION GAMBITS'** The teacher sets a situation, e.g. 'in a restaurant', or 'meeting a friend in the street' or 'visiting a friend in hospital' or gives the first	_____ _____ _____	**'GLUG'** Similar to Twenty Questions, except that 'glug' stands for an action, e.g. dance. Questions like 'Do you like glugging?', 'Have you glugged today?' 'Do you glug in the kitchen?' etc. can be asked.	_____ _____ _____ _____

See Unit 12 for STOP. For other games and variations on these games, please refer to the Further reading section.

2 Questions eliciting extended responses

See also Unit 14, Section **d**.

Find some large pictures, wall charts, maps or diagrams, or similar visuals in textbooks your students have access to, perhaps even short texts on interesting subjects.

Work out ways of phrasing elicitations or questions about these pictures that will encourage the students to give longer responses.

For example, questions beginning 'Why' or 'How' or 'What is_____ like?' usually require a longer answer. Also useful are elicitations beginning

'How do you know————'
'Tell your neighbour about————'/'Why————'/'How————'
'Describe————'.

Practise in twos or threes asking and answering questions like these, that can be used to promote freer production.

3 Role play opportunities

Look through your coursebooks to see what opportunities there are to adapt existing dialogues for role play, or to use parts of stories or reading passages for students to dramatise.

Choose one possible situation and work out how to explain it to a class. Practise giving out roles to your friends, explaining what they each have to do. Write brief details of characters and the roles they play on cue cards for future use.

Finally, get your friends to perform the role play activity, while you watch, and diagnose areas of language your students might need extra help with before being asked to perform the activity.

e Teaching practice

1 Planning

– Split into groups of three or four, with each group taking a different section or unit of your English Language coursebook. If you have teaching practice with genuine students, make sure the material is easy enough for them.

– Think of two activities that could be used after the presentation and practice stages of the Unit to help students *use* the language they have learnt, in order to communicate in a meaningful situation, as close as possible to real life.

– For example, if the passive voice has been taught, a description of a process might be suitable, e.g. 'How rice is grown in Thailand'. Or if question forms have just been practised, a guessing game might be a good idea.

– Isolate any words or phrases that may need revising or pre-teaching. Plan how you would do this.

– Plan also how to stage the teaching; introduction, rehearsal, activity. Divide the lesson up between 'teachers'.

2 Teaching

If you are peer teaching, make sure your 'students' know what they have previously 'learnt'; i.e., tell them what language items they would normally have just been practising, prior to the introduction of the role play activity.

If you are teaching genuine learners, make sure the pre-teaching and rehearsal stages are thorough, before letting them attempt the production activity on their own.

During the last stage, i.e. when students are role playing or playing games etc., the 'teachers' can listen in, in order to diagnose problem areas for future lessons, but without interrupting to correct.

3 Evaluation

Groups should split up and re-form in order to report back to others how their production activity went.

Discuss the following points:

(a) What do you think students feel like when they are told to act a role, play a game or discuss something on their own in groups?

(b) Could the teachers' directions or instructions have been clearer or briefer? If yes, suggest how.

(c) How much teacher talking time was there, as opposed to student working time?

(d) What areas would your students have most difficulty with linguistically? How could you help them beforehand?

Write up and have copies made of any useful ideas for production activities, including details like cue cards, page references etc., for distribution to other teachers.

f Further reading

Donn Byrne (1976) on guided production pp. 70–77, on organising discussion pp. 82–92, on role playing pp. 93–97, on games pp. 99–108.

Andrew Wright (1976) on visual materials to cue oral work pp. 21–23 and pp. 75–82.

W M Rivers and M S Temperley (1978) pp. 47–56.

Helen Moorwood (ed) (1978) pp. 96–98.

18 FOCUS on listening

See also Unit 7, for using a tape recorder, etc.

LISTEN! HOW?
Extensive (general idea)
Intensive (for details)

LISTEN! TO WHAT?
discussions descriptions talks dialogues
stories advertisements
interviews lectures
pop songs
directions
folk songs
news
broadcasts
instructions
telephone conversations

LISTEN! FOR WHAT?

LISTENING

ENABLING SKILLS

1 predicting what people are going to talk about

2 guessing at unknown words or phrases without panicking

3 using one's own knowledge of the subject to help one understand

4 identifying relevant points; rejecting irrelevant information

5 retaining relevant points (note taking, summarising)

6 recognising discourse markers, e.g. 'Well', 'Oh, another thing is,' and 'Now, finally . . .'

7 recognising cohesive devices, e.g. 'such as', 'which', including link words, pronouns, references, etc.

8 understanding different intonation patterns, and uses of stress, etc. which give clues to meaning and social setting

9 understanding inferred information, e.g. speakers' attitude or intentions

PURPOSES

● general information – main points
● specific information – particular items
● cultural interest – general
● people's attitudes and opinions
● organisation of ideas
● sequence of events
● lexical items – words expressing noise/movement
● structural items – their use and meaning
● functional items – their form and use

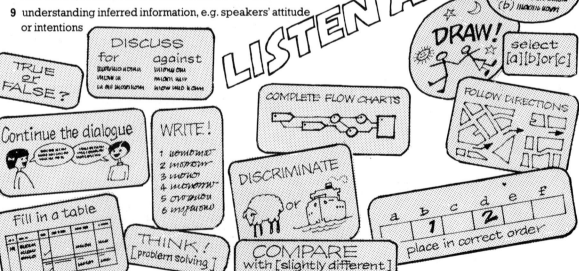

LISTEN AND-

identify who

take notes
(a) ....
(b) ....

DRAW!

select [a][b]or[c]

TRUE or FALSE?

DISCUSS
for against

COMPLETE FLOW CHARTS

FOLLOW DIRECTIONS

Continue the dialogue

WRITE!
1 ....
2 ....
3 ....
4 ....
5 ....
6 ....

DISCRIMINATE
or

Fill in a table

THINK! [problem solving]

COMPARE with [slightly different] reading text

a b c d e f
1 2
place in correct order

Unit 18 Listening skills

The aims of this Unit are **1** to make teachers more aware of the enabling skills involved in the process of listening, and how to TEACH listening rather than TEST their comprehension **2** to practise the language needed for various types of listening activities, at the planning stages and in the classroom **3** to give practice in reading out loud and 'acting' dialogues

(a) Preliminary discussion

1 Speaking and writing are productive skills*. Listening is receptive* rather than productive, but it is an equally important skill. Students need to learn *how* to listen, and to get the chance to listen to different types of English, so they will be able to listen with understanding to spoken English outside the classroom.

(a) What types of spoken English will your students need to understand outside their English classrooms? See the FOCUS page 'LISTEN TO WHAT?'

(b) What will they need to *do* while listening? Take notes, or talk in reply?

(c) How far will their listening exercises in class help them in the future?

2 What types of activity can your students *do* while listening, or as a result of listening? See the FOCUS page and discuss the activities mentioned in 'LISTEN AND?' How suitable would they be for your students?

3 (a) Reading out loud to your students reading passages from books (that were written to be read, not spoken) may not give them the type of listening practice they need. Why not? What about reading dialogues out loud? (See also Unit 14, Section **a**, 1.)

(b) How can taped materials be used to help students to learn how to listen?

4 In real life, when you meet someone, or speak to a friend in the street, or go to hear a lecturer, you usually know what they will talk about; sometimes you can predict what they will say. In the classroom how much help do you think we should give students *before* we give them a listening comprehension exercise?

5 Is it easier or more difficult to understand someone speaking a foreign language when you can *see* him talking? Why?

So what about the use of tape recordings of English people talking? What help can we give students before or while playing them a tape which will make up for the fact they cannot see the people speaking?

6 (a) Sometimes a teacher simply reads a passage two or three times while the students listen and answer questions on it. Is this teaching or testing?

(b) What does a student need to learn in order to understand a spoken text?

(c) It is possible to break 'listening' down into smaller skills, *enabling skills* – the mastery of these skills *enables* students to listen with more understanding. Some elements of these skills can be taught, e.g. discourse markers; others, e.g. predicting what people will say, guessing at new words, must be practised under the teacher's supervision.

Discuss which of the ENABLING SKILLS on the FOCUS page can be taught, and which need to be practised with the teacher's guidance.

(d) Discuss which ENABLING SKILLS your students need most practice in.

(e) Do their coursebooks provide suitable types of listening exercises to help them practise the listening skills they need? Could you adapt more relevant material from other sources for listening exercises?

ⓑ Lesson extracts

The two extracts in this Unit are suitable both for children and adult learners. Extract One is based on an exercise involving street directions which gives practice in intensive listening as a prelude to practice and production, whereas in Extract Two, the listening exercise is an end in itself. It is based on a news bulletin and is designed to give students practice in listening for the general gist only, and rejecting irrelevant information. Listen to both, and if you have time, practise repeating the teacher's parts. Notice the contrast between the *informal* tone in ONE and the more formal tone in TWO.

Extract One

Intensive listening

Late Elementary.
The listening exercise here serves as an introduction to something the class will go on to practise orally in pairs. It is not an end in itself. Before the teacher teaches the class how to give street directions she gives them various sets of street directions to listen to. First she checks they know the places on the map, and the English names. The students already know prepositions like near, etc. The students merely listen and work out which place Ali wants to go to.

T: Today we're going to learn how to give street directions, to ask the way to someone's house, or to a bank. Look, I've got a street map here, to pin up. OK. Who can show me the hospital? Where's the hospital on this map? Point to it! Yes. Good. On South Street. Now then. What about the Station? Where the trains stop. The Railway Station. Where's that? Yes? Point!

S: Near Hospital, down. South Street.

T: Yes. It's near the hospital, isn't it ...? *(Teacher points out all the main buildings and practises street names)* *(Later)* So now we'll do a listening exercise. Will one of you come out? Ali! Whisper where you want to go, just tell me. Ssh! Don't tell the others.

S: *(Ali tells the teacher he wants to go to the Post Office)*

T: We are at the Station now. Ali has no map and he is lost. He asks me the way to somewhere. You listen and look at the map. You must find out *where* Ali is going. Ready? Listen!
'Well let's see, you go out of the Station and turn right, and right again into South Street. You go past the Hospital and turn left at the crossroads. There are traffic lights there; you can't miss it. Then, let's think, it's the second street on the left, near the – Oh no! Sorry. Second on the *right*. It's just down that street on the right.'

T: OK. Who knows where Ali wants to go?

S: Market?

S: No.

T: No! Shall I do it again?

S: Yes.

T: Now listen. Which is your left? Which is right? Yes. OK. Now listen again and follow the map.

Follow up
Teacher waits till they have guessed Post Office, then she repeats the exercise giving directions to different students to and from different places, about 5 or 6 times, the class writing the answers each time until they are all getting them right. Then she will get the class to repeat and practise giving the same directions.

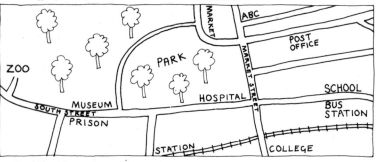

🧍 or 🧍🧍   TEACHING HINTS (a) Why does the teacher ask Ali to come out, and stand at the front? **(b)** Why does she make a mistake on purpose and correct herself? **(c)** Why does she give the class these listening exercises before she teaches them how to ask for and give directions themselves?

Extract Two
Extensive listening

In this lesson extract, notice especially the difference between the way the teacher speaks to his class and the way he reads the news item. Practise repeating the news item, paying attention to the intonation patterns.

Text: Listening exercise
'Bad weather has caused chaos in many parts of Britain today. From the South, reports have come in of an oil tanker, carrying thousands of tons of crude oil, running aground in the channel. It was making its way through heavy seas in poor visibility when it struck rocks, off the French Coast. The Officers and crew have been rescued by helicopter but the vessel itself is badly damaged. Oil is spilling out from the tanker into the sea, and attempts to stop the oil leak were stopped by the chronic weather conditions and rough seas. The French are worried that the oil will drift onto their coast and spoil their beaches, endangering wild life and harming their summer tourist trade....'

Late Intermediate.
The teacher knows that this news bulletin will be difficult for his class to understand in detail. His aim is to get his students to listen for the gist, for a general understanding only, in order to prepare them for real life situations where they cannot expect to understand everything and cannot interact with the speaker.

T: Today we're going to start off with a listening exercise, and then go on to discuss it. I'm going to read you part of a BBC World News Bulletin that was broadcast on the radio one winter, during a spell of very bad, stormy weather. Who knows what stormy means? or what a 'storm' is?
S: er, wind, and rain . . .
S: sea – er – very er, like this . . .
T: rough! yes. When it's windy the sea gets rough, good. And the ships? Well, we'll see. . . . Now, there are lots of words you won't understand. It's not an easy exercise. But it doesn't matter. If you listen you'll get the general idea, the main points, and that's enough. Don't worry about the details. I want you to

tell me *what* happened and *why*. OK? And I'll write one other question on the board that I want you to answer as well. So, *(writes)* 'What happened?', 'Why?' 'How do the people on the French Coast feel?' Right, before we begin, there's one word I'll tell you. The Channel. Look. *(draws)* Here's Britain, England, London's here, the South Coast is here. And here's France, the French Coast. And this bit of sea is called the Channel. OK? There is always a lot of shipping on the Channel. What kind of ships do you know?
S: Motor boats.
T: Yes, but bigger than that?
S: Oil tankers.
T: Yes, good. Passenger ships, oil tankers. Right. Ready to listen? Close your books. Pencils down. Remember what the weather has been like? OK! 'Bad weather . . .' *(See text on left)*
(Later) (After getting the answers to the three signpost questions) Good. Well done. And what do you think the news reader will go on to next? I'll read it again. What's he going to say next? See if you can work it out!

TEACHING HINTS (a) Why does the teacher warn his class that they will not understand every word? **(b)** Why does he give them these particular three questions to find answers to? **(c)** Why does he ask them what they think the news reader will say next?

© Classroom language

Review the FOCUS page at the beginning of this Unit; the tables refer to many of the points presented there. The tables in this Unit can be supplemented by several of the tables in Unit 19 on Reading.

Have in front of you some specific listening materials to which you can refer while practising the language you need from these tables. Work in pairs, helping each other with pronunciation and fluency whenever possible.

Introducing the topic

1

| We | 'll be listening
're going to listen | to a | section
part | of a | story told by_____
lecture given by_____
conversation between_____
news bulletin
radio discussion
'phone call between_____ | about_____ |

| and then | complete a worksheet.
discuss it.
answer some questions on it.
talk about it.
construct a flow chart from it.
wite some notes on it. |

Stating your aim

2

This is to give you practice in listening for			the general idea. the key points. specific details. relevant information. the organisation of the text. the sequence of events.	
And you	don't need to probably won't may not	understand know	every	word. phrase. sentence.	It won't matter. Don't worry!

Making predictions

3

Who knows something Who can tell us something What do you know	about this topic?	What could the passage be about?

(See Unit 19. Tables 11 to 16; substitute 'listening' for 'reading'.)

Revision of listening skills

4

Remember last	week lesson time		different intonation patterns. link words. 'marker' words like 'Well!'	
Don't forget what		we learnt about	words which introduce	an example. stages. a reason. a list. a change of subject.

(See also Table 9.)

Prepare to listen

5

So,	are you ready you're going	to listen and	answer these questions. fill in the flow chart.	I'll	start the tape. begin reading. begin my talk.

After listening

6

Well. That's it.	We'll hear I'll read	it again later, but	first finish _____. now get on and _____.

Going over the activity

7

Would	someone one group	write their answers put their solutions	on the board? Do you	all agree? think these are right?

8

Alright. Let's	go over that. check your answers. have your ideas.	Good. You've got	some of most of nearly all all	the	information ideas points details.	I asked for. you needed.

More intensive practice

Now listen again and	pick out the words which introduce _____ (continued by Table 4 above).					
	notice how tell me why	his my	voice	rises changes falls	when after	he says I say ' _____ '.

(See Unit 19, Tables 21–23.
See the FOCUS page at the beginning of this Unit, LISTEN AND …)

Listen to this	sentence short piece extract	and pick out	a	word phrase	which	show(s) that _____. mean(s) _____. refer(s) to _____.
			any words			denote(s)	colour. movement. noise. attitude.

How else could	he she	have said	that? ' _____ ',	Could you	explain say it	in your own words?
	you say					

To summarise

Could	anyone tell me you in pairs tell each other	quickly briefly	what	that was about? might be said next?

ⓓ Teaching skills

1 Reading out loud for listening comprehension

In pairs

Find two lots of materials you will use for listening comprehension, one mono-logue, e.g. a story or a 'mini-lecture', and one dialogue. Choose topics that will interest your students.

Prepare to read them out loud by carrying out the following tasks:

(a) Decide how it should be spoken and what type of people, attitudes, events etc. are portrayed.

(b) With the dialogue can you consistently 'do' two different voices for the different speakers? How else could you make it clear who is speaking when?

(c) Break the passage or dialogue up into 2, 3 or 4 chunks, each of which stops at a sensible point. You will use these divisions for the intensive listening work at the second stage, so as not to put too large a burden on the students' memories.

(d) Isolate the more difficult sentences after which you may want to leave a longer pause, to give students some thinking and catching up time. Mark thus //.

(e) Mark thus / the ends of all the 'sense groups'* within sentences, so that you phrase your reading naturally without breaking up the continuity of mean-ing.

(f) Underline the word(s) which carry the main stress within each sense-group, and remember to keep all other weak forms neutral.

E.g. He wandered slowly back tò his village, / hoping that his mother would not punish him / fòr what he had done.

(g) Mark in the margins places where you could vary things like volume of voice, speed of delivery, quality of voice, expression; also places where you might mime or act or refer to a visual to make it clearer.

Practise reading chunks out loud to your neighbour, standing at least three metres apart; project your voices but still speak as quietly as is possible; the danger is that you distort vowel sounds if you try to make it too clear and slow.

After each chunk, ask two or three questions to check general understanding of what your neighbour has heard you reading. Then change over. Help each other with pronunciation problems.

2 Questions for listening comprehension

(a) Revision (*in pairs*)

Revise Units 13 and 14, Teaching Skills Sections, on QUESTIONS. Test each other on basic points.

(b) Purposes of questions for teaching listening (*in groups*)

Using the listening material you found for 1, write questions on each passage to fulfil the following purposes:

(i) Two sign-post questions, to promote purposeful listening. (See Section **b**, Extract Two)

(ii) Some general comprehension questions, including one or two very easy ones, to check students have grasped the main ideas.

(iii) Some more specific questions to be answered after a second hearing of the passage, to practise information retrieval. These should only require short answers of one or two words, at this stage.

(iv) Some questions to focus attention on grammatical relations, cohesive devices. (See Tables 9 and 10)

(v) Some more testing questions for the brighter pupils, e.g. on inferred meaning, attitudes etc.

(vi) follow-up questions to promote oral work based on the same topic.

3 Exploiting listening materials (*in groups*)

Revise the list of 'ENABLING SKILLS' on the FOCUS page at the beginning of this Unit.

Find suitable passages which you could adapt or simplify if necessary for your students (not necessarily from their English coursebooks) which are suitable for the practice of different skills. For example, a verbal description of a process would be likely to contain discourse markers like staging words, i.e. 'First', 'then', 'after that' etc. A dialogue between two people trying to agree on plans for a holiday could be suitable material for students to learn: to recognise ways of expressing attitude; to pick out the main arguments for or against one particular plan; the ways of expressing suggestions or disagreement in English, and so on.

If there is time, suitable materials could be discussed, annotated, polycopied, and pooled, together with teaching notes on ideas for which enabling skills could be practised with each passage.

4 Activities for listening

See the FOCUS page at the beginning of this Unit, 'LISTEN AND . . .'

(a) *In groups*

Which of the activities suggested here require a non-verbal or one word response? (e.g. listen and draw, or listen and re-arrange jumbled main points or putting in order a series of pictures?)

Make a list of the activities that would be suitable for your students.

(b) *In pairs*

Find, adapt or invent a short listening exercise to suit one of the activities on the list, then practise explaining in English to the rest of the group how to do it.

For INTRODUCING a LISTENING EXERCISE, read Unit 19, Section **d**, **2**, on Introducing a Reading Passage and pick out the principles which apply also to listening comprehension.

(e) Teaching practice

1 Planning

In groups of three or four, plan two or three 'mini' lessons each including a different type of listening activity, and focusing on three or four of the enabling skills listed on the FOCUS page at the beginning of this Unit. You could use some of the materials you used in 'Teaching Skills' if they are of a level suitable for the students you will be teaching. Divide the lesson up between teachers, so that each gets a chance to give the listening exercise, either for the first or second reading.

(a) Practise reading out loud or saying or acting the material for each listening exercise, making it sound as natural as possible. Follow the steps in Section **a**, **1**.

(b) Isolate any new words that will need pre-teaching. (See Unit 16, p. 115, on selection of vocabulary to pre-teach.)

(c) Plan how you will introduce the topics in such a way as to arouse students' interest. Decide which activities you will get them to do, while or after listening, which will show they have understood.

(d) Write a series of questions as detailed in Section **d**, **2**, most of which focus on the enabling skills you aim to practise.

(e) Think of a suitable follow-up activity which integrates listening with other skills, such as speaking or reading or writing, and plan exactly what you will say, in order to set it up. It need only be very brief, e.g. a minute's pair practice and two minutes' class discussion.

2 Teaching

If peer teaching, groups should split up and re-form so that each person has the benefit of experiencing a different lesson. If teaching students, take care to time the lesson carefully so you each have a turn.

3 Evaluation

Discuss in groups, then as a class.

(a) How much did the students learn or practise during this lesson that will help them in another listening exercise, even if it is on a different topic?

(b) What did they learn that may *not* necessarily help them with another listening exercise on a different topic?

(c) Which of the parts of lessons you saw or experienced would you consider to be the most successful and why?

(f) Further reading

Andrew Wright (1976) on teaching: Chapter 1 pp. 2–13; on testing: Chapter 6 pp. 53–55

Donn Byrne (1976) on listening in general: pp. 8–9; on teaching listening: Chapter 3 pp. 13–19

Julian Dakin (1973) Chapters 3 and 6.

Helen Moorwood (ed) (1978) Section 4.

W M Rivers and M S Temperley (1978) Chapter 3 pp. 64–110.

READ-WHY?

PLEASURE
magazines
holiday brochures
letters from friends

SURVIVAL
forms official notices
bills and receipts
labels directions
bus and train
timetables
place names
street signs

headlines
newspapers
photograph
captions

literature
novels plays
poetry

dictionaries
text books
indexes

glossaries
bibliographies
library catalogues
abstracts

READ WHAT?

Job adverts
instructions for use
contracts
phone directories

charts
diagrams
reference
works
graphs

STUDY

reports articles
catalogues
workshop manuals
notice boards
minutes of meetings
professional journals
advertisements
business letters

WORK

Oh, dear. I can read O.K., but it takes such a long time to read in English!

Ah! So you haven't practised your reading skills. You don't have to read *every* word to get the meaning. You can skim and get the gist and predict what he's going to say next...

A DIFFICULT TEXT? HELP students BY
- More background information!
- Pre-teach key words the day before!
- Divide text into short chunks!
- Sign-post questions for main points!
- Add discourse markers where helpful!
- Ask easy questions!
- Paraphrase difficult ideas!
- Set easy tasks like matching questions and answers!
- Praise and encouragement!

READING ACTIVITIES

AFTER THE EARLY STAGES
(Reading for meaning)

Arrange jumbled sentences into a paragraph.
Answer the questions. Complete the sentences.
Is this information TRUE, FALSE or NOT STATED?
Choose the correct answer from a, b, c or d.
Note taking for summary. Jumbled key points.
Complete a table or chart of information.
Label a diagram. Fill in missing information.
Find a — sentence which tells you that _____
word which shows that _____
Cloze passages, words given below.
Fill the blanks.

Match questions to answers,
jumbled sentence halves.

EARLY STAGES
(word/sentence recognition)

Match words to pictures.
Sort words into lexical sets.
Match sentences to pictures.

READING SKILLS

1. Recognising words and phrases in English script.
2. Using one's own knowledge of the outside world to make predictions about and interpret a text.
3. Retrieving information stated in the passage.
4. Distinguishing the main ideas from subsidiary information.
5. Deducing the meaning and use of unknown words; ignoring unknown words/phrases that are redundant, i.e., that contribute nothing to interpretation.
6. Understanding the meaning and implications of grammatical structures, e.g. cause, result, purpose, reference in time (e.g. verb tenses; compare: 'He could swim well' – past, 'He could come at 10 a.m.' – future).
7. Recognising discourse markers: e.g. therefore + conclusion, however + contrast, that is + paraphrase, e.g. + example.
8. Recognising the function of sentences – even when not introduced by discourse markers: e.g. example, definition, paraphrase, conclusion, warning.
9. Understanding relations within the sentence and the text (words that refer back to a thing or a person mentioned earlier in the sentence or the text, e.g. which, who, it).
10. Extracting specific information for summary or note taking.
11. Skimming* to obtain the gist, and recognise the organisation of ideas within the text.
12. Understanding implied information and attitudes.
13. Knowing how to use an index, a table of contents, etc.
14. Understanding layout, use of headings, etc.

Unit 19 Reading skills

The aims of this Unit are **1** to help teachers develop a deeper understanding of the process of reading itself **2** to show that by breaking 'reading' down into 'enabling skills' we can be more successful in teaching students how to read with understanding and efficiently **3** to practise the language needed for meaningful reading activities in class **4** to help teachers prepare worthwhile reading materials for students of all levels

a Preliminary discussion

1 Reading is a receptive skill, like listening (See Unit 18, Section **a**, 1). **Students need to learn how to read efficiently.**

(a) Which of the two skills, listening or reading, will be most useful to your students? Why?

(b) Which do they find easier, listening or reading? What are the differences between listening and reading from your students' point of view?

2 (a) What type of things will some of your students need to be able to read with understanding, outside school or college? Why? See the FOCUS page at the beginning of this Unit, READ WHAT?

(b) Do their textbooks contain interesting reading passages on topics relevant to their needs?

(c) Do you have access to simple readers that are easy enough for your students to read for pleasure? What about a school or class library? How is it organised?

3 (a) What about reading out loud? If a teacher or student reads out loud how far does it give the students practice in understanding written English?

(b) Which is the best way of checking that students have really read the text and tried to understand it, (i) by getting them to read it out loud, or (ii) by asking them questions after they have read it silently?

(c) What other activities can students be asked to do to show they can understand the text? Explain briefly how students should use them. (See the FOCUS page at the beginning of this Unit).

4 In what ways is teaching elementary reading to beginners different from teaching reading at an intermediate level? (See the FOCUS page at the beginning of this Unit).

5 How can pictures, flash cards (with writing on) and other visual aids be used in the teaching of reading (i) at elementary stages? (ii) at intermediate and advanced stages?

6 (a) Look at FOCUS on LISTENING, Unit 18 p. 134, and discuss which of the *purposes* and *enabling skills* are also relevant to the teaching of reading. What other enabling skills can you think of that would help students develop efficient reading techniques? (for example, scanning). Finally refer to the FOCUS page at the beginning of this Unit, 'Reading Skills'.

(b) Which of these enabling skills do you think *your* students need most practice at?

(c) How far do the reading exercises in their coursebooks help them practice the reading skills they need?

(d) How can you give them practice in other skills not covered in their textbook?

143

ⓑ Lesson extracts

Both lesson extracts are suitable for both school and college. They refer to the reading passage opposite. In Extract One, the teacher makes the class read rapidly to get the general idea (extensive reading) whereas in Extract Two, the teacher is treating the passage in more detail (intensively). Repeat the teacher's part; notice especially the pitch change in the words that carry the stress.

Extract One
Extensive reading

Intermediate.
The teacher has already discussed aquariums with his class in preparation for this lesson. He begins by making them predict or guess what the passage will be about. He then asks them to read the first paragraph quickly and find out two items of information which will show him whether the students have understood the general idea.

T: Look at the passage, the first time, and the picture, and tell me what you think it will be about.
Ss: Tanks. Pipes. Water . . . tube.
T: Who can remember what we talked about last week? Look at the first line.
S: Aquariums.
T: Yes, now look at the diagram, and the title. How do they fit in with aquariums?
S: Filling with water.
T: Perhaps, or? Yes?
S: Empty water . . . er . . . it dirty?
T: Perhaps! Let's find out now what the author wants to tell us.

S: Please, what does 'algae' mean?
T: 'Algae'? Umm – well, if you read the first paragraph you might be able to guess that. It doesn't really matter if you don't understand every word. So, I want you to read the first paragraph silently and complete these two sentences. I'll write them up.
1 To clean the bottom of an aquarium you need a _____
2 Algae makes an aquarium _____ (clean/dirty)
Just write the two words *not* the whole sentence, OK.
Alright! Read it quickly. Silently! Start now. Only the first paragraph! I'll give you one minute.

Follow up
The teacher checks that most students have written the right words, he discusses them, then asks them what the next paragraph could be about; cleaning an aquarium or making a siphon. They then read it quickly to see which is correct.

👤 or 👤👤 **TEACHING HINTS (a) Why do you think the teacher discussed aquariums last week? (b) How does he help them to predict what the text will be about? (c) Why doesn't he explain the word 'algae'? (d) Why does he answer 'Perhaps' twice, rather than 'Yes' or 'No'?**

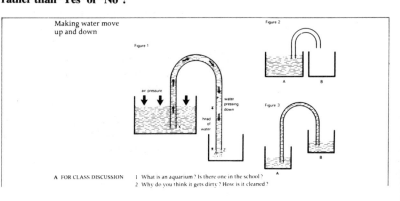

B QUICK READING FOR
INFORMATION

Find out:

1 What is the name of the action that helps you clean the bottom of an aquarium? Write it down.
2 Why do you make the sand in an aquarium slope down to the front?

The glass of an aquarium gets covered in algae, and the sand and pebbles at the bottom get covered with waste matter such as decayed leaves and fish droppings. You can scrape off the algae quite easily with a razor blade. It is also easy to clean the bottom if you know how to use a siphon.

To make a siphon take a piece of rubber tube and hold it under the water in the aquarium until all the air has bubbled out. Keeping one end (end X) under the water, cover the other end (end Z) tightly with your thumb and bring it over the edge and down the side of the aquarium. When end Z is below the level of the surface of the water, release your thumb grip and the water will flow out. Unless you let air into the tube or raise end Z above the water level in the aquarium, the water will continue to flow.

By moving end X around over the bottom of the aquarium you can suck up all the pieces of waste matter. It is a good idea to make the sand slope towards the front so that all the dirt collects in one place.

How does the siphon work? Look at Figure 1. Air presses on the surface of the water in the aquarium. Your U-shaped tube is empty of air and in position. As soon as you open end Z the water in the tube presses downwards and pulls more water behind it. When water is pushed and pulled through a U-shaped tube like this, we say it is being siphoned.

The depth of water pressing downwards is the distance between the surface of the water and the water outlet (end Z of the tube). The greater this distance is, the greater the water pressure will be. This depth of water pressing is called a head of water . . . .

D QUICK ORAL QUESTIONS

1 How does an aquarium get dirty?
2 What is it quite easy to do?
3 Who can demonstrate the action of *scraping*?
4 When is it easy to clean the aquarium bottom?
5 When is it not so easy to do this?
6 Why do you need a piece of rubber tube?
7 How do you drive the air out of the tube?
8 What things have happened when the bubbling stops?
9 Can you think of other ways of driving the air out of the tube?
10 How do you keep the air out of the tube?

Extract Two
Intensive reading

This extract also refers to the reading text above, but this time the teacher is treating it in detail, more intensively.

Intermediate.
The teacher has checked that they have got the general idea, and that they can follow the text using the diagram to help them. The students have guessed the meanings of 'siphon', 'release' and 'thumb grip', and the teacher showed them what 'surface' meant. They have just read the whole text a second time, knowing that they would have to answer the questions below the text afterwards.

T: So you've all read it again, now. Finished? Good. OK. Now in pairs ask each other the questions under the text. Just questions 1–7. See if you can agree on the answers. One to seven. In pairs. In twos! Start now. I'll give you two minutes.
(Teacher wanders round)
Right, before we check your answers, I want you to answer *my* questions. Ready? Think, then put your hands up. Er–First two lines–which words show you there is . . . an example given, an example? . . . . . Yes?

S: Such as?
T: Do you agree? Is he right?
S: Yes.
T: Yes good. Such as. So what *is* waste matter? Is it clean or dirty?
Ss: Dirty, old leaves . . . fish droppings . . .
T: Yes. Good. Right! Line 8, 8, 'bring *it*', what does *'it'* refer to?
S: Thumb?
T: What do *you* think?
S: The other end of the tube?
T: OK – which? Read it carefully.
S: Other end . . .
T: Yes. Now. Last sentence, paragraph two. Two. Got it? How can you stop the water flowing? How can you stop the . . .

Follow up
The teacher asks three or four more detailed questions to draw attention to grammatical relations, then goes on to lexical items, e.g. 'Look at paragraph two and pick out:
(a) all the words to do with water
(b) words which refer to the tube'

TEACHING HINTS (a) Why do you think the teacher got them to ask and answer the questions in pairs? (b) Does the teacher tell the students immediately if their answers are right or wrong? Why not? (c) Why does he pick 'such as' to ask a question about? (d) How easy is the question 'What does "it" refer to?'

Sample reading passage

Back-nestling

A FOR CLASS DISCUSSION

1 How are babies carried in your country?
2 Do you know any other ways of carrying babies?
3 Do men carry babies? Why (not)?

B QUICK READING FOR INFORMATION

Find out:

1 Does the writer think that back-nestling is a good way of carrying a child?
2 Does the writer think that a child should stay on the back of its mother all day?

Many African mothers carry, or nestle, their babies on their backs. This custom has advantages for both mother and child. A working mother who has nobody to look after the baby, knows he is safe on her back, while her hands are free for her work. Meanwhile, the baby stays in close contact with his mother and feels warm and safe. This sense of security may be suddenly broken, however, when the child can no longer be carried. He may be put down and expected to behave like a grown-up child. But he has been over-protected for so long through nestling that he now feels very insecure and may behave like a baby.

Children need freedom and the chance to use their limbs. They need to be able to observe and explore their environment. They also need to learn how to make and do things on their own. [1] *Therefore* even when mothers must carry their babies everywhere, they should try to set them free whenever possible. [2] *Moreover*, in the hot months, the less back-nestling the better.

Many women, [3] *however*, prefer to carry their children all day long. They feel the children are safe, sleep longer, keep quieter and do not make a mess! I once visited a friend's home where the mama-nurse was nestling my friend's eleven-month-old child. Seeing he was restless, I asked the mama-nurse to put him down. [4] *At first* she didn't want to because she thought the child would make the room untidy. When she [5] *finally* agreed I asked for some kitchen pots, spoons, unopened tins and boxes since there were no toys to play with. [6] *Immediately* the child started examining them one by one. [7] *Then* he started banging the pots and boxes with the spoons. The different sounds fascinated him. [8] *But* mama-nurse didn't like the noise or the mess.

The extracts on pages 144, 145 and above are from *Junior English Reading,* a reading course for secondary schools in Africa. See Bibliography, page 190.

The last paragraph of this reading passage would be suitable for a 'Jumbled Paragraph' exercise, see page 152.

This passage is also referred to on pages 153–4, and in the lesson extract, Unit 21, page 166.

Classroom language

Tables 1–9 deal with ELEMENTARY reading activities, (word and sentence recognition etc.)

Tables 10–22 deal with INTERMEDIATE and more ADVANCED reading comprehension lessons (training in reading skills, understanding texts etc.)

All suitable tables should be practised, in pairs, *in conjunction with* the relevant flash cards, pictures, reading texts, so that you get used to handling the lesson materials and speaking about them simultaneously. The text opposite, 'Back Nestling', could be used with Tables 11 onwards.

Elementary reading tasks
Flash cards or blackboard

1

I've got We'll use	some flash cards with	your names words and pictures sentences questions and answers	on. Look!

2

Give me Show me Point to Pick out	the	card word sentence picture	which says '_____'. which goes with this word/sentence.

3

I want you to read	the cards these	out loud to me silently to yourselves to your neighbours in your groups	and then ... (See Table 4)

4

Match the words to the right pictures. Find the sentences about **this** picture. Match the questions to the right answers. etc.	Like this _____ (and write them).

(See Unit 20, Section **c**, Tables 2, 3 and 5.)

5

No? Well,	what	does this	word start with? bit of the word say?	
		is this	letter sound	here?
		do these two letters together sound like?		
	read the **rest** of the sentence and guess.			

6

Could you open your	reading text work	books and find	the story called '_____' in the index. page 91. the lesson we are on at the moment.

7

What does it say Tell me what it says		at the	top bottom	of the page.	
Look at the	exercise writing	in the middle.			
		under by	the	picture photograph	on page _____.

8

Can you read the instructions What do you have to do	for this exercise?

9

You have to	match the questions to answers. find the right word for each gap. arrange the sentences into a good paragraph.

(See the FOCUS page at the beginning of this Unit for further activities.
See Units 12 and 20 for setting homework, Section **c**.)

Checking students have understood

10

Alright.	Do you all know	what to do? how to read this?
	Does anyone have any questions? Any questions? Any problems? Shall I go over it again?	

(See Unit 20, end of Section **c** for STUDENT QUERIES.)

Intermediate and advanced reading comprehension

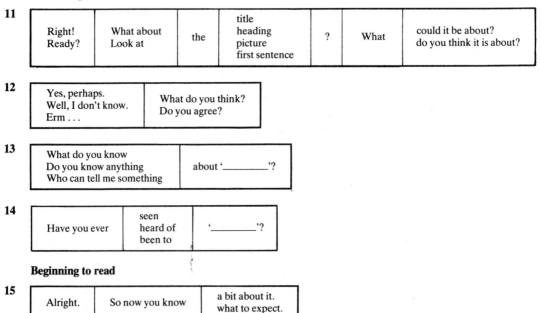

Find a reading comprehension passage in your textbook and adapt the language in the tables to refer to *your* text, filling the blanks with relevant words from the text. Try to imagine what the teacher is doing at each stage, and why. Use the passage on page 146 if you do not have a suitable text available.

Still in pairs, take turns to be the teacher! Practise rephrasing your instructions, using two or three alternative expressions from each table. If the 'teacher' is not 100% clear, the 'student' should interrupt and ask.

Introducing the text

11

Right! Ready?	What about Look at	the	title heading picture first sentence	?	What	could it be about? do you think it is about?

12

Yes, perhaps. Well, I don't know. Erm . . .	What do you think? Do you agree?

13

What do you know Do you know anything Who can tell me something	about '_____'?

14

Have you ever	seen heard of been to	'_____'?

Beginning to read

15

Alright.	So now you know	a bit about it. what to expect.

(See Unit 18, Table 2, but instead of 'listening', use 'reading' or 'skimming'.)

Before	you begin reading	you'll need to understand '_____'. tell me what '_____' means. could someone explain '_____'.
		look at this question. make a note of these questions.

Student: | But I don't understand '_____'!

'_____'?	Well	'_____'	doesn't matter now! is not important here. you can guess later on.

Now read the	first paragraph 2nd section	silently	and	find the answer to this. pick out important points. jot down relevant information.

Finished?	So	then discuss it/them with your neighbour. Write down a question to ask the class.

Now	will you all	think of write down	some 2 5	questions to ask	me. your neighbour. the other group.

(See Part One, Unit 9, Section **d**, Exploiting a reading passage.)

Talking about the text in detail

In line 4, The 10th line from the top, The 2nd line in paragraph 2, Near the bottom, The sentence beginning '_____',	what	does the author mean by '_____'? **can** he mean by '_____'? do you think 'which' refers to? does the word 'however' tell us?
	Why does he	use the word 'moreover'? repeat the words '_____'?
Can you say/explain that in your own words?		

Difficult? You don't know?	Never mind.	Look at the sentence	after. before.
		See if you can guess. What **could** it be? Guess.	
Try to	think work	it out for yourselves. Think!	Is it '_____' or '_____'?

(See Unit 18, Tables 10 and 11. Change 'Listen to' to 'read'.)

Let's recap quickly.		
So what	do you think the author	wanted to tell his readers? will say next? will go on to say next?
	kind of people is the author writing for, do you think?	

24   A game to play

In groups! Each group writes down 5 questions to ask the other group.

If *they* get the answer right, they get 2 marks. If not, *you* get 2 – (if your question was a good one).

(See also Part One, Unit 8 for language for team games, and Unit 9 for language for group work.)

(d)   Teaching skills

Do Exercises 1 and 2 in full, then *select* from 3, 4 and 5 the activities which will be most useful for your classes. Pool the work you do which will be useful to others. Have it duplicated and distributed to all teachers.

1   An experiment

Read the nonsense passage on the left and see how many of the questions you can answer.

> The grifty snolls cloppered raucingly along the unchoofed trake. They were klary, so they higgled on, sperately. 'Ah, chiwar kervay,' they squopped rehoply, 'Mi psar Quaj!' 'Quaj!' snilled one, and filted even jucklier.

(a) Where did the snolls clopper?

(b) What was the trake like?

(c) Why did they higgle on?

(d) Why did they clopper raucingly?

(e) Why did they higgle sperately?

(f) Would an unchoofed trake be easy or difficult to drive a car on?

(g) Did the snolls travel quietly or noisily? How do you know?

(h) What was the name of the place they were going to?

Did you understand the passage?

How many of these questions were you able to answer?

Discuss in groups why you were able to answer some but not others. Compare especially questions (d) and (e).

What has this nonsense exercise shown about writing comprehension questions on reading passages?

2   Introducing a reading passage

In real life when we pick something up to read, we usually know roughly why it was written and what it is going to be about. We rarely read anything in a 'vacuum', i.e. knowing nothing whatsoever about the subject. Reading passages in language textbooks are taken out of their normal contexts, so we have fewer clues as to what they might be about, and the task of reading with understanding is, therefore, more difficult. Pictures and titles help us to predict the subject matter, but students need both guidance and motivation in order to read with purpose and satisfaction. The way a teacher introduces a reading passage can be vital. A good introduction should, (a) make the students want to read the passage, and make it worth their while to read it, and (b) get the students' minds working on themes close to the one in the passage, to make them read the text in the light of what they know already about the topic.

An introduction in the form of a teacher monologue is less likely to motivate the students than one which involves the students in a discussion. An introduction which poses questions is more likely to make students want to read than one which gives all the answers and summarises the story or information; then there is no point in the students reading it for themselves.

(a) In groups of three, choose a reading passage from your textbooks and discuss how you would introduce the passage to the class, bearing in mind the points made above. Allow about five minutes for the introduction. When you have decided how to introduce it, split groups up and re-form. Then take it in turns to introduce your passage to the two new group members, as if they were students in a class.

(b) Write down the name and page number of your passage, and briefly your ideas for an introduction. Collect everyone's ideas together, and get them duplicated and circulated.

3 Preparing elementary reading activities[1] — word cards

Aims

At the early stages it is important to make the task of learning to read as easy and interesting as possible. Students need lots of practice before they are able to recognise words and phrases quickly, and even the most interesting reading book or textbook gets boring if they have to read the same things more than once.

Materials

If you use different types of reading cards, like those illustrated here, it is possible to set up a variety of games and activities that your students will enjoy. At the same time they will be learning to recognise words and phrases, to read with understanding and develop speed. The cards can be used again and again in different games and with different classes, and once they are prepared, there is no further preparation or marking to be done. The fact that the students have successfully completed the task set shows that they have understood. When they finally read from their books they will find it easy.

Preparation

You will need light colour card or strong paper; folders or envelopes large enough to store sets of cards in, rulers, dark coloured felt tipped pens or markers and scissors. Decide how big each card should be: large enough to be read clearly in groups but small and neat enough to store. When deciding what to write on the cards, remember that students should only be asked to read words they can already say and understand, so you will need to use only words and phrases with which they are familiar.

Activities and word games

(a) Matching word to picture

Students match the word to the correct picture as quickly as possible.

To make: Prepare 6 pairs of small cards, a word on one card, a picture illustrating it on the other, using words your students will need to be able to read in their textbooks. Mix each set up and store in a labelled envelope. Write the words the envelope contains on the outside of the envelope, with the instructions to the students: 'Find a picture to match each word, then write the words down'.

(b) Word families (or lexical sets)

Each envelope can contain any number of words on separate cards belonging to one word or family lexical set, e.g. names of animals, kinds of food, colours etc. The teacher mixes words from two or three envelopes (i.e. different lexical sets) together; the students read them and sort them out back into sets as quickly as possible. This can be done competitively.

To make: Complete the sets below with familiar words or phrases then copy them on to cards. Store each set in a separate envelope, clearly labelled. Pictures can also be added, to make a combination of both games (a) and (b).

Places	Food	People	Clothes	Colours	
(to) the shop	rice	the doctor	shirt	_____	_____
(at) school	sugar	Mr Jones	sandals	_____	_____
_____	_____	My father	_____	_____	_____
_____	_____	_____	_____	_____	_____
_____	_____	_____	_____	_____	_____

[1] Also suitable for WRITING practice. See Unit 20, Section **d**.

To make: Complete the sets above with familiar words or phrases then copy them on to cards. Store each set in a separate envelope, clearly labelled. Pictures can also be added, to make a combination of both games (a) and (b).

4 Preparing reading activities[1] — elementary to intermediate — sentence cards

(a) Matching sentences to pictures or wall charts

Two or more pictures or wall charts are displayed, and students read and sort sentences into two columns, according to which picture they are about. This can be done with small pictures, e.g. magazine pictures, or wall pictures or maps etc.

To make: Find suitable pictures to suit the vocabulary your students know orally and need to read. Write 6 sentences about each picture on cards. Store them in labelled envelopes, containing or referring to the correct picture.

To use: Mix the sentence cards from two or more envelopes; students sort them as quickly as possible according to the picture they refer to.

(b) Matching questions and answers (based on a picture or short text)

Students look at the picture, or read the text, then find all the question cards. Then they find a card with a suitable answer for each question. This gives students practice in recognising referential words like 'he', 'she' etc. and discourse markers like 'because', 'in order to' etc.

To make: Choose a suitable magazine picture or short text. Mount it on card the right size to fit in the envelope. Write, on separate cards, 6 questions and 6 or more answers. The answers should be natural sounding answers, not too long; because to have long answers that repeat or look like the question would make the matching too easy. It is a good idea to provide two extra 'answers' that do not match any questions, then students cannot get the last ones right unless they really understand all of them.

An example is shown here:

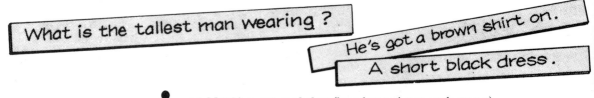

(c) Matching sentence halves (based on a picture or short text)

This is the same as matching question and answer except that you split sentences in half and write half on each card. An example is shown here:

(d) Jumbled paragraphs or texts

Students read the sentences on the cards, then re-arrange the cards in the best way to form a coherent paragraph which they can check by looking up the original paragraph in their textbooks. This gives them practice in reading for meaning, seeing how a text is organised, and reorganising link words and words which refer back or forwards. Rearranging paragraphs of a text is also useful.

[1] Also suitable for controlled WRITING practice. See Unit 20, Section **d**, **1** (a).

To make: Choose a short interesting paragraph from the students' course-books or reading books, part of the passage on page 146 might be suitable. Rewrite each sentence on a separate card. Shuffle the cards and store them in an envelope marked with the book title and page number of the paragraph.

Alternatively, to make a *class set* of the same exercise, you can write or type the sentences in the wrong order, each sentence beginning on a new line. Have the page duplicated. The students then cut the page up, and arrange the sentences into the right order, thus making a sensible paragraph. Remember you can also 'jumble' a *longer text*, dividing it into 3–6 *paragraphs* or *chunks*.

5 Other reading exercises on reading passages

A different reading passage should be chosen by each person. All the exercises suggested in (a)–(d) below can be based on this one passage. At the end of the session, all material can be written up, duplicated and distributed to all teachers, for future use. Reference to the book, unit and page number should be made clear and ideas for a suitable introduction outlined briefly. See **2**, above.

(a) True/false/not-stated

Students are asked to say whether a number of statements written about the passage are true or false, or whether there is not sufficient information in the passage for them to judge.

This gives students practice in scanning* for information, and reading with meaning and evaluation.

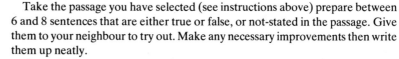

Take the passage you have selected (see instructions above) prepare between 6 and 8 sentences that are either true or false, or not-stated in the passage. Give them to your neighbour to try out. Make any necessary improvements then write them up neatly.

Example: See text on page 144.

State whether the following sentences are True, False or Not-Stated in the passage.

(i) The first paragraph is mainly about algae. F

(ii) You have to clean an aquarium regularly. NS

(iii) The author mentions two main things needed to clean out an aquarium. T

(b) Jumbled key points

Write a list of the main ideas or key points in the passage. Copy them out in the wrong order. Label them A, B, C, etc. Students must number them in the order they are expressed in the passage. Be careful to disguise the wording of the main ideas so that students cannot recognise a similar sentence in the passage, and perhaps get the right order without understanding the passage.

(c) General comprehension questions

Remember Exercise 1 (the nonsense passage), and how easy it can be to get the answers right without understanding the passage!

Write 5 or 6 general comprehension questions on your passage and then try them out on your neighbour. Discuss how he or she knew how to find the right answers; exactly what words/phrases/referential words etc., had to be understood?

(d) Intensive questions

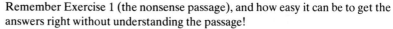

First refer to the list of reading skills on the FOCUS page at the beginning of this Unit, then read these questions, based on the reading passage about aquariums on page 144. Write beside each question the number of the particular skill or skills being practised here as the students find the answers.

_____ (i) Are *decayed* leaves fresh, new leaves or old leaves?

_____ (ii) Does the author think it is difficult to clean an aquarium?

_____ (iii) When using a siphon, how do you stop the water flowing once it has started?

_____ (iv) What must you hold under the water for some time?

_____ (v) Why must the siphon be full of water?

_____ (vi) Why is it a good idea to make the dirt collect in one place?

Which of these enabling skills can be practised by students reading the passage *you* have chosen? Write one or two questions to practise each relevant skill, then try them out on your neighbour. Make any improvements necessary before you write them up neatly, to follow on from the general questions you did in (c).

(e) Cloze exercise (intensive reading)
First, try out this cloze (or blank filling) exercise yourselves. The passage is taken from a textbook so that the students can check their own work. There are more words than blanks to make students think hard even for the last blank. In order to carry out the task successfully students must recognise the relationship between parts of sentences as well as understanding the gist of the passage. Discuss why these particular blanks were left, and why these particular extra words were chosen for the box.

Fill each blank with one suitable word from the box on the right. When you have finished, discuss your work with your neighbour. Then check your work by referring to the same paragraph on page 146 of this book.

Back nestling
Many African mothers carry, _____ nestle, their babies on _____ backs. _____ custom has advantages _____ both _____ and _____
A working mother, _____ has nobody to look after _____ baby, knows _____ is safe on her back.

she	the	or	their	mother
he	this	people	his	child
who	that	for	her	also

Write a short cloze exercise in the same way, based on a meaningful extract from the comprehension passage you have been working on. Make sure you leave enough words in the extract to enable the students to get the gist. Often the first paragraph is the best and clearest for this type of exercise. Perhaps you will need to leave the first one or two sentences complete before you start leaving blanks. Decide what type of words to elicit. Try it out on your neighbours to make sure it is not too difficult, then write it up neatly.

Teaching practice
1 Planning
In groups. Select a suitable text for your students and choose one short section of it for this lesson. (Make sure you can get enough copies of the text for your students to have in the lesson.)

(a) Decide what your lesson objectives are. These will depend on what the passage has to offer. Decide which reading skills, which words you will teach.

(b) Plan an introduction to the topic and prepare any visuals you need.

(c) Decide which words (if any) are vital to pre-teach, and which are not. See Unit 16, Section **c**, Tables 7 onwards, and this Unit, Section **c**, Tables 16 and 17.

(d) Make up one or two sign-post questions, so that students read with a purpose.

(e) Then three comprehension questions or True/False/Non-Stated items, to check general understanding.

(f) Write these down, and add a few quick oral questions to check that most main points are understood.

(g) Prepare some questions using Table 21 for more intensive reading, and practice in reading skills.

(h) Decide on patterns of student/teacher interaction and how to vary the lesson. Is there any opportunity for a short spell of pair work0

(i) Discuss but do not plan in detail the type of follow up activity that would be appropriate for this passage, e.g. jumbled key sentences to arrange. See the FOCUS page at the beginning of this Unit for more ideas, and Unit 20 or 21 on WRITING.

2 Teaching

Remember when teaching this lesson that you are not simply teaching or explaining *this* passage, but are using this passage as a means of developing your students' reading skills for *future* texts. Make your students do the work of finding out the meanings of words by prediction, careful guess work, evaluating other students' replies etc. so that they can learn to apply the same methods when reading on their own.

If peer teaching, split up and re-form groups so you can 'teach' 'students' who are new to the passage.

3 Follow up and evaluation

In groups. Discuss whether teachers used their own classroom language as effectively as possible, i.e. getting their *students* to think for themselves, or did *teachers* do too much explaining?

As a class

(a) Write up on the blackboard which reading skills were practised by each groups' students. To do this think back to the *questions* you asked your students.

(b) Which words were learnt by your students? Which of these words will be most useful for further reading tasks?

(c) Discuss how you could improve your students' reading ability. Do they need more extensive reading, reading for pleasure? What kind of skills do they need to pass their final exams? How could you help?

🄵 Further reading

On reading activities at various levels Andrew Wright (1976) Chapter 3, pp. 31–37.

On testing reading comprehension J B Heaton (1975) Chapter 7, pp. 103–111, 125.

On aims and method Malcolm Cooper and Michael Fox (1978) Introduction for the Teacher, pp. vii–xi.

C Brumfit and K Johnson (1979) pp. 117–142.

Donn Byrne (ed) (1980) pp. 122–6, 132–3, 169–171.

A Davies and H G Widdowson in 'The Edinburgh Course in Applied Linguistics' Vol. 3, Chapter 6.

W M Rivers and M S Temperley (1978) Chapters 6 and 7.

20 FOCUS on writing practice

(Early stages of writing)

For Intermediate and Advanced Writing see Unit 21

Difficult?
Before students write make sure that they
- can say it
- can read it
- can understand it
- know what you want them to do
- know how you want them to do it
- know why they are doing it

WRITE WHAT?

WHY WRITE in class?
to learn the motor skills of handwriting; to develop neatness, clarity and speed
to learn spelling and punctuation, etc.
to reinforce vocabulary and structures already mastered orally
to keep a written record of what has been learnt and achieved
to practise for end-of-term achievement tests

WRITING ACTIVITIES

1 Match then copy

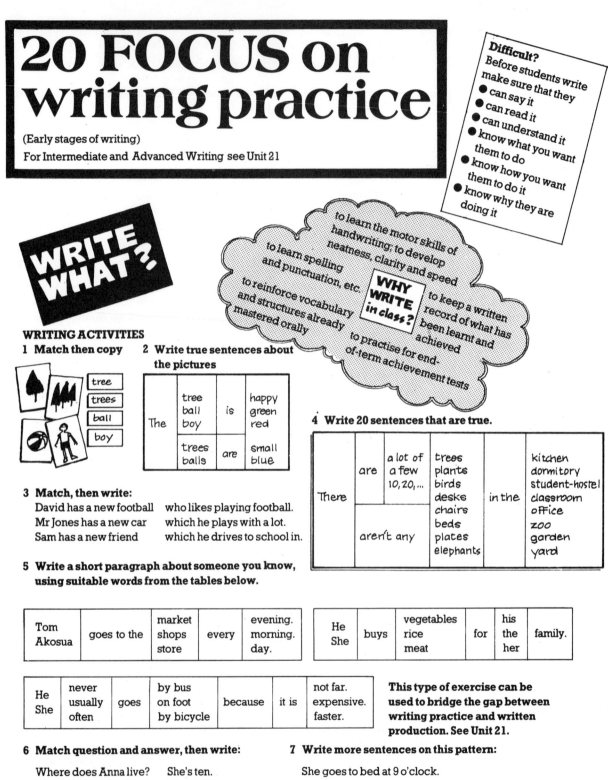

tree
trees
ball
boy

2 Write true sentences about the pictures

The	tree ball boy	is	happy green red
	trees balls	are	small blue

3 Match, then write:

David has a new football   who likes playing football.
Mr Jones has a new car   which he plays with a lot.
Sam has a new friend   which he drives to school in.

4 Write 20 sentences that are true.

There	are	a lot of a few 10, 20, ...	trees plants birds desks chairs beds plates elephants	in the	kitchen dormitory student-hostel classroom office zoo garden yard
	aren't any				

5 Write a short paragraph about someone you know, using suitable words from the tables below.

Tom Akosua	goes to the	market shops store	every	evening. morning. day.

He She	buys	vegetables rice meat	for	his the her	family.

He She	never usually often	goes	by bus on foot by bicycle	because	it is	not far. expensive. faster.

This type of exercise can be used to bridge the gap between writing practice and written production. See Unit 21.

6 Match question and answer, then write:

Where does Anna live?   She's ten.
Where do you live?   I live in Keta.
How old is Peter?   She lives near me.
How old is Anna?   He's twelve.

7 Write more sentences on this pattern:

She goes to bed at 9 o'clock.

He / go / school / 7.
They / come / home / 2.
Peter / eat / lunch / 12.

See also Unit 19, FOCUS on READING, page 142. Many of those ideas are suitable for writing too

Unit 20 Writing practice (Early stages of writing)

The aims of this Unit are **1** to discuss the aims and purposes of writing at the elementary stage and the different types of meaningful writing activity that can be set **2** to show how writing can be integrated* with other skills, for example reading and oral work, in order to help students write more accurately

ⓐ Preliminary discussion

1 (a) When we talk about teaching the four language skills (listening, speaking, reading, writing), writing usually comes last. Why?

(b) At what stage in your English course is writing introduced for the first time? How soon after learning to read should students begin to learn to write? Why?

2 What are the purposes of writing English at elementary level? See 'WHY WRITE?' on the FOCUS page. Which do you consider more important?

3 What difficulties do your students have in the early stages of learning to write? Why? Can they understand what they are asked to write? Is there a lack of suitable and interesting guided writing exercises in their textbooks? Is there interference from their pronunciation which hinders their spelling, e.g. writing 'leave' instead of 'live' or 'clisp' for 'crisp'. Have they perhaps not mastered new patterns well enough orally to recognise and write them correctly?

4 (a) What type of writing activities do *you* use in the early stages to give students meaningful writing practice? Describe some.

(b) Discuss the advantages and disadvantages of getting students to copy passages from the board or from their textbooks.

(c) Discuss what the purposes of the writing activities illustrated on the FOCUS page at the beginning of this Unit could be.

(d) Which of these activities are the easier ones? Say why.

5 Preparation for writing tasks can often be achieved through oral work or through reading activities.

(a) Which of the ORAL PRACTICE activities in Unit 15, on pp. 110–113 could lead into useful elementary writing tasks?

(b) Which of the READING ACTIVITIES outlined in Unit 19, on pp. 150–5 could lead into written tasks suitable for elementary students?

6 (a) 'There is no point in students producing a bad piece of writing.' Discuss.

(b) You can help students to produce good writing by doing adequate oral and reading preparation before the writing task, by setting simple but meaningful tasks, and by giving very clear instructions. What instructions would you give for some of the tasks on the FOCUS page?

(c) Another way of helping them is to set writing exercises in class where you can watch them write, encourage them and stop bad habits early on. You can also help them to learn to spot and correct their own mistakes. What would you say if a student wrote this:

My brother ~~live~~ leave in manchester.   Is nice town.

157

ⓑ Lesson extract

There is only one extract in this Unit. It is suitable for both children and adult students who are beginning to read. It is an extract of a lesson which progresses from oral work, to reading and finally writing.

The picture and tables below are the ones the teacher refers to in this lesson.

Patsy				
George!	I've lost Where's Where are	my	pen keys school bag watch English books	! ?

George				
Your	Keys watch English books school bag pen	? .	It's They're	on the in the	table. bookcase. floor. cupboard. drawer.

The teacher began the lesson revising questions and answers with 'Where is' and 'Where are', using a large wall picture. She then sets up the situation where Patsy is always late for college because she loses things, and George gets impatient. The teacher has worked out the tables before the lesson, so after the students have practised dialogues similar to the ones from the tables, she begins to copy the tables up on to the blackboard.

T: Good. You did those dialogues really well. Now some reading, and later we'll do some writing. Still the same picture. See if you can read these words as I write them. Oh! No – pens down! Don't write anything yet. You're going to read it first. Pens down. OK. Remember the things in the picture. What do these words say? (*Teachers begins with the three columns of nouns*)

Ss: Pen.

T: Pen, yes.

Ss: School ... er ... school bag.

T: Schoolbag, good. etc.... (*She finishes the tables and draws the lines*) Now we've got two tables; this table is what Patsy says, and this is what?

Ss: George!

T: Yes. What George says. Good. So you read across, choosing the right words, like this: 'George! Where are my keys?' and George says, 'Your keys? They're on the table' see the picture. Two keys, right? So we take 'they're', not 'it's' from here. Alright, tell me if this one is good. Listen hard! 'George! I've lost my watch.' 'Your watch? They're on the

Ss: No! ... er. *it's* ... not *they're*!

T: Good! So, you see, you must make *good* sentences. Let's hear you say some ... (*Teacher hears several*

students read) OK. Now, some writing! In pencil. Very neatly, in your exercise books. I want you to write three dialogues. Three. Each sentence on a new line. Right. Someone come and do one on the board, to show the others. You, Kumah? I'll draw some lines for you. OK? Start here.

T: You others watch. Don't write yet. Pens down. Capital letter for George. That's right. (*reads*) Where are ... my ... English books. And do you need a question mark or a full stop? This or this? Ah good. You've put a question mark. New line, now. Capital Y. Good! ... (*Silence as student writes*) Everybody, is that correct? Has he forgotten anything? Full stop? Apostrophe?

S: Full stop.

T: Yes, good. Like this. A full stop. Good. Well. That is good writing. Just be careful of your gs and ys. They sit *on* the line and their tails hang down like this. That's better. Well done. Thank you very much. Now could you all write three dialogues, different ones, and then check them carefully? Ask your neighbours to help you check them. OK? Start writing now. In your exercise books.

Follow up
The teacher wanders round while students write; she points out where mistakes are but does not tell them what is wrong; they have to correct their own mistakes themselves. Then she gets some students to read one of their dialogues out. Some students' writing is shown to the class. Then she rubs off the columns of nouns and asks the class to write another two dialogues quickly on a piece of rough paper to check how well they can write without copying. She asks them to learn the spellings for homework.

TEACHING HINTS (a) How does the teacher make sure the students understand what they are copying from the tables? (Two ways) (b) Why does she ask someone to write a dialogue on the board before they write it in their books? (c) Why does she make them try to correct their own mistakes?

ⓒ Classroom language

Practise the language from the tables in pairs or small groups, referring to suitable writing exercises on the blackboard, or in your textbooks or from the FOCUS page at the beginning of this Unit. Remember to rephrase instructions and speak clearly but not unnaturally slowly.

For Tables 6–9 you could each produce two or three lines of handwriting making three or four deliberate mistakes. Then, using the language from the tables you can 'correct' each other's writing.

Whoever takes the student's part should ask whenever something is not 100% clear; see Tables 11–13, for STUDENTS' QUERIES. These are useful queries that you should gradually teach and encourage your students to use. See also Appendix B.

See Part One, Unit 5, Section **c**, for ways of introducing a writing stage.

Preparing to write

| Before you | begin to write do any writing write anything | let's see if you can I want you to | tell me say | what you're going to write. |
| | | | do it orally first. read this first. | |

Who can	tell me this one? read this one	Hands up Put your hands up	if you	know. can do it.		
What does this say?						
Hossein, Rosa,	can you	read do	this one?	Everyone, All of you,	put your hands up if	she he	is right.

Careful!	This is That's	a	new hard	phrase. word. sentence.	Listen to how I	read say	it. OK?
					Watch how I This is how you	write spell	
			new exercise.		Watch how to do		

| You'll need You need Could you take | your | pens pencils | out. | And Also | your | note books, exercise books, | please. |
| | | | | | some rough paper, | | |

Giving instructions

| So, you | match these make five good find ten true sort out these fill the blanks in these complete these   etc. | sentences, then | copy write | them | neatly. carefully. | |
| | | | | | taking care with and watch your | spelling. punctuation. capital letters, etc. |

Details

6

Make sure See that	your	'g's', 'y's', and so on	sit on the line. have tails which hang down.
		'k's', 'l's' and so on go right up. 'u's' are different from your 'v's'. spaces between words are clear.	
Don't forget to		cross your 't's' and dot your 'i's'. put capital letters where needed. spell correctly. write neatly. lay it out neatly.	

Helping students to spot their mistakes

7

| That's | quite good,
good
much better,
very neat, | but | what's wrong
there's something missing | in this | line
word
phrase
text | ? |
| | | | you've | forgotten something
left something out | here. | |

8

| Check
It's
What about | your | spelling of '_____'.
punctuation.
handwriting.
grammar.
capital letters. |

9

| Is that a | true
good | sentence? | Can you read it to me?
Could you read what you have written please?
Does it make sense, or is it silly? |
| What do you all think?
Think what that means! | | | |

Setting simple homework

10

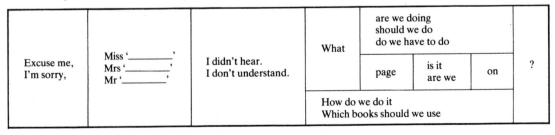

| At home
For homework
Tonight | not now, | can
could
will | you | finish writing this?
write this out again neatly?
learn how to spell the new words?
practise writing_____? |
| and give | your | books
papers | in
to me | tomorrow morning by 8 o'clock.
next lesson, at_____. |

(See also Part One, Unit 12, Section **c**, Tables 5 to 8.)

Student queries

11

Excuse me, I'm sorry,	Miss '_____' Mrs '_____' Mr '_____'	I didn't hear. I don't understand.	What	are we doing should we do do we have to do			?
				page	is it are we	on	
			How do we do it Which books should we use				

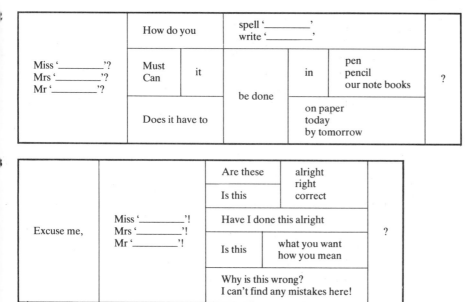

		How do you	spell '_____' write '_____'				?
Miss '_____'? Mrs '_____'? Mr '_____'?	Must Can	it		in	pen pencil our note books		
	Does it have to		be done	on paper today by tomorrow			

		Are these	alright right		?
Excuse me,	Miss '_____'! Mrs '_____'! Mr '_____'!	Is this	correct		
		Have I done this alright			
		Is this	what you want how you mean		
		Why is this wrong? I can't find any mistakes here!			

(See also Part One, Unit 12, 'Ending a lesson', Section **c**, since writing is often the final stage in a teaching sequence or lesson.

Appendix B contains more relevant student language, see QUERIES ABOUT TASKS SET, especially Tables 14 and 15.)

ⓓ Teaching skills

Select the writing tasks which are most relevant to your teaching situation. The first are examples of very controlled writing exercises, suitable for beginners. The tasks in **2** are more demanding.

1 Simple writing practice

(a) Writing words/handwriting/spelling

See Unit 19, Section **d**, **3** (a) and (b).

Matching words to pictures or sorting words into sets and then writing them down ensures that students read and understand what they are copying. If you only ask your students to write a *few* words, you can insist on their handwriting being perfect.

  What problems do your students have with handwriting and spelling? List them. Think of some easy words containing the problem items, write them on cards, and either add them if possible to the 'Matching words to pictures' or 'Word family' sets that you made in Unit 19, or devise similar ways to use them in class. (Spelling competitions? group handwriting competitions?)

(b) Substitution tables

Students can be asked to write *true* sentences from a substitution table, like numbers 2 and 4 in the FOCUS page at the beginning of this Unit. Students should always be asked to read sentences out loud first, to make sure they understand and can read all the words. After writing ten or so, they can give their sentences to their neighbours to check for them, to make sure they are true and spelled correctly.

  (i) In pairs, each pair taking a different unit from the Elementary English textbook, make up one or two substitution tables for each lesson.

(ii) Practise writing one table neatly on the blackboard. Pool your work, so you each have a copy of all the tables.

(c) Substitution tables – progressive deletion

See **1** (b) above.

After students have *copied* a number of sentences from the table, one column, (then later another column) can be rubbed off the board (or covered up). Students begin writing on a new page to see how many sentences they can remember. Finally, they can write a few whole sentences from memory.

 Look at the tables you wrote for **1** (b) and decide which column(s) you would erase (or cover up) first.

(d) Substitution tables for paragraphs

The tables on the FOCUS page give students some choice in what they write, and practice in selecting meaningful combinations. There is little chance of error, so students feel satisfied at completing a task well. Marking is simple.

Look at the topics set for writing tasks in your early intermediate textbooks. If the tasks set are too difficult, and result in students making a lot of mistakes, try preparing some of the writing tasks in this way.

 In pairs, each pair should select a different topic. First write a 'model' paragraph. Then see which words could be varied and suggest variations. Finally build up a chain of substitution tables like Example 5 on p. 156.

2 Elementary to intermediate writing tasks

(a) Read then write (Miscellaneous activities)

Study the activities suggested in Unit 19, Section **d**, 4 for reading, and discuss which ones would lead into useful writing practice. See also the FOCUS page at the beginning of this Unit for more examples.

Which of the basic writing skills could you focus students' attention on for each task: handwriting, spelling, punctuation, layout, speech? What instructions would you give your students immediately before each writing task (after they had done the necessary reading)? See Tables 1 to 5. What might your students need to ask at this stage? Practise in twos or threes, one being the teacher, others being students who are a bit slow to grasp what they should do and therefore need to ask. (See Tables 11–12 for student language. Add to it where you can.)

(b) Speak then write

(Expansion sentences – following a pattern)

See the FOCUS page at the beginning of this Unit. Do Activity 7 orally in pairs and discuss what makes it difficult.

This technique can be used to introduce or revise the written form of a structure. Sentences should be prepared orally in class before they are written. This will help you to diagnose where the difficulties lie and help you remedy mistakes before they are written down.

In pairs, prepare sets of six sentences to practise patterns that your students often get wrong. (One pattern per pair.) Try them out on someone else. Write them up neatly and pool your work. This work will be useful in Unit 21, Section **d**, 3 (b).

(c) Oral practice activities for writing practice

Look at FOCUS on ORAL PRACTICE, Unit 15, page 104.

Which of the activities there would be useful also for writing practice? List them. (Remember we do not normally write spoken English; so activities like 2 are not very suitable for writing).[1] Write clear, simple instructions in English for each activity, so that your students can read the instructions and write the exercise without needing to ask anything. Check your instructions with your neighbour.

---

[1] This applies less to the really early stages, when students need to write to reinforce their oral work.

e Teaching practice

1 Planning

Groups of three or four.

Split the time allowed for the practice lesson between you. Choose one different type of writing activity for each 15 or 20 minutes worth of lesson, and decide on the aim or purpose of each one.

Choose your material very carefully. With only 15 or 20 minutes, you have no time to present a *new* item orally and proceed through oral practice, oral production and reading to the written stage. It must be language your students are already familiar with orally, and can read without too much difficulty. If your last lesson with them was reading (Unit 19) you could base the writing exercise on those reading materials.

(a) Write down the tables, sentences etc. you have prepared for the writing task.

(b) Plan a quick spell of oral work to introduce the class to the theme of the writing material.

(c) Decide how you will present the written form for them to read and practise orally before they write.

(d) Diagnose any difficulties that might crop up, e.g. spellings? and decide how and when to deal with them.

(e) Practise the instructions you will give them before they write. (Revise Section **b** and relevant tables in Section **c**.) Which example(s) will you do for them on the board before they start? How long will you give them to write it?

(f) How and when will you correct their work?

2 Teaching

If you have real students, make sure there will be spare pens, sharp pencils and paper available.

The first teacher should introduce the lesson and explain what will be happening in the lesson.

If peer teaching, split groups and re-form so you teach your micro* lesson to some different people.

3 Follow up and evaluation

The test of the success of a writing lesson is to see how well the students actually wrote, and to ask yourself if they could write it the next lesson as well, or even better.

(a) If you taught genuine students, discuss the following points:

What did the students *learn* during the lesson? Was it useful?

What mistakes did your students make? How could you have prevented them?

What extra preparation or guidance could you give next time?

Do they have any specific difficulty in common that you could plan a remedial writing lesson on? How would you do this?

(b) If peer teaching, discuss: how clear and logical was the staging of the lesson? Were the instructions really clear?

What mistakes might students have made? How would you have dealt with these?

(c) Final points: How useful and meaningful was the writing task? Which types of writing activity were the most successful? Why?

f Further reading

Donn Byrne (1979) Chapters 1–4 and Appendices 2 and 3.

Helen Moorwood (ed) (1978) Section 5.

W M Rivers and M S Temperley (1978) Chapter 8.

Writing skills

1 Handwriting: forming and joining letters.

2 Mastering spelling, punctuation, sentence construction, referential words (he, who).

3 Linking sentences, using connecting words, relatives, etc. Connecting paragraphs.

4 Being aware of different demands of written English (contrast with spoken).

5 Organising information logically and clearly with a specific type of reader in mind.

6 Using discourse markers appropriately to indicate main points, developments in a theme, change of topic, examples, conclusions, etc.

7 Using variation in normal sentence patterns and word order to develop a theme clearly and emphasise the main points at each stage.

8 Selecting vocabulary to convey attitude and implied meaning.

21 FOCUS on written production

WRITING – WHAT? WHY? WHO FOR?

STUDY

biographies
stories
people
places
description
narrative
information
process
facts
reports
instructions
reported events
arguments
for/against
further education
application forms

selling
enquiring
ordering
business letters
minutes of meetings
references
jobs
testimonials
rotas/schedules

adverts
notices

to newspapers
semi-official
letters
informal
form filling

WORK

DAILY LIFE

WRITING TASKS:

Paragraph writing

1 Hossein's new house is off Kings Street. He moved there because it was quieter. It's next door to a hospital and has a large garden at the back. His wife likes it because it has a modern kitchen.

Sadegh/flat/Park Road.//moved/cheaper.//cinema/small garden/front.//Friends/near/town centre.//

Now write about your friend's house, using the similar sentences.

2 'You think you have seen a man who is wanted by the police. **Write**, for the police, a short description of the man, saying when and where you saw him.'

Begin: The man I saw was coming out of, etc. place, time, date. Description of clothes, briefcase, etc., appearance, manner, possible intentions.

Essay writing

3 'The school leaving age should be 15 minimum' **Discuss.**
Skeleton plan: Advantages: It's a good thing to do x because . . .
Disadvantages: It's not a good thing to do x because . . .
Most people prefer x (or y) because . . .

I think perhaps y $\genfrac{}{}{0pt}{}{\text{as well as}}{\text{instead of}}$ x

because (+ example)

4 Write a letter applying for the job advertised here. Give all necessary details and ask for more information re hours, pay, etc.

> *WANTED*
> JUL/AUG Exp. Sales Assistant, large store. Must speak English. Apply to D. Lee, Waltrex Stores, City Rd, Sidville.

Oh, dear, I can never think of what to write for English Compositions. And I always make so many mistakes.

Well, our teacher discusses what we can write about, we get our ideas together and then we form a plan. We often say it through first, so my marks aren't too bad.

Are your students POOR at WRITING? Try the following:

● Stage preparation carefully: students should speak – read – then write.
● Grade each step; give shorter, simpler tasks until they improve.
● Give practice in planning, organising and expressing information.
● Give model or target essays.
● Practise relevant structures before they write their own.
● Keep a record of common mistakes. Focus on ONE per lesson.
● Insist on corrections. Test them later.
● Make them write in class. Vary the topics set.
● Do writing as group work. (The good help the weak.)

Unit 21
Written production

The aims of this Unit are **1** to define the problems that students face when learning to write English, and to discuss ways of helping them to produce good written English **2** to study the language used in the classroom when teaching writing, and give practice in the different forms of written English normally required by examinations.

ⓐ Preliminary discussion

1 What are the main differences between 'Writing Practice' as in Unit 20 and 'Written Production'? (Cf. Oral practice and oral production.) **Do you think formal accuracy is more important in spoken than in written English? Why?**

2 (a) What are the main differences between spoken English and written English? (See Unit 14, Section **a**, **1**.) **Is normal written English the same as spoken English written down? Why?**

(b) **What about reading English? How can intelligent reading help students to write well? Which of the reading skills in the FOCUS on Reading, page 142 could help with writing? Finally compare these reading skills with the writing skills listed on the FOCUS page opposite.**

3 (a) Which of these writing skills will be most useful to your students, (i) now, as they study? (ii) in the long term?

(b) **What types of writing do your students need to do? Refer to the venn diagram opposite, entitled 'WRITING WHAT? WHY? WHO FOR?'.**

(c) Are the writing tasks in the textbook suitable for all your students? Why?

4 How far do the examinations your students will take influence your teaching of writing? **Could any of the examinations be made more relevant to students' needs? Would you still teach composition if it was not needed for the exam?**

5 Since even English-speaking students find it difficult to write clear, concise essays and summaries, your students are also likely to have problems writing English.

(a) The suggestions on the FOCUS page, see 'Poor Writing' may help them. Discuss these and add your own.

(b) **Discuss the advantages and disadvantages of guided or controlled writing with special reference to, (i) student satisfaction (ii) the teacher's marking load (iii) giving back students' work (iv) making students do corrections (v) reinforcement of correct forms (vi) gradual progression from controlled writing to freer writing, up to free writing in exams only.**

6 (a) Discuss what types of written production tasks are possible and profitable? (See FOCUS pages Units 15, 19 and 21.) **Which of the tasks shown are easier? Which would be suitable for your students at different levels?**

(b) **What preparation would you need to do between the oral production and/or reading stage and the writing stage? Discuss briefly with reference to tasks suitable for your students.**

(c) **What instructions would you give your students (after adequate oral and reading preparation) for each of the above tasks?**

(d) **How would you train them to find and correct their own mistakes?**

ⓑ Lesson extract

This extract is taken from a late intermediate lesson based on the reading text 'Back Nestling' reproduced on page 146, in Unit 19.

It is suitable for classes approaching examinations, in school or college. Notice the amount of preparation already completed before this extract. Listen to the tape and practise repeating the teacher's part, especially the instructions and elicitations.

The teacher has already completed these steps:

1 Students have read the reading text; made notes on the organisation of information in the passage, and studied the use of discourse markers like 'however', 'moreover' etc.

2 They have summarised orally the advantages and disadvantages of back nestling giving their own personal anecdote to follow, parallel to the example in the text.

3 The topic under discussion now is 3 on the FOCUS page at the beginning of this Unit. Students have listed the pros and cons of leaving school at the age of 15, and discussed them orally.

4 The teacher has supplied some vocabulary, on the board, e.g. 'independent', and has drilled the first conditional ('If you leave school . . .') Now the planning begins, basing it on the skeleton plan from 'Back Nestling'.

T: Stop discussing, now, please, and look at your main points. You've all got some advantages (Pros) and some disadvantages (Cons) written down, haven't you? About 5 or 6 points?

S: I've got 7.

T: Good. Now, we've got to organise these points, rearrange them, so they will make two or three clear paragraphs. And it's got to sound like written English, not spoken English. OK?
Let's have a look at the skeleton plan we did for that reading passage. How did the passage begin? . . . Yes?

S: Many African mothers.

T: Oh yes. Many people do x.⎫ *(writes* It's a good thing to do x ⎬ *on board)*, and then what does the author do?

S: er . . . gives us a reason, 'because . . .'

T: Very good. 'We do x because . . .' *(writes)* Right. Make a sentence like that about leaving school before 16.

S1: Many people leave school before 16 because . . . er . . . they er . . .

S2: want to earn money

S3: get job

T: get a job, yes, good, both of you. You could also use this word here.

S1: Oh, because they want be independent.

T: Sorry?

Ss: *to* be

S: they want to be independent.

T: Good. Who else can say that?

S: because they want to be independent.

T: Yes. Tell me what you could write, then for a first paragraph. Listen the rest of you, and check for mistakes. . . . *(Later . . .)*

T: How can you introduce the disadvantages, then, to let your reader know you're going to begin something different? . . . Yes?

Ss: But . . . On the other hand . . . however . .

T: Good. Alright then, how can you express these* in written English? *(Points to main points* on blackboard)*

S: If you will stay at school . . .

T: If you? Remember the tables we did?

S: Oh. If you stay at school.

T: umhm.

S: after you're 16, you can study . . . er . . .

T: anyone?

S: You can take the examinations and you will go to University, . . .

S: You can get a better job . . .

T: Fine. Now start with 'People who . . .'; same sentence, but 'People who . . .' etc. *(Later . . .)*
So I want you to write that now. Two paragraphs, OK? With your own examples put in. Well, what order will you put these points in? And how can we link these? . . . Can *you* tell me . . .

Follow up
Students write, then check their own work for mistakes, then change and check each others, so they get practice in correcting mistakes. The teacher acts as advisor. Then on to the third paragraph — a personal experience of someone who did or did not stay at school and succeeded . . . Prepares orally, pair work, then a final writing session.

👤 or 👤👤   **TEACHING HINTS (a) In what ways does the teacher help the students to produce a clear, well organised essay that sounds natural? (b) Why does he make the students write in class and not at home? (c) Why does he not prepare all three paragraphs together, instead of letting them write two and then preparing the third?**

Ⓒ Classroom language

The writing tasks covered in these tables progress from fairly controlled, early intermediate tasks, Tables 1 and 2, to longer more complex tasks, Tables 3 to 11, and finally to practice in teaching 'free' writing and essay writing for examinations, Tables 12 to 22.

See also Unit 20, Section **c**; most of the language there will be useful also at this higher level, too, expecially Tables 7 to 9, and the student language in Tables 11–13.

In pairs, select only the tables which relate to the level at which you teach and the type of writing task your students need to do.

Select from your textbooks or from the FOCUS pages some specific writing material to refer to while you practise. (For example, Tables 12 to 18 could refer to writing task 4 on the FOCUS page at the beginning of this Unit.) As you practise in twos, keep the *aim* of the teacher in mind all the time; 'students' should query if something is not clear.

Writing based on simple reading work (See Reading Activities, Unit 19, Section **d**, 5)

1

When you've chosen As well as choosing	True, False or Not Stated the best order of the key points/sentences the best word for the gap	I want you to write out

the sentences,	the **true** ones, and correct the false ones. to form a paragraph.
the paragraph,	filling the gaps.

2

So First	let's practise orally tell me exactly	what the sentences	you're going to write.

Using a model paragraph/essay as a reading text

3

I want you to	read study	this	paragraph. essay. letter.	It's	like similar to nearly the same as	the one you're going to write.

4

Now	read it again study it	and	see how it is planned. Jot down the plan. pick out the main points. Write them down.	
			underline the	phrases which introduce new ideas. link words. discourse markers, like '_____'

5

Done that? Finished? OK?	Let's	discuss what you've written. see if we agree.	I'll write	a plan the points	on the blackboard.
		Could you tell me what you've got?			

6

Now But	instead we are going to	do an essay called '_____' write about '_____' change this a bit and do '_____'	which is similar.
	So what will our main points be?		

7

| Let's work out how | this author planned his | text.
information. |
| | you could plan your piece of writing. | |

| What | does he
could you | do first? Think of our main points. |

8   (Practise this table with a reading passage in front of you to refer to.)

First Then Next Finally	he she you can we could	introduce(s) the	story, topic, idea of '_____'	by	telling us about_____. describing_____. explaining_____.
		describe(s) the	process of_____, how to_____. place where_____. characters who_____. history of_____. what happens when_____.		
			differences similarities	between_____.	
		state(s) explain(s) give(s)	the	advantages disadvantages	of_____.
			the	cause result purpose	of_____.
			some	examples reasons	of_____. for_____. why_____.
			his opinions why_____.		

(See Table 15.)

Expanding key points (see Section d, 2 (c) linking answers to questions (Section a, 2 (e)

9

| Now you've | answered all the questions in full,
got all your key points here, | you need to | expand them.
write a bit more about them. |
| What could you say about
Who can suggest something for | this one? | | |

10

| Good.
Now. | How can you | join
link | these 2 sentences to make | it sound better?
one longer sentence?
them follow on? |
| | What other changes will you need to make? | | | |

11

| Half
The first part of
The first and last parts of | this | essay
letter
paragraph | is
are | done for you. | You read | it
them | then |

| plan
discuss
write | the | rest.
second half.
other part. |

Essay writing (Tables 12–18 should be taken in the order they appear here.)

Read the	title instructions	carefully.	What	form of writing is it? Descriptive? etc. could you write about? **must** you include? information do they want? is the purpose of writing this? style is appropriate?
			Who will be reading it?	

What type of	words structures organisation plan	would be	appropriate suitable	for this topic?	Jot some ideas down. Arrange your points. Plan your paragraphs.
How many paragraphs					

(See Part One, Unit 9, Section **d**, Exploiting written assignments.)

Get together in groups, discuss	your	plans. ideas.
	what goes into each paragraph.	

(For subsequent discussion, see Table 5. For outlining the plan, see Table 8, but add to it.)

What exactly	could you	say for this?
How else	could you	express that?

Well,	that	is not quite right, does not sound very good is quite an important structure,	so let's practise that pattern orally.
	you'd better get that right,		

(See FOCUS on Oral Practice, Unit 15, page 104, 1, 3, 10 for ways to practise structures.)

Let's	go through each paragraph once more make sure you know what you're going to say	before you start writing.

Back into groups	each person can write one paragraph in turn. discuss what you want to write, then dictate it for one of you to write. choose your first secretary.

Examination practice

Read Study	the instructions. Find out	how	many questions you must answer. long the essay must be. much time you have per question. you will divide your time.
		what form/style of writing it requires. See Table 12.	

20

| By yourselves!
No talking!
Books closed! | This is practice for the exam.
You've got 40 minutes to write this. | | Start now. |
| | Don't | forget to leave time at the end to check your work.
make any silly mistakes. | |

(See Unit 20, Tables 7, 8 and 9 on checking their own work.)

Returning work

21

| You can have
I'll give you | your | homework
work
tests
essays | back today; | you did it | fairly
quite
very | well. |
| | | | | but first I'll go over | a few
some | points.
errors.
mistakes. |

22

I've given you	grades A–E, marks out of 20.	A 16 and over B	is very good, excellent.
		11 and over C	is quite good.
		8–10	is just satisfactory.
		Well, below that is not good enough.	

ⓓ Teaching skills

Select the teaching skills you feel you need most practice in. If you are teaching examination classes it would be useful to have a set of past exam papers to refer to.

1 Syllabus and examination requirements

 As a class.

(a) **List the kinds of written tasks** apart from essay or composition that your students *have to* perform for the final school leaving examination.

How far can these be practised in class using the kinds of written tasks outlined in Units 19, 20 and 21?

Discuss any other techniques you personally have found practical and successful.

(b) **Composition** is generally the most difficult task. If, however, students have had plenty of guidance in class covering the kinds of topics they may get in the examination and if they can recognise which *form* of writing is relevant and suitable, they stand a better chance of success. Together, plan a pre-examination programme of essay writing revision as follows:

(i) List the typical *forms of writing* required by the essay topics on past examination papers. (Take into account any changes in the future syllabus.) Forms of writing include things like *describing places, giving instructions, narrative in the past, the language of argument* etc.

(ii) What specific grammatical structures and other language items can be used for each form of writing? (e.g. instructions: 'you'+present simple tense, or simple imperative, or passive voice, depending on context and setting; discourse markers denoting stages, i.e. 'first', 'then', etc.) Do any of the forms of writing use similar structural items? (e.g. giving street directions: similar use of 'you'+present simple as instructions)

(iii) What types of essay could be planned or organised in similar ways? (Some topics, like describing a process or giving directions are usually linear and can be written using markers like 'first', 'second', 'then,' 'later'); others use a comparisons technique comparing advantages with disadvantages, different opinions etc. and need markers like 'however', 'on the other hand'.)

(iv) To summarise the above – what have different forms of writing got in common? If you revised one or two different forms of writing each week (or more, if they have structures etc. in common) how many weeks before the exam would you need to begin revision? (Allow two or three weeks at the end for *timed* exam practice.) What order would you tackle them in? You would need to show your students how *one* form of writing might be useful in three or four different essay topics; this is useful when they select exam questions.

(v) Another area to revise for essay work might be vocabulary. Vocabulary depends on the *topic,* not so much the *form* of writing; e.g., a description of a place may include some of the same vocabulary as giving street directions but not the same grammatical structures, as we've seen in (ii) above. List areas of lexis which may be needed for the examination, e.g. places/towns/buildings, biographical details etc.

See Teaching Skills 5 and 6 for further suggestions on teaching 'free' writing and training students for examination essay writing.

2 Early intermediate writing. Model paragraphs, guided production

If students can be shown a model paragraph, they know more exactly what their target is, i.e. what is wanted of them. They are, therefore, far more likely to write better, learn more and feel more satisfied. Model paragraphs can be used in many ways:

(a) Read/expand/write

See the FOCUS page at the beginning of this Unit, Task 1 about Hossein's house. This is in three stages; reading, writing practice, on to written production. Do this exercise quickly, orally in pairs. What problems might there be at the third stage for your students? Write another short model paragraph, giving biographical details about a (famous) person you all know. Then think of someone else, similar, and write prompts as in stage 2. Finally, think of someone else for students to write about by themselves, keeping to the same patterns. Perhaps they could do an autobiography, with some extra help.

(b) Cloze paragraphs

Write another short model paragraph at a level simple enough for your students to imitate, using a different form of writing. Give it to your neighbour to check. To use this in class you would write it on the board[1] leaving out every 6th word or some of the verbs or subjects etc. Write below it more than enough words to fill the blanks. (These must include the missing words, obviously.) When your students can say and write it correctly, you could delete more words, or perhaps every 5th word instead, and not give them words below to choose from. They then write this on a new page (so they cannot see what they have just written.) By this method, students practise one form of writing intensively, and you only have to write the model *once* on the blackboard.

(c) Expanding from key points

This is more difficult than expanding sentences, since students have to not only expand each point into a sentence but also provide something to go before and

[1] O.H.P. transparencies are useful for this and similar exercises, then you can keep the model and use it again.

after. Adequate oral planning is essential. Structural and lexical items need revising too; so do suitable discourse markers and connecting words. Preparation must be thorough if students are to produce good writing and feel satisfied.

Practise in pairs getting each other to expand the points in Task 2 on the FOCUS page at the beginning of this Unit, to the length and form it should be written in. Then practise with a different topic taken from your textbook, making sure the expanded version sounds like written English. Finally write down the difficulties your students may find with this type of excercise (e.g. linking ideas, punctuation, short jerky sentences etc.). If you do one version for them on the board as a target text, then rub it out bit by bit, they will get the idea better.

(d) Jumbled key points (based on key points from a reading text)
See Unit 19, Section **d**, **5** (b).
When students have arranged the key points in the correct order, they can be asked to join sentences, using link words, relatives etc., and make any other changes necessary to make it sound like good written English. Then, after preparing it orally first, they can write it down.

In pairs, discuss possible alternative ways of linking the sentences in the activity 'jumbled key points' that *you* prepared.

(e) Answering questions on a reading text (to form a summary)[1]
Answering, in full, questions designated to elicit the main points of a reading passage is another way to get students to write a guided paragraph. Suggested link words can be shown, in brackets, beside the questions.

3 Correcting written assignments

(a) Avoiding 'pitfalls'
If the writing task has been prepared thoroughly, there should not be too much correcting to do. If there are a lot of mistakes in many students' work you should ask yourself what went wrong at the preparation stage. Maybe there were some problems you had not foreseen.

In groups. Tell each other about any notable 'pitfalls' or 'disasters' you have experienced, (we have all had them!) so that other teachers can learn to avoid them!

NB It helps you to diagnose the problems if *you* write the essay you want your *students* to write, *before* you prepare the preparation lesson.

(b) Training students to spot and correct their own mistakes
In the early stages students find this difficult, and so they need guidance in correcting their own work. Gradually, this guidance should be withdrawn, until by examination time, students are better at checking their own work and correcting their own mistakes. See the stages suggested in (c) below.

In pairs. Make a quick list of common careless errors that you could train your students in examination classes to look for and correct for themselves. They should always leave five or ten minutes at the end of the exam time to do this.

(c) A method of marking
If you let your student know what kind of mistake he has made, he has more chance of correcting it correctly!

On the left are some symbols that have been found useful:
You can withdraw your help in *stages* throughout the course, thus:
Stage 1 – (elementary) underline the mistake and write the symbol in the margin.
Stage 2 – underline the whole word/phrase and write the symbol in the margin.
Stage 3 – do *not* underline the word or the mistake; only write the symbol in the margin.

S – spelling

C – concord (agreement: subject and verb)

S/P – singular, plural

W/O – word order

T – tense

V – vocabulary, wrong word or usage

app – appropriacy (inappropriate style or register)

P – punctuation (including capital letters)

Ir – irrelevant information

?M – meaning not clear

∧ – word missing

[1] *Warning*: writing a summary *without* thorough guidance should never be set except to advanced students. Even native speaker students find this a very difficult task and often do it badly.

Stage 4 – (exam classes) put a dot or x in the margin for each mistake.
Which of the above stages would these be?

T S   [i]   *I am not liking my new skool.*   STAGE ....

S V   [ii] My freind arrived to͜ station.   STAGE ....

S s p [iii] *I'm writeing to ask your advise*

T (app.) *Please be helping me .*   STAGE ....

(d) Marking practice

 Each person should write four or five lines of 'intermediate' level English making three or four typical mistakes. Give the writing to your neighbour. Using the above scheme (make any adaptations you think suitable), correct your neighbour's work. (Stage Two.)

(e) Awarding marks or grades for compositions

There are two main ways of grading a piece of writing: 'impression' marking and 'split' (or analytic) marking.

Impression marking: you read the written work through quickly and give it an 'impression' mark. In an exam, at least two, preferably three, people independently should give an impression mark for each essay, keeping a record on a separate mark sheet, not writing the grade on the essay itself.

Split marking: you 'split' total marks, and give a proportion for each of the following: organisation (i.e. plan, paragraphing, etc.) accuracy (grammar and spelling), appropriacy (style, register) and content (relevance). Depending on what form of writing it is you adjust the proportion of total marks given for each category. For example, out of 20, a business letter would need a low proportion of marks for content, say 3, and higher than usual for appropriacy and accuracy, say 7 and 6 respectively, leaving 4 for organisation of ideas (in the case of a letter, layout would be included here). You could also add or subtract a few marks for neatness, layout etc.

This method is still subjective but easier to grade. In an exam it would still be preferable to have three or so markers.

The marks are recorded on the student's work thus:

org. 3/4   acc. 3/6   appr. 2/7   content 3/3   (11/20)

What can the student deduce from these marks?

Discuss the advantages of each type of marking,
(a) from the teacher's point of view, (b) from the students' point of view.

How would you split 20 marks between the four categories for each of the topics on the FOCUS page at the beginning of this Unit?

A third type of marking, one which I could not recommend for marking essays, is where the student begins with 20 marks and one mark is deducted for each mistake.

Why is this not a fair way to grade a piece of written work?

(f) Discuss ways of eradicating important common *careless* errors that your students repeatedly make when writing.

Penalty points? Writing out the correct version 5 (10) (20) times? Refuse to mark any work with a particular mistake in? Regular but quick testing? Short quizzes? Any other ideas?

4   Basing composition work on reading texts/skeleton plans

Refer to Section **b** in this Unit, the lesson extract on page 166 and 3 on the FOCUS page at the beginning of this Unit.

Study the steps taken by the teacher to draw up a skeleton plan from the text, to adapt it to quite a different topic, to turn to the text as a model to find suitable ways of expressing ideas like 'Many people think that', ... 'Many, however,' ... etc.

Are there any suitable reading passages in your textbooks that would be suitable for this type of essay planning lesson? In groups, each taking a different section of your textbooks, identify the passages that would be suitable, and write a skeleton plan for each.

Example – based on the passage on 'Back nestling' reproduced on page 146. ('x' in the plan = 'back nestling')
Skeleton plan: Para. 1: Many people do 'x', + advantages.
'x', however, has disadvantages, too.

Para. 2: Reasons for 'y'.

Para. 3 'Many people prefer 'x', + reasons. Anecdote/example of such a person. Conclusion, 'x' as well as 'y' is perhaps the answer.

Other topics that could be written on the base of this plan:
'x' could stand for driving to work by car, instead of walking,
or living in a town, not a village, etc.
i.e. many other 'discussion' or argument style essays. Alternative skeleton plans could also be discussed by the class.

5   Training in exam techniques

In the year or term of the examination, practice in examination techniques is essential. Give students exam practice *in class*. This has two advantages:
(a) they get used to being timed and working under pressure
(b) you can see where they are likely to go wrong and devote more time to that area in another lesson.

Techniques specific to exams: students are usually expected to
(a) read and carry out instructions on the exam paper
(b) work to time, on their own and silently
(c) select (the right number of) questions
(d) interpret the essay title – meaning, purpose, aim
(e) select relevant information and appropriate style or register for task
(f) plan, organise clearly and logically
(g) leave time to correct own mistakes.

At what stage in the exam year will you begin to give your students exam practice? (See also Section **d**, **1** (b).) How do you think is best to do this for (a) (b) and (c) above?

How about (d) (e) (f) and (g)? These should have been practised already at lower levels. See **6** on the next page.

6 Essay/paragraph writing (preparing students for 'free' writing)

When teaching 'free' writing, i.e. paragraph or essay writing, it's a good idea to take in class the same steps as your students should take when writing for an examination. Then they will get into good habits and are less likely to go wrong in the exam when there are so many things to think about that accuracy is certain to suffer, unless a good deal of the thinking (i.e. steps 1–8) has been done beforehand.

There are ten steps to follow in order (after reading the instructions, planning out the time and selecting a title).

STEPS
1 Read the title, underline the key words, identify what form of writing is required.
2 What is the purpose of the piece of writing? Who is it for? What style is appropriate, formal, informal?
3 List possible *main* points – note form.
4 List *necessary* subsidiary points – to back up the main points, examples, anecdote, opinion, etc.
5 Express (to yourself or in written form) each main point in full, as simply and clearly as you can.
6 Jot down any useful words, phrases, structures, idioms you think you might forget when actually writing.
7 Select and organise relevant main points into a *plan*, with relevant subsidiary points – note form – (try different ways of arranging if the first plan does not seem clear). Do not include any information that is *not* asked for.
8 Add link words, phrases, discourse markers to plan (trying to say the whole thing through to yourself in your head).
9 Write it, clearly and simply.
10 Check it through, once for relevance, again for accuracy (subject/verb agreement, tenses, spelling, punctuation etc.).

When first preparing students for 'free' writing you will need to show them how to tackle each step you'll be working *with* them. Later, you can tell them, 'OK. What's the first step? Study the title. Right, do that first ...' Then get them to tell you what they think the key words are, etc. They do the work, in groups, or by themselves, then discuss it. Nearer the exam, you can get them to do Steps 1–5 on their own before you discuss anything, and so on, gradually withdrawing guidance.

Plan the above steps using topic 4 on the FOCUS page at the beginning of this Unit. Write the letter yourself first, as simply and clearly as possible. Compare letters with your friends.

NB Never ask a *student* to write an essay that *you* haven't written (or at least fully planned) yourself. Titles that sound deceptively simple and interesting to write sometimes are the hardest of all. Some titles are conceptually difficult for children to grasp, e.g. 'Politics and sport' would be impossible for young teenagers.

See Section **e**, Teaching Practice. The material prepared above may be suitable for the task you set your students.

Teaching practice

1 Planning

In groups of three or four. Together prepare *one* 40–60 minute lesson, suitable for intermediate students of 14 or over. The teaching of the lesson can be shared between teachers thus:

(i) introduction, title, form of writing, main points, paragraphing.

(ii) language work, expanding main points, linking sentences within the first paragraph(s).

(iii) same as (ii) above for the second half of the essay; giving instructions for the actual writing.

All teachers can help out with group work.

Use one of the topics you prepared in Section **d**, **4** or **6**, or choose a suitable essay title from one of your textbooks.

Plan and write the essay yourselves first, using language simple enough for your students to produce. As you write, discuss which language points your students may need to revise and practise orally. Consider also alternative ways to write the same essay.

Your aim, when teaching, is to take your students through the 10 STEPS outlined in Section **d**, **6**, seeing how much of the work they can do themselves, and giving help with language where necessary. Notice the language in the relevant tables in Section **c** is nearly all in question form; this is to get the students to think for themselves.

STEP 6 gives the teacher a chance to slot in necessary structural practice and other words or phrases. Plan what you will practise here, and be prepared to cope with other problems, too.

Write down roughly how long each stage should take. Allow plenty of time for the essay (or one paragraph of the essay), to be written in class, and checked over by the students themselves. If teaching real students, allow some time for social chat at the start of the lesson, and remember to announce your intentions.

2 Teaching

Remember your aim is to get the students to do as much of the work (i.e. thinking and planning) as they can. Help only when necessary. Accept their ideas whenever they are relevant and suitable. It doesn't matter if their essays are different from yours as long as they are relevant, appropriate in form and language, and fairly accurate.

As you watch each other teach, jot down each time a student's suggestion is considered by the teacher. Notice also how many students *are* actually thinking and trying to work, rather than waiting for someone else to answer and produce the ideas. Does the teacher try to include everybody? Are all instructions clear?

3 Follow up and evaluation

In groups. Discuss the points raised above. Were the aims of the lesson fulfilled? i.e. did most students write reasonably well? Why?

As a class. Each group should report on how their lesson went, what problems cropped up, etc. Also discuss how these lessons, and also the materials in these last two Units could be adapted to suit your own students.

Further reading

Andrew Wright (1976) on teaching composition pp. 41–47.

J B Heaton (1975) Chapter 8.

Donn Byrne (1979) Chapters 5–8 and Appendix 1.

W M Rivers and M S Temperley (1978) Chapter 9.

Appendix A
List of language items

This is a list of possible language teaching items occurring naturally in or arising out of the language used in the classroom in particular circumstances, see Part One, **EXPLOITATION SECTIONS**.
You can use or exploit a classroom situation to practise a structural item, lexical items or the realisation of a function or notion that you have already presented to the class in a recent lesson. You can also use or exploit a genuine classroom situation to introduce and present a new teaching point, or revise an old one.

Unit 1 The beginning of the lesson
(a) Greetings (formal, informal) – Elementary
(b) Ways of addressing people (formal, informal) – Elementary
(c) Past simple tense (question forms, negative forms, short answer tags, irregular forms)
(d) Lexis. (I went climbing/skiing/walking/shopping)
(e) Prepositions e.g.
    I went *for* a walk/picnic/drive
        on an outing/expedition
        to the cinema/football
        round to my friend's house
        out for a walk/meal/drink
(f) Opinions. (Intermediate) Did you like the film/enjoy it? What did you think of the programme? What was it like?

Unit 2 Checking attendance
(a) Present of verb 'to be' – is/are, questions
    short answer tags to practise he/she/they forms, e.g. 'Is Mary here?' 'No, she isn't.' (Elem)[1]
(b) Singular verb with 'everybody', 'who', etc. (Elem or Inter)[1]
(c) Indirect questions, e.g. 'Do you know where Peter is?'. (Word order!) (Inter or early Advanced).

[1] Elem = elementary, Inter. = intermediate.

(d) Contrast in usage of the past simple and the present perfect, e.g. 'You've been away twice. You were away last week.' (Inter).
(e) 'You'll have to', e.g. 'You'll have to work extra hard.' (notion of necessity) (Inter).
(f) Illnesses. (If a lot of people have been away). Lexical set – 'I had a cold, a cough, a bad tooth' etc. (Elem or Inter).
(g) Speculative language – the notion of uncertainty and possibility, e.g. 'Perhaps he's ill.' 'He might have gone to Isfahan.' 'She may be coming later.' 'I'm not sure. Maybe she'll come later.' (Inter).

Unit 3 Physical conditions in the classroom
(a) Adjectives referring to climate, weather, seasons etc.
(b) Weather, e.g. It's hot/cold/raining/etc.
(c) Too v. very, e.g. 'It's *very* hot today but it's not *too* hot to work.' 'It's *too* noisy in here; you can't hear what I say properly.'
(d) Making polite requests, e.g. 'Would you help me please?' 'Would you mind + ing . . .' 'Please could you say that again?'
(e) Ask v. tell. '*Tell* him to come and see me', e.g. '*Come* and see Mr X' or 'Go and . . . *Ask* him to come over', e.g. '*Could you come* over some time?'
(f) Comparatives, e.g. 'It's better now/quieter/cooler/warmer'/etc.
(g) Statements with tags, e.g. 'It's got very hot today, hasn't it?'
(h) Discussion topics: disturbances outside the room: traffic, building site activity, people passing, playground noise, aeroplane noise etc. – attitudes to the weather; advantages of different types of climates, etc.

Unit 4 Getting organised
(a) Polite requests with 'Would you mind + ing . . .' and appropriate acknowledgments. (Appropriate for adult students or in less informal situations.)
(b) Prepositions of place ('in front of, next

to' etc.) and adverbs and prepositions denoting movement ('along, forwards' etc.).
(c) Giving instructions for moving things or organising people into positions. (Probably this will involve talking to people of a slightly lower status than you, e.g. house owner to furniture removal men; football coach to players.)

Unit 5 Using visual aids
(a) Need, e.g. 'He needs X to do Y.'
(b) Lexical set – drawing pins, sticky tape, glue etc.
(c) Expressions of place, e.g. 'on the right/left, in the middle/centre, higher up, lower down, too high/low'
(d) Offers, e.g. 'Can I help you?/Shall I do it?'
(e) Polite requests, e.g. 'Could/would you put this up for me?'
(f) Verbs with pronoun object, e.g. 'put it away/up, take it down'
(g) Expressions of lack, e.g. 'We've run out of,' 'There aren't any Xs left.'

Unit 7 Tape recorders and other electrical equipment
(a) Lexical sets: terms for operating electrical equipment, e.g. 'plug in, switch on, adjust the volume/focus, play back, rewind.'
    terms for control devices: e.g. 'knob, switch, button, key, lever, control.'
(b) Infinitive of purpose, e.g. 'Turn this knob to adjust the volume.'
(c) Result clauses, e.g. 'If you don't set the counter to 000 you won't be able to find the beginning of the dialogue you want to hear on the tape.'
(d) Giving instructions, e.g. 'First you turn the tape recorder on . . .' 'You have to turn it on . . .' 'It has to be turned on . . .'
(e) Following instructions, e.g. 'What do I/you do when/if . . .' 'What should I do next?' 'What happens if . . .'
(f) Things going wrong, e.g. 'This won't work/adjust properly.' 'I can't make this work/go.' 'It doesn't seem to be working properly.' 'Something's gone wrong with the . . .'
(g) Present perfect tense for checking up,

e.g. 'Have you plugged it in?'
(h) Staging words, e.g. 'first, second, next, after that, then, finally.'

Unit 8 Dividing the class up: choral/individual and teams
(a) Cardinal numerals (for adding up points) (including 0 – zero)
(b) Ordinal numerals, e.g. 'first/second/third/last' etc. (winning teams)
(c) Time, e.g. 'It took you 1 minute 35 seconds.'
(d) Comparatives, e.g. 'You did it *faster than* them.'
(e) 'Whose' as an interrogative
(f) Possessive pronouns, e.g. 'mine/hers/yours' etc. e.g. 'Whose turn is it?' 'Mine.'

(g) Making objections, e.g. 'But they cheated!' 'It isn't fair.'

Unit 10 Interruptions: latecomers, things lost
(a) Apologies and acknowledgments, e.g. 'I'm sorry . . .' 'Oh, that's alright.'
(b) Making excuses (reasons for delayed arrivals), e.g. 'I had to go to the doctor's.' 'I got stuck in the traffic.' etc.
(c) Past simple tense question forms, either/or questions, e.g. 'Did your bus come late or was the traffic bad?'
(d) The notion of obligation 'should (have)/shouldn't (have) ought to', e.g. 'You should have got up earlier.'
(e) Suggestions/advice, e.g. 'Why don't you get a new car?' 'You'd better . . .'

Unit 12 Ending the lesson or a stage in the lesson
(a) Expressing the planned future, e.g. present continuous, or with 'going to'
(b) Expressing the unplanned or uncertain future, e.g. 'I'll probably go' 'Perhaps I'll . . .' 'I might . . .'
(c) Suggestions, e.g. 'Why don't we/you . . .' 'What about . . . ing . . .' 'We could . . .'
(d) 'It's time to', e.g. 'It's time to stop now.' (general meaning)
(e) It's time you/we + past verb form, e.g. 'It's time you went now' (more personal use)
(f) 'Have to' for tasks set, e.g. homework.
(g) Ways of saying goodbye and taking leave, e.g. 'See you Monday. Have a good time!'

Appendix B Summary of basic student language

Usually in the classroom it is the teacher who initiates or begins an exchange, and the student who responds.

Sometimes, however it is the student who needs to interrupt the lesson, to make a query, or ask permission to do something.

The following tables summarise student-initiated language that may be needed in the classroom. (Obviously it cannot all be taught at once, but the teacher can introduce it gradually as the need arises, and by the end of the first year, students should at least be able to use the simpler forms and not feel shy about asking questions.)

Interrupting politely

In a formal classroom situation:

1

Excuse me, Please, Sorry,	(Mr_____) (Mrs_____) (+name). (Miss_____.)	Could I	ask say add	something?

In a less formal situation or a small group:

2 Yes and_____ (if agreeing)
What about_____

3 Yes, but_____ (if about to disagree)
But what about_____

Queries about meaning

4 What's the meaning of_____?
What does_____ mean?

5 I don't understand_____

Can you explain { what you said about_____
the sentence beginning_____

You said something about_____ but I didn't understand.

6 What's the difference between_____ and_____?
Is_____ the same as_____?
Is it something to do with_____?

Making requests/asking permission

7

Mr_____ Mrs_____ Miss_____	may I could I can I do you mind if I is it alright if I	go out for a minute? go to the toilet? (children only) go and get a drink? leave now? go early? open the window? change places? move and sit in the shade? share with (name of friend), I've forgotten my book, sorry. do my homework tonight, I didn't have time yesterday?

Making apologies (See Unit 10)

8

I'm sorry I'm terribly sorry	I'm late. (+reason/excuse) I've forgotten to bring my book/homework. (+excuse) I've lost my book. (+explanation) I haven't done my homework. (+reason why) I haven't got a pen/pencil, can someone lend me one?

9 **Queries about tasks set**

What are we doing?
What must we do?
I'm not sure what we have to do.

10

Which	page exercise	are you on? is it? must we do?

11

When	do we have to do must we do is	our homework for?

12

When	are we having is are we going to have	our	test? dictation? exam?

13

What	do we have to learn must we learn	for it?

14

Are these Is this	alright? right? correct?
Have I done this alright?	

15

I've	finished checked done	this. these.	What	should shall can	I do	now? next?

16

Which room	should we must we	go to	next lesson? now?

(See also Unit 20, pages 160–161, for more **Student Queries**.)

Appendix C Tapescripts of 'Sample Exploitation' taped materials Part One

Unit 1   Section b
Language activity

T: Well, today, I thought we'd talk a little bit about what you're going to do at the weekend, because today is Friday, tomorrow is . . .? What day?

S: Saturday.

T: Saturday, good. So can you find out, in twos, you can be in a three, can you ask each other what you're going to do . . . Can you make that question? How do you make that question? To find out what you're going to do tomorrow morning, Saturday morning. How will you ask? Ask me! Ask me what I'm going to do tomorrow morning.

S: . . . are you going to do tomorrow morning?

T: That's very good, Abdullah. Can you all say that? Listen! What are you going to do tomorrow morning?

Ss: What are you going to do tomorrow morning . . . *(very ragged)*

T: That wasn't very good, was it? Listen again and all together, right? What are you going to do tomorrow morning?

Ss: What are you going to do tomorrow morning?

T: That was much better, good.

T: OK, so in twos, I want you to ask each other, what are you going to do tomorrow. Have you any plans? What are you going to do tomorrow? OK?

S: What are . . .

T: and you! . . . PAIR WORK . . . .
. . . .

S: . . . After that? After that, I'm going to go . . .

Unit 1 Section d
Exploitation

T: Hello, hello. Hello everyone, come in. Could you get a chair from over there? Hello, good morning, come in and sit down. Good morning.

Ss: Hello. Good morning.

T: That's right, you sit here. Good. Where's everybody else? Are they coming? They're being a long time, aren't they?

T: And what about you, are you well? Are you all well?

Ss: Us?

T: Are you all well?

Ss: Yes, thanks.

S: Yes.

T: OK.

S: Perhaps half and half.

T: Quite well. Quite well.

S: Quite well, yes.

T: Quite well. Are you tired, because it is the end of the week? Are you tired?

Ss: Yes, of course. Yes.

T: Because today is . . .? What day is it today?

Ss: It's Friday.

T: Yes, so you've had Monday, Tuesday, Wednesday, Thursday, Friday, lessons every day, so now you are tired.

S: Yes, a little.

S: And we will have Sunday and Monday . . . (laughter)

T: Where's Mohammad this morning? Where's Mohammad? Is Mohammad coming?

S: I don't know.

T: You don't know.

S: I think Mohammad is sick.

T: Oh! Why? Was he ill yesterday?

S: I saw I saw he this morning . . .

T: Yes,

S: And he said me, he said me, I'm sick. I think she . . . mm . . . he went to hospital.

T: Has he gone to hospital? Oh, poor Mohammad! I hope he gets better over the weekend.

Unit 2 Section b
Language activity

T: Abdullah, ask Cecilia.

Ab: Ah, Cecilia.

C: Yes.

Ab: How long are you staying in England?

C: Perhaps I'll stay here until August.

T: mm

C: Yes.

T: Good, until August. And then what? Then what?

Ph: I couldn't understand. We couldn't understand.

T: Didn't you understand? Philip. OK so you didn't understand, so what must

you say to Cecilia? If you didn't understand?

Ab: Please, again.

T: Please can you say it again.

Ph: Please can you say it again?

T: Yes.

C: Perhaps I'll stay here until August.

T: Yes.

S: It's alright?

T: Very good. Did you understand, Philip?

Ph: Yes.

T: Is she definitely staying? Is she sure to stay until August?

Ph: Yes.

T: Philip, is she definitely staying till August? Or might she leave before?

Ph: Not definitely.

T: Good, well done, not definitely. OK.

Unit 2 Section d
Exploitation

T: OK. erm . . . I just wanted to check your names. Erm Fransi? She hasn't come yet. Is she coming, Fransi?

Ss: Yes, yes, she's coming. She's coming now!

T: Oh, she's here, Hello, Fransi.

F: (Whispers) Sorry I'm late.

T: That's alright. Aino? Yes. Mohammad . . . No.

Ss: No. Maybe. Mohammad's absent. He's ill.

T: Mohammad's away, yes, he's ill, that's right. Cecilia?

C: Yes.

T: You're here. Abdullah. Yes, Abdullah's here. Abdullah, why are you wearing your scarf? Are you cold?

Ab: Sometimes. (laughter)

S: Are you happy?

T: I don't mind what you wear! But it's very warm in here.

Ss: Yes.

T: And if you are wearing your scarf you'll get very warm, and then you'll fall asleep and you won't listen to the rest of the lesson.

S: Abdullah everyday has a scarf on . . . (laughter)

T: Right, Khosrow?

K: Yes.

T: You're here. Are you cold, Khosrow? No? You're alright, good. And Philip, you're OK. . . .
OK. Right!

Unit 3 Section d
Exploitation

S: Today is fine, sunshine, er . . . brilliant . . .

T: Yes, the weather today is lovely, isn't it? It's like Spring. Very nice. Is it warmer today, than yesterday?

Ss: Yes, yes, than yesterday.

T: In fact, don't you think it's hot in here? Don't you think it's warm in here?

S: It's warm, yes,

T: Do you think . . . er . . . Do you think you could open a window? Ahmad. Could you open a window, please? Thank you. That bottom window, over there . . . What's he doing? What's Ahmad doing?

Ss: He's opening the window.

Ah: Is this enough?

T: Yes, yes that's lovely, thank you. Why is he opening the window? Why has he opened the window?

Ss: Because it's warm in the classroom.

T: Yes, good. It's too warm in the classroom. It's a bit stuffy isn't it. There's not enough air in the classroom. Good. So what must I say to Ahmad, now? He's opened the window, what should I say to him?

Ss: Thank you.

T: Good. That's right. Thank you Ahmad! That was very kind of you.

C: Don't mention it!

T: Oh, very good. (laughter) That's good, Cecilia.

Unit 6 Section d
Exploitation
Extract 1

T: OK. Now. Who can come and put a picture on the board for me? I've got a nice picture here, I'm going to tell you what he's going to do, OK? Can someone put it on the board for me? Could someone pin it up for me? Can you?

S: (nods)

T: What does he need to pin it up on the board? What does he need?

S: Celo . . . ta . . .

S: He need . . . He need . . . er . . .

T: He needs

S: He needs . . . er . . .

T: What do we call this? Blutac. He needs some blutac.
Good, thank you very much, thank you, Abdullah.

Ab: It's OK.

Extract 2

T: First of all, let's clear the board up. Shall we take everything off the board then if I need to write some more words on the board I can do it. So, please, erm Fransi, could you take the pictures off the board for me ? Can you take the pictures down for me please?

F: (nods)

T: Right, what's Fransi going to do?

Ph: She's going to take the pictures on the

T: Off the

Ph: Off the whiteboard.

T: Off the whiteboard, good. She's going

to take the pictures down you can say. Yes, good. Yes, put the, on the table here, Fransi, thank you very much.

F: It's my pleasure.

T: Good. That's alright. You can say, that's alright.

F: That's alright.

T: That's alright, good.
Alright now. Could someone clean the board for me please? Could someone clean the board for me?

Ai: Me

T: Aino, OK, Aino. Abdullah opened the window, you see, so he's already done something for me today, so Aino's going to clean the board for me. That's right.
What's she doing?

Ss: She's cleaning the board.

T: She's cleaning the board. Yes, good, yes...

Extract 3

T: Philip... thank you. Who can tell me what was written on the board? What has Philip cleaned off the board? What was on the board?

Ss: Cecilia is looking forward to Saturday....
(Choral repetition)

T: Forward to Saturday. Good, that's very good... OK...

Unit 7 Section d
Exploitation

T: Alright. We're going to play a tape but first I want you to tell me how to put it on here. We've got a tape recorder here and we've got a tape.

Ss: Open that cover.

Ss: Yes.

T: Good. I've got to open the cover, take the cover off, open the box, and?

Ss: Take the tape out.

T: Take the tape out. Very good. Take the tape out. All of you:

Ss: Take the tape out.

T: Good. And I'll put the box down there. Now what. What do I do?

Ss: First, put it on the record

T: On the recorder. Good. I'm going to put it on the tape recorder. Like that? Is that right?

S: Yes.

T: Good! It has to go round here. No, it doesn't. It has to go through there.

S: Yes.

T: And on to the other... what do we call that?... It's a spool.

Ss: Spool.

T: Spool, yes, on to the other spool, on to the empty spool. And I have to tur –
And what am I doing now?

S: Turning.

T: Yes, good, so I have to turn – ?

Ss: Turn it round.

T: Turn it round. Yes. Good. Turn it round until the brown comes. Alright, now. I've plugged it in, I've plugged it in.

Ss: Yes.

T: What must I do next?

Ss: Switch on, switch it on.

T: Switch it on, good, yes. I must switch it on.

S: Excuse me. I think there is a mistake. When you make the tape... er...

T: When I put the tape round, have I done it wrong? Is it twisted? Come and tell me. Come and show me, Abdullah.

S: It doesn't matter, it doesn't matter....

T: Ah, that should be up, yes, OK, good, thank you.

S: It's alright.

T: Good. Now. I've plugged it in, I've switched it on, what should I do next? What do I have to do next?

S: Start the recorder.

T: Good. How do I start the recorder?

S: You push the switch.
(music)

Unit 9 Section a
Preliminary discussion

(Pair work in progress)
Students are all talking together. Some snatches of conversation follow.

S: OK. OK. What are you doing...

S: Perhaps I'll have some homework.

S: ...picnic...

S: Perhaps I'll do my homework.

T: Khosrow, what are you doing on Sunday?

K: ...Abdullah's...

T: Good, and what are you doing, Fransi?
...

Unit 10 Section d
Exploitation

Ss: *(laughter)*

T: Oh look, come in, come in...

Ab: Good morning.

T: Good morning Abdullah, you're late this morning...

Ab: Oh, I'm sorry.

T: Come and sit here. Or there, that's OK.
Oh, well, who can ask Abdullah why he's late?
Cecilia, can you ask him why he's late?

C: Why do you late agai today?

Ab: Pardon?

T: Why are you late...

C: Why are you late today?

T: Good.

Ab: Yes, because I was in the park.

C: In the park?

Ab: Yes. Car park.

Ss: Why?

Ab: Because I am worried about my car.

Ss: mmm

T: Did you forget to lock your car?

Ab: Yes, but after that I locked it.

T: Aha! What happens if you don't lock your car? What might happen?

S: Didn't start.

S: Maybe someone stolen it.

T: Yes, perhaps someone will steal it.

S: Will steal it.

T: If you don't lock your car, perhaps someone will steal it. Then at the end of the lesson, Abdullah goes out to get in his car, and...?

S: Nothing!

T: and there's no car!

S: No car, yes. *(laughter)*

T: OK. Very good.

Unit 12 Section d
Exploitation

The students are talking about their plans for the weekend, in pairs, at the end of the lesson.

Ss: ...Tomorrow? Why?... Why?... Yes ... I can eat Korean food...

T: OK. Thank you very much.

Ss: *(continue talking)*

T: I can't stop them talking!

Ss: *(laughter)*

T: OK that was very good, you talked together very well.

T: Right we must go for coffee, now, and we'll go on again afterwards, OK? So go and have your coffee now, ten minutes, and then come back and we'll do some more practising, OK? and we'll practise asking each other questions, like that.

S: We are going to miss the coffee time.

T: If you go quickly, quick quick quick. Run, run, I don't think you will, I don't think you'll miss it; are you sure? If you go quickly, right?

S: Thank you very much.

T: Go and have your break and then come back after break, and you won't be so tired then.

Ss: Yes, yes...

Appendix D
Key to teaching hints

Abbreviations: Sch – School dialogue or extract, **Coll** – College dialogue or extract, T – Teacher, S – Student, Ss – Students

Unit 1

Sch: T asks some individual Ss after the choral work to make the interaction more personal and also to keep all Ss alert during choral work in case they get asked a question afterwards ...

Coll: T nominates S *after* he asks the question and pauses so that *all* Ss will think of an answer. T asks Ss to ask their neighbours a question to maximise S practice time. All Ss thus get a chance to speak English. Also, all Ss learn how to *ask* questions as well as answer them.

Unit 2

Sch: T lets Ss know she is going to call the register so that they know what to do – in this case listen, and be prepared to have a chat.

Coll: When speaking slowly and clearly stress patterns are often distorted and no longer sound like normal English. If Ts always speak slowly, their Ss will never learn how to listen to and understand English spoken in real life at normal speed.

Unit 3

Sch: T wants Ss to pay attention, so she uses a form that requires a response from the Ss.

Coll: Situations like these create a lot of opportunities for genuine use of English. Ss learn to understand and carry out instructions. Ss get used to using English communicatively and for a purpose. Ss usually like helping in class; when they are involved in the organisation of their class, it makes them feel they belong.

Unit 4

Sch: T repeats the request for Lisa using the 'you' form which is more common in real life, so that Ss will see how polite requests can be used. Teachers often use polite forms to Ss although they are not obliged to do so. Children however are obliged to use polite forms when talking to adults, and should therefore practise them in class.

Coll: It is less appropriate to ask adult students to do jobs which involve getting dirty. (Chalk dust can be difficult to get off clothes!)

Unit 5

Sch: This is a 'warm-up' stage; the T's aim here is not to practise the past tense form, it is to get her Ss to relax and recall last lesson's dialogue. Over-correction can inhibit Ss' responses and then the T may not find out how much they can remember.

Coll: L¹ could have been used briefly to explain 'suggestions'. See Introduction, Section 7.

Unit 6

Sch: So that all Ss can see it well. By asking rather a short S, the T is creating a situation for some genuine use of English. The short S has to use a polite request in order to get someone to help her! Obviously one would not do this if one was likely to cause embarrassment to the S.

Coll: So that the S would have to use English to say he needed some more. T did not correct S when he said 'finish', he just looked as if he didn't understand and supplied the right phrase, hoping that next time someone might remember it and begin to use it. This is a more encouraging approach than correcting every mistake.

Unit 7

Sch: T involves Ss in setting the tape recorder up by getting them to help and give instructions. By asking them to listen for Unit 10 she is making them listen for one specific item of information. Listening for specific information is a valuable listening skill. (See FOCUS on LISTENING, Unit 18, page 134.)

Coll: T realises Ss have forgotten how to say this in English so she re-activates their latent knowledge by giving them two forms to choose from, in an either/or question. This way Ss can get the answer right more easily and feel encouraged.

Unit 8

Sch/Coll: During chorus work it is difficult to hear small errors or individual mistakes, so after the chorus work, T checks that individual Ss are saying it correctly and can understand. Also if Ts always do this it makes Ss work harder during the chorus work because they know they are going to be checked. T asks Kumah first because he is bright and more likely to get it right. Then Ali, who is not so bright, can copy Kumah and thus has more chance of getting it right himself.

Unit 9

Sch: T helps them by showing one group how to make a six first, then asking the rest of the class to do the same.

Coll: T needs to be free to wander round and hear other pairs practising. This is a good chance to hear and concentrate on the weaker Ss, helping them, without holding up the rest of the class. He can also listen for common mistakes as he walks round, and identify problem areas which he can then deal with after the pair work. T should however make sure that it is not always the same Ss that have to work in a three during pair practice times.

Unit 10

Sch: T uses difficult structures only in a context where the Ss will be able to understand the meaning. Later on when Ss need to produce these structures they will already be familiar with how they are used and they will learn to use them more easily.

Coll: The question 'Did you miss the bus?' can be answered in one word. Here, T wants to give the S a chance to practise his English, so he phrases the question in a way that will elicit an extended reply. (See Section d in Units 13, 14, 15.)

Unit 11

Sch: Hans is evidently a talkative student who tries to answer as many questions as he can. Gustav needs more time to get it right and T does not want him to feel rushed. Besides which, Gustav must learn that it is rude to interrupt.

Coll: Ss can help each other remember and correct each others' mistakes; this way they will learn more. Working in twos is often relaxing and more enjoyable; it also adds variety to the lesson. T only has half the number of dialogues to mark in detail, so his work is halved.

Unit 12

Sch: T checks that all Ss are sure of what they have to do for homework. Also this gives Ss another chance to use their English in a communicative way.

Coll: Ss are obviously finding this exercise difficult and T wants to stop before they get discouraged. By telling them they only have two more questions to do, Ss will work harder at those two and feel happier because the goal is more attainable. A game at this point will liven up the lesson and make learning more fun again. (If Ss are tired, the game should be an easy one that they know already.)

Unit 13

Sch: 'This is' is rarely stressed in everyday speech because it rarely carries new information. If T stresses it in class, Ss will learn the wrong pronunciation and may not understand it later hearing it unstressed as it normally is in conversation.

Coll: Ss will understand more and more classroom English as time goes by. They must get used to not understanding every word; outside the classroom they may always be in a situation where they do not understand all the English they hear. They need practice in guessing the meaning of what is said; here T helps by using gestures and by giving plenty of examples, e.g. 'Listen, like this.'

Unit 14

Sch: (a) by pointing to the picture. (b) ask some individual Ss to say it, to check that they can do it properly. (c) because at the beginning T's aim is to get Ss to practise communicating in English and to tell her what they could about the picture informally and naturally. She will correct Ss later if they get the main teaching point wrong, e.g. when they are practising the set dialogue.

Coll: (a) by giving them a 'sign-post' question before he reads the dialogue to the class. Ss must listen carefully to find out how to say 'tickets finished' in *correct* English. (b) This dialogue is the second dialogue of the lesson and probably contains similar language to the first. The T's aim is to use this dialogue to present the new teaching items 'no _____ left', 'sold out' etc. in a meaningful context and to offer this dialogue as an example of what Ss are to make up for themselves later on. (c) Ss know their own dialogues must be similar to the one they have just done, in content and length.

Unit 15

Sch/Coll: (a) T knows Gustav has been to Hamburg and can answer successfully; also the question 'What's it like?' often follows the question 'Have you ever been to _____?' in normal conversation, so it

prepares Ss for social English in the real world. It also provides an example for the rest of the class to follow. (b) A map of their own country is more involving for Ss. Also few of the Ss will have travelled overseas and so will only be able to answer 'No, I haven't' to questions about UK or USA. (c) The aim of this pair work is practice in communicating and interacting in English. Ss will get a good idea of how to use this new language they have just learnt and will therefore remember it better in the end. (d) Writing can help reinforce what they have learnt orally; also it provides a change of activity for the Ss and a rest for the T.

Unit 16

Sch: By asking Ss to do things with the rice and beans etc.

Coll: (a) 'Keep Fit' and 'jogging' are words that Ss must understand before they read the passage, otherwise they will have no idea of what the passage could be about. 'Sedentary' and 'agonising' are not vital to the understanding of the passage. They could also be guessed from the context or from Ss' knowledge of the outside world (Businessmen – offices – sitting all day . . .) (b) To make sure the Ss recognise the word when they see it in its written form, in the reading passage.

Unit 17

Sch: (a) The aim of this production stage is to give Ss practice in *using* language to communicate, as if in real life. Correction at this stage will only discourage Ss and inhibit them. In real life few people will actually correct Ss if they make mistakes; people will only worry if they cannot understand, i.e. if the S has not communicated successfully. So communication practice in interactive situations is vital in the classroom. (b) If Ss can only have six things, they will need to discuss and argue about which things they will leave out. They will have to give reasons to justify their choices. Therefore this limitation generates more language *use*.

Coll: (a) T is at present playing the role of a businessman; when prompting, he has to revert briefly to his role as T; he does not want this prompt to interrupt the role play situation so he speaks as quietly as possible. (b) Because the aim at this stage is communication practice, practice in *using* English, and mistakes like this will not impede or prevent understanding. (See Key to Unit 17, **Sch**; (a) above).

Unit 18

One (a) Ss feel more involved if one of their friends is at the front, and will listen better. (b) In everyday conversation, people often make mistakes or say the wrong thing and correct themselves; Ss must learn to recognise when this happens and not be put

off. (c) To show Ss the need to learn street directions and how they can be used in everyday life.

Two (a) So that his Ss would know that they were not expected to understand it all; if they did not know this they might well get worried and panic, or refuse to even try to understand anything. (b) These three questions refer to the three main points of the news item and so will guide Ss to an understanding of the gist of the passage which is all the T wants them to do at this stage. (c) Ss should realise that this is only the first part of a larger news item about the effects of the bad weather; the reader talks here about the South, but at the start he mentioned the whole country, so we can predict that the next part will be about other areas where the weather has caused damage. Ability to predict what might follow will help Ss understand quite difficult English in the future.

Unit 19

One (a) To familiarise Ss with the topic beforehand. (b) By asking them to look at the pictures and the first line; also to think back to their own experience. (c) She wants them to guess what 'algae' means from the context. (d) If T tells them the right answers, Ss will then have no real need to read the passage to find out for themselves. If they read it knowing exactly what information it contains, they will read it with closed minds and will not get the practice in 'interpreting' the meaning of the passage as they read, as people do in real life.

Two (a) By working in pairs, all students have to think and try to work out the answers for themselves. They can help each other. (This could be done in L[1], see Introduction, 7) This technique helps to make the Ss less dependent on the teacher. (b) No. The T wants *all* students to evaluate replies, to keep all Ss involved and thinking. (c) 'Such as' is used in a great variety of texts and is a common way of introducing an example. Words like these will help the Ss to understand the organisation in many *other* texts as well as the text they are reading at the moment. (d) Not very. Ss must understand the connection between 'rubber tube'/'one end'/'other end' and not be sidetracked by the nearest singular noun, 'thumb'. The question shows the T whether or not the Ss have understood the sense of the paragraph.

Unit 20

Sch/Coll: (a) Ss must relate the words to the picture *and* select an answer that matches the question in order to get it right. (b) To diagnose what problems the Ss might have when writing the dialogue in their own notebooks. By correcting one S's work on the board, before the class writes, a lot of mistakes may be avoided. Also, this method shows all Ss exactly what they have to do for themselves; they can all feel confident that they are doing the work in the right way. (c) To help them become independent and to train them to be critical of their own work.

Unit 21
Sch/Coll: (a) Once the Ss have got their main points, T helps them to organise the points; she suggests ways of linking sentences and introducing the paragraphs. (b) T can make sure that good writing habits are learnt and put into practice. The ideas are fresh in the Ss' minds so they are less likely to forget and make mistakes. T

can spend some time helping the weaker Ss with their work. T can set a time limit so they get used to writing essays to time, as they will have to do in examinations. (c) A period of writing in the middle helps to make the lesson more varied. Also three paragraphs might be too many for some Ss to remember well.

Glossary

Words and phrases used in a specialised sense in the context of English language teaching.

acceptable Acceptable English is English that the hearer can understand and which does not cause offence. In spoken English, it does not necessarily mean 'perfectly accurate'; a speaker can make mistakes in grammar but the hearer will not mind. English that is not appropriate in social register is more likely to be unacceptable and cause offence.
See appropriate.

(to) acknowledge To say something in answer to someone. You can acknowledge someone's arrival by a nod of the head. You can acknowledge a 'thank you' by saying 'Not at all' or 'That's alright'. How can you acknowledge an apology?

(to) activate *See active control.*
If a student understands a language item but cannot use it actively, the teacher will need to give him more oral practice in order to 'activate' it so he can say it and use it when he needs to.

active control If the students have *active* control of a structure or some vocabulary they can say it, *use* it, where relevant. A lot of school students leave school with only a *passive* control of English, as they have had no practice in communicating in English or actively producing any English for themselves. Their English needs to be *activated*.

activities Things you *do* in the classroom. E.g. (i) listening comprehension (ii) teacher questions, student answers (iii) pair work – enacting dialogues in twos.

advanced *See level.*

aim What the teacher wants the students to be able to do by the end of a certain length of time. See Unit 13, Section **e**, for an example. You can have: (i) *long term aims* (e.g. By the end of this year my students will be able to write at the paragraph level, with reasonable accuracy.) (ii) *short term aims* (e.g. In this next 5 minutes I will make the students practise short answer tags, e.g. 'Yes he did', 'Yes I was', so they can produce them accurately and automatically. (iii) Sometimes short term aims are called *objectives*. (iv) *'Goal'* is another word usually for long term aims.

appropriate Suitable.
Language that is suitable for, or appropriate when talking to children or close friends is often not appropriate when speaking to someone you are meeting for the first time. E.g. 'fag' in English is slang for a 'cigarette'. If you said to a King 'Have a fag, your Royal Highness,' it would lack appropriacy; you cannot be informal and formal in one utterance. The King would be highly offended. Because of his status, you would address him politely and formally.

audio Something you can hear. Audio-visual means something you can hear and see. You can have audio tape and video tape.

chaining Forward chaining and backward chaining are techniques you can use if a sentence is too long or complex for the students to repeat or practise in one go. See Unit 7, Section **b**, for examples.

(a) chunk If a paragraph is too long for your students to read or study all at once, you can divide it up into smaller sections which are still meaningful. These are known as chunks.

consolidation To consolidate a student's knowledge of a language item is to practise all aspects of the item so that he is able to use it in all possible circumstances with no problems. Consolidation means to have a thorough knowledge of the item concerned.

(a) cue Cues can be words or pictures which tell the student what he is expected to answer or say next. You can give cues for a drill, e.g. T: I like dogs. CATS. S: I like cats. Here, CATS is the cue word. It's a verbal cue, not a picture cue. You can write one or two cue words for each line of a dialogue that the students are about to practise in pairs, to help them remember what to say next.
See flash cards.

(the) cultural aspect Peoples' social habits and attitudes differ from country to country. E.g. In Britain, people stand in orderly queues at bus stops, or to buy tickets etc. In some countries it is the same, but in others, you just push forward. In

Britain, especially in London, it is normal for a woman to go and have a drink in a pub alone. In many countries this would not be accepted. These are cultural differences. Some English Language coursebooks are written for foreign students studying in Britain and are very culture bound. Books with a high emphasis on cultural aspects of British life are not necessarily suitable for learners living in their own country and not intending to go to Britain. Such books may well be culturally inaccessible to the learner if he knows little about British culture to start with.

discrimination The ability to discriminate or distinguish between, or to tell the difference between two (or more) things. See FOCUS on Oral Practice, Unit 15, page 104. Students can be asked to discriminate (i) between two sounds, like w and v, (ii) between two intonation patterns, (iii) between two different time references, like 'Did he go?' and 'Does he go?' or two different meanings, like 'He's been there' and 'He's gone there.' Games which practise language discrimination are useful for contrasting meanings, establishing patterns, and checking understanding. They help students develop a passive control of the language.

distortion Sometimes the natural stress patterns and sounds of English become distorted and no longer sound natural or recognisable. This sometimes happens when a class does a lot of choral work which gets a rhythm of its own, or when a teacher speaks too clearly, stressing every word, even the words not normally stressed. *See stress and weak forms.*

drilling Making students practise intensively. There are many kinds of language drills, oral and written, they normally aim to practise the form or the structure of an item, but often do not attach much importance to what it means. E.g. A substitution drill, to practise the present simple tense forms – T: I go to market every day. HE. Ss: He goes to market every day. T: THEY. Ss: They go to market every day. T: DO THEY. etc.

(to) elicit To encourage the class to give a reply or say something; e.g. (i) the teacher wants his student to say 'Yes, he is'. In order to *elicit* this, he asks 'Is John well today?' If he wants to elicit the answer 'No, she hasn't,' he might ask 'Has Mary got £3,000?' (ii) To elicit a sentence expressing uncertainty or possibility, the teacher could say; 'Peter isn't here yet. Do you think he's ill, or could he have missed the bus?' Students could answer 'He may be ill' or 'He might have missed the bus'. See Units 15 and 16, Section **d**.

ELT English Language Teaching.

(to) establish To *establish* the *meaning* of a word means to illustrate the meaning of the word and make it clear so that the students can understand.

(an) exchange An exchange is one small stage of a conversation, e.g. A: Thanks for a lovely party. B: That's alright. I'm glad you enjoyed it. A: Oh, we did! An exchange is usually made up of at least two utterances. *See utterances*.

exploitation To exploit a situation is to use the situation to its full advantage, to make the most of a situation. A teacher should *use* every opportunity he can get for meaningful and genuine language practise. E.g. If the blackboard is dirty, ask them, (i) if it is clean, (ii) why it isn't clean, (iii) if they can clean it, (iv) why they haven't cleaned it before etc.

(a) flannel board Made of rough flannel stuck on to cards hung on the wall; figures of people or objects made of felt or card backed with sand paper stick on easily and can be moved around on the board.

flash cards In a classroom, students usually wait for a sign from the teacher before they speak. The sign can be a gesture, a nod of the head, an air of expectancy, a verbal cue or sometimes a picture cue. Verbal cues can be oral or written. It is effective if picture cues or verbal cues are on flash cards that can be held up briefly or 'flashed' in front of the class to cue an answer or a response. They can also be called cue cards. *See cue*.

fluently Quickly and smoothly; pausing at the end of each phrase, not after every word in a jerky or stilted way.

formal You speak more formally to people you don't know well and who are of a higher status than you. You would also speak in a formal way to a person you knew well if you were in a formal situation like a business meeting. *See register.*

(alternative) forms Here 'forms' means patterns, e.g. grammatical patterns. You can *either* say 'You were absent for 3 days', or you can say 'You have missed 3 days school'. These two sentences mean the same, so we call them alternative forms. You can say either.

(the) function e.g. (i) The phrases 'Be quiet' 'Stop talking' 'That's enough talking now' all have the same *function*. Their function is to make the class be quiet. They have different forms, but are similar in function, e.g. (ii) 'He *may* be ill' 'He *might* be ill' '*Perhaps* he's ill'. The words in italics

all have the same function. They all express the idea or notion of uncertainty or possibility, e.g. (iii) the word 'could' can have many different functions. 'Could' can express all the ideas or notions below. (a) *asking permission:* 'Could I go now?' (b) *making a suggestion:* 'We could have a party next Saturday. Let's!' (c) *past ability:* 'I could read when I was 5.' (d) *uncertainty:* 'He could be ill. I don't know.'

gist The gist of a dialogue or reading passage is the general idea of the meaning. Often you don't need to understand every word, understanding the gist is enough. If you read quickly, you'll get the gist.

hardware E.g., tape recorders, cassette players, overhead projectors (O.H.P.s), etc. – in other words, the equipment, usually electrical, found in classrooms. *See software.*

informal Casual, friendly. You should speak formally to a stranger, but you act informally with friends, unless you are in a formal setting. *See formal.*

information gap An information gap occurs when one person has information that the other person does not have, but needs. (The information can be from a visual source – a picture, or an audio source – a tape, or from a reading passage.) Problem solving activities like 'Find the difference', p. 124, Guessing games, p. 104 and Simulation activities work well because there is a genuine information gap which should promote real communication between students. See also p. 131, Tables 19 and 20.

integration Integrated skills is when the main language skills are practised in conjunction with each other; e.g. when oral practice leads into reading and then into written work on the same theme.

interference Interference is when language habits usually of the mother tongue are transferred to L^2 where they are incorrect; e.g. French, 'Il a 10 ans' (literally 'he has 10 years') compared to English 'He is ten'. A French child is likely to say 'He has ten years', making an error which is due to *interference*.

intermediate See *level.*

intonation The way the voice rises and falls is called intonation. At the end of a sentence, it usually falls. In a question, like 'Are you ready?' it normally rises. If the voice rises when you say 'Coming?', you can *infer* that 'Coming?' is a question. If it falls, 'Coming', it is a statement.

(an) item A language point; it can be a structural item like the present perfect, an item of vocabulary, a phrase or an idiom.

key words The most important words that carry the meaning of the sentence.

L¹ The mother tongue or the native language.

L$^{2, 3, 4,}$ etc The second, third and fourth language, one of which may be English.

TL The target language that a person is acquiring.

levels Obviously the meaning of the words 'elementary', 'intermediate' and 'advanced' (with regard to the level of English language being taught), will differ from country to country, depending on the status of English, the local examination system, and so on. In Britain, roughly speaking, 'elementary' covers true beginners, and remedial beginners, up to students who have had about a year (approximately 120 hours) of English, working from the first book of a standard course. 'Advanced' students are those who have passed the Cambridge First Certificate or RSA II examinations and who are preparing for the Cambridge Proficiency on RSA III examinations. They should be already fairly fluent. 'Intermediate' students are in between, roughly those in their second, third and fourth years of study, who have done between 150 and 600 hours of English, up to and including the Cambridge First Certificate or RSA II examinations. N.B. (i) 'When teaching *at* elementary *level,* you . . .', (ii) 'When teaching the present simple tense *to* elementary *students* you . . .', (iii) 'At the *early* (or *late*) intermediate stage, you . . .'

lexis Vocabulary. It is a collective term meaning 'words'. You cannot make 'lexis' or 'vocabulary' plural by adding 's' because they are collective nouns. If you want to be specific you have to say 'a word', (plural – 'words'). 'An item of vocabulary' (plural – 'items of vocabulary'). A lexical item (plural 'lexical items').

(a) magnet board A magnetic board on to which you can fix pictures, or cut-out figures, using magnets (either stuck on the back of the paper or card, or placed on top of the paper to hold it in position). Using magnets makes it easy to move the pictures or cut-out figures around. Most whiteboards are magnetic too.

micro Small or short. Micro-teaching means teaching one small *part* or stage of a lesson only, i.e. teaching for a very short time.

motivation (to motivate) The desire to learn, the desire to please. e.g. (i) If a student wishes to learn, if he is motivated, he will make progress. If, however, he lacks motivation, if he has no desire to learn, he will probably not make progress. (ii) A teacher should try to *build up motivation* in his students. He must try to motivate them, to make them *want* to learn.

(to) mount To cut out and stick pictures or photos on to larger pieces of card. Pictures from newspapers and magazines are apt to tear and look old and shabby very quickly, because they are on such thin paper. If you cut them out and stick them on to pieces of card they last much longer and are pleasant to handle. They are also easier to store and select from and you can make lists on the back of the cards of the language items you have practised with them.

(a) notion The concept or meaning expressed by language. Notions can be *conceptual,* e.g. the notion of likes/dislikes can be expressed using several different structural and lexical items. I like tea, but I dislike strong coffee. I'm fond of tea, but I hate coffee. I prefer tea to coffee, or *semantico–grammatical,* e.g. ways of expressing past action using the verb systems, or ways of expressing continuous or progressive action, in past, present or future time.¹

a notional/functional coursebook One based on a notional/functional syllabus, rather than a structural syllabus, i.e. one which divides language up according to a sequence of notions and functions, as used in real life conversations (e.g. how to *offer* someone something, how to *refuse* an offer politely and give a reason or excuse, how to offer an alternative, etc.) rather than according to grammatical structures based on grammar books (e.g. present continuous tense, formation of adverbs). With a notional/functional syllabus, grammatical structures must still be taught, but the ordering and grouping of these is determined according to functions and notions. The emphasis is on the communicative use of the language in real life, how conversations are built up, and how people interact in English.

objectives *See aim.*

pace When a teacher spends a long time introducing a new item, the pace is slow. When a lot of new material is introduced or practised in a short time the pace is fast. A variety of pace and activities within a lesson is a good thing when teaching a foreign language.

¹ See D A Wilkins (1976) (1979).

pair practice Pair practice is when two students practise speaking together, each taking one part in a dialogue that the teacher has presented to them. Massed pair practice is when all the class pairs off and all the pairs practise, quietly, simultaneously. This technique gives every student a chance to speak, and gives the teacher a chance to walk round and check to see if they have learnt it. Pair practice can be controlled (where students practise a set dialogue) or less controlled practice (where they make up their own dialogue from cue words or a series of pictures) or fairly free production (where the teacher gives them a situation, or shows a picture of people talking and asks the students to act the roles of the people in that situation and make up an appropriate dialogue). This is nearer to role play. This technique produces very good results, as it maximises the students' oral production time and helps them to communicate in English.

paralinguistic features include sounds like 'er', 'ah', and facial expressions, gestures, all of which can communicate something without actually using words.

parrot-fashion When students repeat parrot-fashion, they repeat automatically the sounds they hear without understanding their meaning, like a parrot imitates, with no understanding.

passive control Students usually have a greater passive control of L² than active. In other words, they can understand more than they can say or write. Passive control refers to their comprehension, or how much they can understand. *See active control.*

pattern Usually means the same as 'structure', e.g. a grammatical pattern; two sentences on the same pattern, two sentences with the same grammatical structure.

patterns of response (of interaction) If a teacher wants to ask some questions, she can ask either the whole class; one section of the class; an individual student; or anyone at all, to respond, or she can ask students to ask each other to respond, in groups or pairs, instead of always interacting with the teacher. The use of varied patterns of response and interaction makes a lesson more varied.

phonology The study of the sound system and includes pronunciation, intonation, stress and weak forms.

(the) pitch A high pitched voice sounds squeaky. If you called 'Help!' you would say it loudly, beginning on a *high pitch*, and then with falling intonation. You might begin on a low pitch if you were apologising about something you felt bad about. 'Look I'm sorry I forgot.' You would say 'look' in a low voice, with a low pitch. Pitch is the level or height of your voice at any given time, compared with your usual level. Intonation is the tune or pattern of connected pitches.

(the) practice stage When the students begin to repeat the new item, to complete or make sentences, from prompt words or from picture cues, and perhaps learn a dialogue containing that item so that they get some practice in using the new item in conversation. The practice stage progresses from very controlled work to less controlled work, which in turn leads on to the production stage, where students can make up their own dialogues, do role play etc. without much help from the teacher.

(the) presentation stage The introduction of the form and meaning of a new language point, which the students do not know yet. The presentation usually involves the teacher talking, repeating, demonstrating, showing pictures, illustrating the new point until the class has grasped the meaning, and have some idea of the form. Then the teacher goes on to the practice stage.[1] Can also refer to the presentation of a new text or reading passage.

procedure Classroom procedure really means the techniques you use in order to achieve your objectives.

to produce (production) To speak or write English. Oral production is when the student speaks. Written production is when he writes. Controlled production is when he speaks or writes with the teacher helping or guiding him. Free production is when he produces oral or written English with very little help from the teacher or the textbook in a situation very near to real life. Even if students make mistakes at this stage they should be allowed to continue, because it is only by using the language and saying what they want to say that they will learn how to use English and communicate with confidence. The teacher's role at the production stage is to sit back and let his students try to communicate on their own.

productive skills The main skills of speaking and writing. *See receptive skills.*

(to) project (one's voice) (voice projection) To speak out clearly and distinctly (not necessarily slowly or very loudly).

[1] For more detail on these three stages, read pages 1–3 of *Teaching Oral English*, Donn Byrne (1976).

pronunciation The way you pronounce individual sounds and words. Often the sounds 'v' and 'w' are pronounced badly by learners, e.g. 'invite' is often mispronounced to sound like 'in white'. The pronunciation of vowel sounds can cause problems, especially the weak forms of unstressed vowels.

rapport A good friendly positive relationship between the class and the teacher. Students and teacher feel happy and relaxed together and enjoy working together. Teachers who *lack rapport with* their class may find their classes do not work well for them, and there is a cold atmosphere in the room. Good rapport increases motivation.

realia Real objects, real things that you can bring into the classroom to illustrate the meaning more clearly or to use as aids to make a situation more meaningful and therefore more memorable. Realia are good for role play. They make the acting easier and more real.

recall To remember something. To aid recall, you can use visual aids, to make something memorable.

receptive skills i.e. listening or reading and understanding. The receptive skills are different to the productive skills (speaking and writing). The discrimination game on p. 104 helps students develop receptive skills or in other words their passive control of the language. Look at this table of the skills:

	Oral	Written
Receptive	listening	reading
Productive	speaking	writing

In a teaching situation, students should listen before they speak, speak before they read, and read before they write.

redundancy When listening or reading you often only notice the key words, the most important words that carry the meaning. A lot of the other words and sometimes even sentences are what we call redundant: we don't need them. A text with densely packed information is often harder to grasp than one with a lot of redundancy, because we have less time to process and retain the closely packed information.

register Has two very different meanings. (i) You take the register every lesson (or call the roll every day) to check if all the students are present. This register is a list of names. (ii) *Social register* is the degree of formality of language; it ranges from very formal (e.g. a king to an ambassador from abroad) and formal (two company directors who had not met until now) to

informal or casual register (between friends). It also depends on the comparative *status* of the two people. *Example*: (Mrs Smith is a secretary, married with one child.) *Mrs Smith to child*: 'Hurry up and finish that book, Peter.' *Mrs Smith to husband*: 'Finish that book soon, could you please?' *Mrs Smith to boss*: 'Would you mind finishing that book as soon as possible, please?' *See pp. 98–99.*

(to) reinforce to practise or use a particular structure or language item again, so that students will find it easier to remember and use for themselves.

(to) rephrase To say the same thing again but in a different way, e.g. 'Can you tell me where Jim is?' ⟶ 'Where's Jim?'

role play Members of the group pretend they are different people (like actors in a play in the theatre) and act their roles, play their parts and speak according to which role they are playing. It is a very useful activity when encouraging students to produce English suitable to a particular situation. *See simulation.*

(to) scan To read rapidly through a text looking for specific items of information (not necessarily the main points).

sense groups When splitting a sentence up into sections to make it easier for students to repeat you make the divisions at meaningful points; e.g. Mr Smith/the retired policeman/, put the light out/ and left/. NOT: Mr Smith, the retired/policeman, put the light/out and left/. The same applies when dividing paragraphs into chunks. *See chunks.*

simulation activities similar to role play situations except that participants take part in simulated situations *as themselves* instead of acting a part. e.g. (i) giving directions to each other's homes, as if they were going to visit each other. (ii) Students are asked to agree on what seven articles they would choose to have with them if they were shipwrecked on a desert island, and finally to arrange the articles in order of importance. See p. 129, Tables 13 and 14. This involves using language to explain, to suggest, to give reasons, to justify one's choice, to persuade others, to agree, disagree, etc., and is closer to real-life use.

skills This is used in two ways: (i) the four main language skills are listening, speaking, reading and writing (ii) 'enabling' skills, which are sub-skills; e.g. the ability to pick out the main points in a reading text is just one of the skills that helps you to read efficiently. See the FOCUS pages of Units 18, 19, and 21. *See also receptive and productive.*

(to) skim Skimming is when you read the whole text rapidly to get the gist.

software e.g. books, papers, and additional materials like games, magazine pictures, homework sheets, class worksheets, and supplementary reading materials. Also tapes. *See hardware*.

(a) stage Here 'stage' means part of the lesson. A lesson can normally be divided into several stages. The beginning of the lesson where you chat informally and take the register is the first stage. The second stage might be correcting homework, or revising the last lesson. The third stage might be your presentation of a new language item.

stress You normally stress the important words in a sentence, the words which carry most meaning. You place the stress, or emphasis on 'now' and 'later', in the following sentence 'Is John coming now or later?' In words of more than one syllable, one (or occasionally more) syllable bears the stress, e.g. important (the stress is on 'por'), before (the stress is on 'fore'), dinner – the stress is on the first syllable.

(a) structure A pattern = a grammatical item = a structural item, e.g. the present simple tense.

(to) substitute To put something different in the place of the original item. To change one item for another; e.g. (i) Tony went to market. (substitute Mary for Tony) = Mary went to market. (ii) In your textbook perhaps there is a shopping situation. If Angela is buying *fruit*, you could substitute *vegetables* without too many necessary changes. Hower if you substitute 'a new dress', this would involve a whole new set of vocabulary, a different social register and it would be an entirely different exchange.

(to) subvocalise Students who subvocalise when reading silently go through the motions of reading out loud, moving their lips and tongue but making no noise. Subvocalising slows up the pace of their reading.

(a) syllable One section of a word; e.g. 'Dinner' has 2 syllables, 'accuracy' has 4 syllables.

TEFL The teaching of English as a Foreign Language.

TESFL The teaching of English as a Second or Foreign Language.

(a) technique A teaching technique is the method you use when teaching. It refers to how you teach.

tone of voice You often show your attitude or your feelings by the expression you use in your voice, by your tone of voice. Your tone can convey more meaning than the words you use. Practise saying the name *Peter* as if you were (a) going to ask him a favour (b) angry with him (c) surprised he was there (d) sharing a joke with him. Can your friend tell which way you are saying it?

transfer Students often seem to have learnt an item very well in class, but when they are outside the classroom they seem to use very little of what they have learnt in class and lapse back into bad English. This is due to lack of language *transfer*. Such students have been given too little guidance and insight into the usage of the language they 'know'. They have no idea when to use it, once they are in a real life situation. To obtain this transfer is one of the most difficult things in TEFL.

tune in To get used to hearing English spoken again. Their last lesson may have been in L^1, or they may have been speaking L^1 among themselves. 'Warm up' is also used in a similar way.

(an) utterance Something which is spoken. It could be a question, an answer or a statement. An utterance is usually short, two or three sentences at the most, perhaps one small part of a dialogue. An *exchange* is made up of various utterances, e.g. a question, an answer and a comment.

(the) value You say words like 'Right!' and 'OK!' when you want the class to pay attention. 'Right' does not mean 'correct' here; it shows the class something new is going to happen. It has the 'value' of attracting their attention, it does not mean anything by itself. E.g. 'Yes?' (with a rising intonation) does not *mean* 'Yes' (not 'No') but it can encourage a student to speak. It has the value of showing a certain student you are waiting for him to answer.

visual aids Things which the students can *see*. E.g. pictures, wall charts, diagrams, models (e.g. toy animals), realia, and even the view from the window, and which therefore help them to understand. (Audio – is something that can be *heard*. Hence an audio-visual course – is a course that has tapes and slides, or tapes and pictures, or, of course film or video tape, that can be heard and seen.) Visual material in class adds variety and keeps students interested in the lesson.

weak forms Sometimes the vowel sound in a word changes if it is not stressed, and becomes (ə), a neutral sound, or a weak form. Look at 'was' and 'to' and 'too' in this dialogue, when are they weak or unstressed?
Read it out loud. 'Katy was going to the *cinema* tonight.' 'What about Peter?' 'Oh yes, Peter was too.' In the first sentence they are unstressed or weak, but in the last, they are stressed.

Select bibliography

See also suggestions for Further Reading, in most Units.

1 General background reading on ELT theory and methodology

Note: Only certain sections of each book will be of immediate relevance. In some cases, specific references are given to page or chapter numbers. Where no references are given, you should check through the Table of Contents and the Index in the book itself. Only a limited number of the most useful works are listed here. Most books, for example Donn Byrne's *English Teaching Perspectives*, themselves contain suggestions for further reading and bibliographies.

ALLEN, J P B and CORDER, S P *The Edinburgh Course in Applied Linguistics* Vol 3 (Oxford University Press 1974) Chapters 4, 6 and 9.

BROUGHTON, G et al *Teaching English as a Foreign Language* (Routledge and Kegan Paul 1978)

BRUMFIT, C J and JOHNSON, K (Eds) *The Communicative Approach to Language Teaching* (Oxford University Press 1979) pp. 183–205 for general methodoloy.

BYRNE, D *English Teaching Perspectives* (Longman 1980) a collection of extracts from British and American writers on the theory of ELT.

FINOCCHIARO, M *English as a Second Language* (Regents 1974)

FINOCCHIARO, M and BONOMO, M *The Foreign Language Learner* (Regents 1973)

HARMER, J *The Practice of English Language Teaching* (Longman forthcoming)

HAYCRAFT, J *An Introduction to English Language Teaching* (Longman 1978), a very basic guide for inexperienced teachers.

JOHNSON, K and MORROW K *Communication in the Classroom* (Longman 1981)

JOINER, E G and WESTPHAL P B (eds) *Developing Communication Skills* (Newbury House Publishers, Inc 1978)

MOORWOOD, H (Ed) *Selections from MET (Modern English Teacher)* (Longman 1978). Full of practical ideas that can be adapted to most ELT classrooms.

PIT CORDER, S *Introducing Applied Linguistics* (Penguin Education 1973), a theoretical account.

RIVERS, W *Teaching Foreign Language Skills* (University of Chicago Press 1968)

RIVERS, W and TEMPERLEY, M S *A Practical Guide to the Teaching of English as a Second or Foreign Language* (Oxford University Press Inc 1979)

VINCENT, M *English Teachers' Handbook* (Voluntary Service Overseas, London 1978). A very practical handbook, intended for British teachers working in developing countries, but useful for any English teacher anywhere.

WIDDOWSON, H G *Teaching Language as Communication* (Oxford University Press 1978)

WILKINS, D A *Notional Syllabuses* (Oxford University Press 1976)

WILKINS, D A *Grammatical, situational and notional syllabuses* in BRUMFIT and JOHNSON 1979 above, pp. 82–98.

2 Recommended works on specific areas of ELT

Grammar

THOMSON, A J and MARTINET, A V *A Practical English Grammar* (Oxford University Press, new edition 1980)

QUIRK, R S and GREENBAUM, G *A University Grammar of English* (Longman 1973)

LEECH, G and SVARTVIK, J *A Communicative Grammar of English* (Longman 1975)

ZANDVOORT, R W *A Handbook of English Grammar* (Longman 1957)

LEECH, G *Meaning and the English Verb* (Longman 1971)

PALMER, F R *A Linguistic Study of the English Verb* (Longman 1965)

Testing

HEATON, J B *Writing English Language Tests* (Longman 1975)

MORROW, K *Communicative Language Testing: revolution or evolution?* in BRUMFIT and JOHNSON (1979) see above, pp. 143–157

Aids

McALPINE, J *The Magazine Picture Library* (George Allen & Unwin 1979)

MUGGLESTONE, P *Planning and Using the Blackboard* (George Allen & Unwin 1979)

WRIGHT, A *Visual Materials for the Language Teacher* (Longman 1976)

Listening and speaking

BYRNE, D *Teaching Oral English* (Longman 1976)

DAKIN, J *The Language Laboratory and Language Learning* (Longman 1973)

BROWN, G *Listening to Spoken English* (Longman 1977)

WRIGHT, A et al *Games for Language Learning* (Cambridge University Press 1979)

Reading and writing

BYRNE, D *Teaching Writing Skills* (Longman 1979)

COOPER, M and FOX, M *Junior English Reading* (Longman 1978) *Introduction*. *Senior English Reading* (Longman 1980) *Introduction*.

JOHNSON, K *Communicate in Writing* (Longman 1980)

MUNBY, J *Read and Think* (Longman 1968) *Introduction*.

WHITE, R *Teaching Written English* (George Allen & Unwin 1979)

English for Special Purposes

KENNEDY, C *English for Special Purposes* (Macmillan Press 1980)

MACKAY, R, MOUNTFORD, A *English for Specific Purposes* (Longman 1978)

Index of
teaching skills

Index of language games for teachers